Education in a Competitive and Globalizing World

Arts Education: Assessment and Access

EDUCATION IN A COMPETITIVE AND GLOBALIZING WORLD

Additional books in this series can be found on Nova's website under the Series tab.

Additional E-books in this series can be found on Nova's website under the E-book tab.

EDUCATION IN A COMPETITIVE AND GLOBALIZING WORLD

ARTS EDUCATION: ASSESSMENT AND ACCESS

OLIVIA M. WILSON
EDITOR

Nova
Nova Science Publishers, Inc.
New York

Copyright © 2010 by Nova Science Publishers, Inc.

All rights reserved. No part of this book may be reproduced, stored in a retrieval system or transmitted in any form or by any means: electronic, electrostatic, magnetic, tape, mechanical photocopying, recording or otherwise without the written permission of the Publisher.

For permission to use material from this book please contact us:
Telephone 631-231-7269; Fax 631-231-8175
Web Site: http://www.novapublishers.com

NOTICE TO THE READER

The Publisher has taken reasonable care in the preparation of this book, but makes no expressed or implied warranty of any kind and assumes no responsibility for any errors or omissions. No liability is assumed for incidental or consequential damages in connection with or arising out of information contained in this book. The Publisher shall not be liable for any special, consequential, or exemplary damages resulting, in whole or in part, from the readers' use of, or reliance upon, this material. Any parts of this book based on government reports are so indicated and copyright is claimed for those parts to the extent applicable to compilations of such works.

Independent verification should be sought for any data, advice or recommendations contained in this book. In addition, no responsibility is assumed by the publisher for any injury and/or damage to persons or property arising from any methods, products, instructions, ideas or otherwise contained in this publication.

This publication is designed to provide accurate and authoritative information with regard to the subject matter covered herein. It is sold with the clear understanding that the Publisher is not engaged in rendering legal or any other professional services. If legal or any other expert assistance is required, the services of a competent person should be sought. FROM A DECLARATION OF PARTICIPANTS JOINTLY ADOPTED BY A COMMITTEE OF THE AMERICAN BAR ASSOCIATION AND A COMMITTEE OF PUBLISHERS.

LIBRARY OF CONGRESS CATALOGING-IN-PUBLICATION DATA

Arts education : assessment and access / editor, Olivia M. Wilson.
    p. cm.
  Includes index.
  ISBN 978-1-61728-266-9 (hardcover)
  1. Arts--Study and teaching. 2. Educational evaluation. I. Wilson, Olivia M.
  NX280.A698 2010
  700.71'073--dc22
                            2010015568

Published by Nova Science Publishers, Inc. † New York

CONTENTS

Preface		vii
Chapter 1	2008 Arts Education Assessment Framework *National Assessment of Educational Progress (NAEP)*	1
Chapter 2	The Nation's Report Card: Arts 2008 - Music and Visual Arts *National Assessment of Educational Progress at Grade 8*	119
Chapter 3	Access to Arts Education: Inclusion of Additional Questions in Education's Planned Research Would Help Explain Why Instruction Time Has Decreased for Some Students *United State Government Accountability Office.*	165
Chapter Sources		201
Index		203

PREFACE

The National Assessment of Educational Progress (NAEP) arts education framework is founded on a vision of a society that believes the arts are essential to every child's complete development. Throughout their lives, they will draw from artistic experience and knowledge as a means of understanding what happens both inside and outside their own skin, just as they use mathematical, scientific, and other frameworks for understanding. This new book examines the results of the 2008 National Assessment of Education Progress in the arts, which was given to a nationally representative sample of 7,900 eighth grade public and private school students.

Chapter 1 - The National Assessment of Educational Progress (NAEP) is the only nationally representative and continuing assessment of what America's students know and can do in various subject areas. Since 1969, assessments have been conducted to provide comprehensive information on student knowledge and skills at ages 9, 13, and 17 and, more recently, for students in grades 4, 8, and 12. Because the information on student performance and related factors is available to policymakers, parents, educators, and the general public, NAEP is an integral part of the nation's evaluation of the condition and progress of student achievement.

NAEP is a congressionally mandated project of the U.S. Department of Education's National Center for Education Statistics (NCES). In 1988, Congress created the National Assessment Governing Board to set policy for NAEP. The 26-member, broadly representative Board selects subject areas to be assessed, develops assessment objectives and specifications through a national process, and sets appropriate achievement goals, among other responsibilities.

Chapter 2 - This chapterpresents the results of the 2008 National Assessment of Educational Progress (NAEP) in the arts, which was given to a nationally representative sample of 7,900 eighth- grade public and private school students. Approximately one-half of these students were assessed in music, and the other half were assessed in visual arts.

The **MUSIC** portion of the assessment measured students' ability to respond to music in various ways. Students were asked to analyze and describe aspects of music they heard, critique instrumental and vocal performances, and demonstrate their knowledge of standard musical notation and music's role in society. One question, for example, asked students to identify the instrument they heard in the beginning solo of "Rhapsody in Blue" that was played for them.

The average responding score for music was reported on a NAEP scale of 0 to 300. Scores ranged from 105 for the lowest-performing students to 194 for the highest-performing students.

The **VISUAL ARTS** portion of the assessment included questions that measured students' ability to respond to art as well as questions that measured their ability to create art. Responding questions asked students to analyze and describe works of art and design. For example, students were asked to describe specific differences in how certain parts of an artist's self-portrait were drawn. The average responding score for visual arts was reported on a NAEP scale of 0 to 300 with scores ranging from 104 for the lowest- performing students to 193 for the highest-performing students.

Creating questions, on the other hand, required students to create works of art and design of their own. For example, students were asked to create a self-portrait that was scored for identifying detail, compositional elements, and use of materials. The average creating task score for visual arts was reported separately as the average percentage of the maximum possible score from 0 to 100 with a national average of 52. In general, students who performed well on the responding questions also performed well on the creating questions.

Chapter 3 - Under the No Child Left Behind Act (NCLBA), districts and schools must demonstrate adequate yearly progress (AYP) for all students. Because schools may spend more time improving students' academic skills to meet NCLBA's requirements, some are concerned that arts education might be cut back. To determine how, if at all, student access to arts education has changed since NCLBA, the Congress asked: (1) has the amount of instruction time for arts education changed and, if so, have certain groups been more affected than others, (2) to what extent have state education agencies' requirements and funding for arts education changed since NCLBA, (3) what are school officials in selected districts doing to provide arts education since NCLBA and what challenges do they face in doing so, and (4) what is known about the effect of arts education in improving student outcomes? GAO analyzed data from the U.S. Department of Education (Education), surveyed 50 state arts officials, interviewed officials in 8 school districts and 19 schools, and reviewed existing research.

In: Arts Education: Assessment and Access
Editor: Olivia M. Wilson

ISBN: 978-1-61728-266-9
© 2010 Nova Science Publishers, Inc.

Chapter 1

2008 ARTS EDUCATION ASSESSMENT FRAMEWORK

National Assessment of Educational Progress (NAEP)

DEVELOPMENT OF THE NAEP ARTS EDUCATION FRAMEWORK

The National Assessment of Educational Progress

The National Assessment of Educational Progress (NAEP) is the only nationally representative and continuing assessment of what America's students know and can do in various subject areas. Since 1969, assessments have been conducted to provide comprehensive information on student knowledge and skills at ages 9, 13, and 17 and, more recently, for students in grades 4, 8, and 12. Because the information on student performance and related factors is available to policymakers, parents, educators, and the general public, NAEP is an integral part of the nation's evaluation of the condition and progress of student achievement.

NAEP is a congressionally mandated project of the U.S. Department of Education's National Center for Education Statistics (NCES). In 1988, Congress created the National Assessment Governing Board to set policy for NAEP. The 26-member, broadly representative Board selects subject areas to be assessed, develops assessment objectives and specifications through a national process, and sets appropriate achievement goals, among other responsibilities.

The Arts Education Framework and Assessments

This framework was used to develop the 1997 and 2008 NAEP Arts Education Assessments. For 2008, NAEP tested students in music and visual arts based on a nationally representative sample of eighth-grade schools. Results of the 2008 arts assessment will be released in spring 2009. Due to budget constraints and the small percentage of schools with theater and dance programs, these arts disciplines were not assessed in 2008.

In 1997, the NAEP arts assessment was conducted nationally at grade 8. For music and visual arts, representative samples of public and nonpublic school students were assessed. For theater, a special targeted sample was selected from eighth-grade schools that offered theater courses and from students who took those courses. Dance was not assessed because only a small percentage of schools had regular dance programs.

Findings from the 1997 arts assessment were reported in several ways: a brief Highlights Report, a comprehensive Arts Report Card, a CD–ROM containing sample tasks and student responses, and an online report of the test development process. Additional information on these materials is available at http://nces.ed.gov/nationsreportcard.

The Framework Development Process

In January 1992, the Governing Board issued a request for proposals to develop an assessment framework and specifications for a planned 1997 Arts Education Assessment. The contract was awarded to the Council of Chief State School Officers (CCSSO), with the College Board and the Council for Basic Education as subcontractors. The 18-month project began in September 1992 and concluded in March 1994.

The purpose of the contract was to develop and recommend a framework and other design features for an arts education assessment that includes dance, music, theatre, and the visual arts. The recommended form of the assessment was designed by a 32-member planning committee with guidance from a steering committee. The planning committee was responsible for recommending the content and contributing to the assessment framework and other design documents. Composed of K–12 teachers, arts educators from higher education, practicing artists, assessment specialists, and lay persons, the planning committee was chaired by Frank Philip of CCSSO.

The 29-member steering committee was co-chaired by Ramsay Selden, director of the State Education Assessment Center at CCSSO and project director; and A. Graham Down, president of the Council for Basic Education. The committee included representatives from professional education organizations, parent groups, artist organizations, business, policymakers, and the public at large. The steering committee provided policy and procedural guidance during the project.

NAEP and National Standards: Cooperation and Coordination

The development of the NAEP Arts Education Assessment Framework coincided with the development of the *National Standards for Education in the Arts (National Standards)*. This confluence of a standards-setting process and its immediate application in creating a national assessment provide an unprecedented opportunity to align standards and assessment in a model for arts education.

The two projects—NAEP and the *National Standards*—have a special role in establishing the importance of the arts in the education of all American students.

The leadership of both groups has ensured that the projects will be coordinated in every aspect of the work, from crafting a common vision through matching schedules and sharing personnel. From the project's inception, the process has been predicated on the assumption that the *National Standards* and the NAEP assessment should reflect a common vision of arts education.

At the leadership level, A. Graham Down, chair of the oversight committee for the standards project, also co-chaired the steering committee for the assessment project. Seven members, or approximately one-fourth of the standards oversight committee, were also invited to serve on the steering committee for the assessment project. Frank Philip and Joan Peterson, who co-chaired the National Council of State Arts Education Consultants task force for the standards project, served as coordinator for the NAEP Arts assessment Project and consultant for the College Board (a subcontractor to CCSSO), respectively.

Each of the four subcommittees of the NAEP assessment planning committee included representatives from the writing task forces of the standards project and either the presi- dent or the president-elect of the national arts education professional organizations. Each executive director of the major national arts education organizations was a member of the steering committee of the assessment project.

The meeting schedule, the dates for hearings, and the release of drafts for the assessment project were aligned to follow similar events of the standards project. The standards project shared the developing drafts of the standards with the planning committee of the assessment project in a regular and timely fashion to ensure a smooth articulation between the two.

Development of the Framework

Issues

Ruth Mitchell and Dennie Palmer-Wolf, consultants to the project, wrote an issues paper that identified the major areas of concern for the assessment design. Published in early January 1993, the paper was designed to be the focus of the national hearings scheduled in February 1993. The paper helped frame significant questions for the assessment and placed them in a broader context for understanding the role and feasibility of a national assessment in the arts.

National Hearings

In considering the design of the proposed National Assessment for Arts Education, the project's management team decided to seek public input at two points in the development process:

- The February 1993 hearings were designed to gather responses and reactions to the issues paper. The San Francisco hearing was held in conjunction with a major arts education conference attended by many prominent writers and leaders of arts education. The Orlando, FL, hearing was scheduled for a time and location that allowed teachers, parents, and students to attend. The New York City hearing attracted the arts community from one of the country's major population centers.
- Hearings were conducted in Seattle, Chicago, and Washington, DC, in October 1993 to solicit input and reaction to a draft of the assessment framework. Appendix B contains a brief description of the hearings; a complete report is available from CCSSO.

STEERING COMMITTEE GUIDELINES

1. The assessment should affirm and articulate the arts as ways of knowing and forms of knowledge with a unique capacity to integrate the intellect, the emotions, and physical skills in the construction of meaning.
2. The assessment should honor the discrete disciplines (dance, music, theatre, visual arts), but should at the same time encourage students to see the artistic experience as a unified whole and make connections between the arts and other disciplines.
3. The NAEP assessment and national standards processes must work hand in hand.
4. Where possible, the assessment should examine and report on developing abilities so younger and older students exhibit stages in the development of the same capability.
5. The assessment should connect with students' real-life experiences so students can use their personal knowledge in areas such as street dance, their everyday experience with TV drama, or their understanding of traditional regional art forms and community arts resources.
6. The assessment should assess students' knowledge, attitudes, and performance in the modalities and forms of expression characteristic of the arts (music, dance, painting or drawing, acting) as well as verbal or written linguistic modes; that is, writing or talking about the arts.
7. The assessment should go beyond quantification to include critical judgment. An effort should be made to ensure that reporting includes descriptive information on student performance as well as numerical data.
8. The assessment should use a common list of background variables to recognize differences and inequities in school resources and the conditions related to achievement, such as teacher qualifications, instructional time in the arts, school structure, cultural and social background of the school community, and incentives. This recognition must be evident in reported data. Results have meaning only in terms of the availability and continuity of arts instruction.
9. The assessment should address both processes and products, and should expand the public's information about the importance of each.
10. The assessment should be based on a comprehensive vision of arts education and should communicate that vision clearly. The assessment should focus on what ought to be in arts education rather than what is, but idealism should be tempered with reality. Hence, exercises should model multifaceted and thoughtful activities without making unreasonable demands on time, materials, and human resources.
11. To stimulate support for arts education, the assessment should produce information useful to a variety of audiences—students, artists, teachers, and administrators; local, state, and national policymakers; and community members such as parents and business persons—and be disseminated in a variety of ways for different audiences.
12. The assessment should sample student performances under two conditions: a general sample reflecting universal expectations and a specialized sample for students in magnet and advanced programs at grade 12.
13. The assessment should reflect a pluralistic view of arts education in terms of both individual products and the cultural bases of the arts. It should be oriented toward the demonstration of student learning, be sensitive to a variety of instructional approaches, include the range of contemporary theories evident in arts education, and include examples of appropriate exercises addressing universal themes.

Next Steps

The consensus process produced the design documents and recommendations. This framework describes the proposed assessment. The specifications document explains the details for developing the assessment instrument. The consensus work also produced documents that suggest the nature and range of background information that should be collected along with the assessment and a set of strategies for reporting the results to the public and to the field. The second phase of the process began with a contract that NCES awarded to the Educational Testing Service in May 1994 to design the assessment exercises. Field testing of the exercises was scheduled for February 1995 and February 1996.

Recent Changes in the Assessment Schedule

A complete and comprehensive assessment in any subject area depends on funding from Congress. Because of a funding shortfall, the 1994 math and science assessments were postponed until 1996. In September 1994, the Governing Board executive committee recommended that the arts assessment be rescheduled for 1997. This would provide the opportunity for a two-stage field test in 1995 and 1996. The expanded field test would allow thorough development of the many complex, performance-based assessment tasks.

Guidelines for the Project

The steering committee's first task was to develop guidelines to inform the planning committee's work on drafting the framework. A major issue confronted the committee: how to balance "what is" in U.S. arts education with "what ought to be." Although the issue cannot be resolved completely, the creative tension it has generated continues to be a source of positive energy for the assessment design.

Another important issue must be mentioned. Early in the process, the steering committee insisted on a policy of inclusion in arts education. This means that the proposed NAEP assessment should reinforce the promise of arts education for all, including those students whose physical and mental abilities need additional support for artistic expression. Engaging the wheelchair-bound child in dance movement, or reviewing the theatrical performance of the hearing-impaired middle school student, for example, are recommended for the administration of the assessment.

NAEP ARTS PROJECT STAFF AND COMMITTEES

Steering Committee
Adrienne Bailey
Educational Consultant
Chicago, IL

John Bonaiuto
Secretary of Education
South Dakota Department of Education
Pierre, SD

Harry Clark
President
International NETWORK of Performing
and Visual Arts Schools
Pittsburgh, PA

Nicolette Clarke
Executive Director
Vermont Council on the Arts
Montpelier, VT

Elliott Eisner
Professor of Education and Art
Stanford University
Stanford, CA

Harriett Fulbright
President
Center for Arts in the Basic Curriculum
Washington, DC

Eduardo Garcia
Arts Education Consultant
Plainsboro, NJ

Keith Geiger
President
National Education Association
Washington, DC

Kay Goodwin
Arts Advocate
Ripley, WV

Michael Green
President
National Academy of Recording
Arts and Sciences
Burbank, CA

Richard Gurin
President and CEO
Binney & Smith, Inc.
Easton, PA

Ronne Hartfield
Executive Director of Museum
Education
Art Institute of Chicago
Chicago, IL

Tom Hatfield
Executive Director
National Art Education Association
Reston, VA

Jerome Hausman
Director, Center for Arts Curriculum
Planning and Evaluation
Urban Gateways
Chicago, IL

Samuel Hope
Executive Director
National Office for Arts Accreditation
in Higher Education
Reston, VA

Rebecca Hutton
Executive Director
National Dance Association
Reston, VA

Joan Katz
Director, Elementary/
Secondary Service
Public Broadcasting Service
Alexandria, VA

Robert Lloyd
Dean
Visual Studies Institute for Teachers
Andover, MA

John Mahlmann
Executive Director
Music Educators National Conference
Reston, VA

Greg McCaslin
Director, Education and Information

New York Foundation for the Arts
New York, NY

Michael Moore
President
Association of Institutes for
Aesthetic Education
Bowling Green, OH

David O'Fallon
Staff Director, Arts Education
Partnership Working Group
The Kennedy Center
Washington, DC

Bethany Rogers
Coalition of Essential Schools
Brown University
Providence, RI

John Terrell Scott
Professor of Art/Artist
Xavier University
New Orleans, LA

Kent Seidel
Director, Teacher Services and Advocacy
Educational Theatre Association
Cincinnati, OH

Albert Shanker
President
American Federation of Teachers
Washington, DC

Carol Sterling
Director, Arts Education
American Council for the Arts
New York, NY

Kathryn Whitefill
President-Elect
National PTA
Pasadena, TX

Barbara Wills
Executive Director
American Alliance for Theatre and Education
Tacoma, WA

Kelvin Yazzie
Artist
Flagstaff, AZ

Washington, DC

Advisors to Planning and Steering Committees

Paul Lehman
Senior Associate Dean
University of Michigan
Ann Arbor, MI

Brent Wilson
Professor
Penn State University
University Park, PA

Planning Committee

Angelique Acevedo
Artist/Teacher, Arts Curriculum
Integration Specialist
Bear Creek High School
Lakewood, CO

Carolyn Adams
Dance Teacher, Harlem Dance Foundation
Director, Dance Program
City College of New York
Chair, Dance/USA's National Task
Force on Dance Education
New York, NY

Marianna Adams[*]
Curator of Education
Museum of Art
Fort Lauderdale, FL

Donna Kay Beattie[*]
Asst. Professor of Art Education

Brigham Young University
Provo, UT

Ellyn Berk
Arts Consultant
New York, NY

Deborah Brzoska[*]
Fine Arts Coordinator
Vancouver School District
Vancouver, WA

Linda Gregoric Cook
Registered Drama Therapist
New Orleans Schools
New Orleans, LA

Jennifer Davidson[*]
Arts Education Consultant
Oakland Schools
Waterford, MI

Meredith Davis
Professor/Head, Department of
Graphic Design
North Carolina State University
Raleigh, NC

Maxine DeBruyn
Dance Chair
Hope College
Holland, MI

Ed Gero
Director of the Ensemble
George Mason University Actor
Shakespeare Theatre
Washington, DC

MacArthur Goodwin
Education Associate
South Carolina Department of Education
Columbia, SC

Robert W. Gross
Multimedia/Assessment Specialist
Fine Arts Department Chair
Carl Sandburg High School
Orlando Park, IL

Mark Hansen
President
National Art Education Association
Arts Resource Coordinator
Forest Lake Public Schools
Forest Lake, MN

Jorge Huerta
Professor of Theatre
University of California, San Diego
La Jolla, CA

Sandra June McCollister
Assistant Professor, Art Education
Southwest Texas University
San Marcos, TX

Claudette Morton[*]
Director
Rural Education Center
Western Montana College
Dillon, MT

Nancy Norwood
Media Arts Instructor
Minnesota Center for Arts Education
Golden Valley, MN

Barry Oreck[*]
Director of In-School Programs
Arts Connection
New York, NY

Nancy Pistone
Arts Education Consultant
Pittsburgh, PA

Theresa Purcell
President
National Dance Association
Dance/Physical Education Specialist

Brunswick Acres Elementary School
Kendall Park, NJ

Janice Ross
Dance Lecturer
Stanford University
Stanford, CA

Nancy Roucher
Co-Director
Florida Institute for Art Education
Sarasota, FL

Laura Gardner Salazar
President
American Alliance for Theatre Education
Professor of Theatre
Grand Valley State University
Allendale, MI

Will Schmid
President
Music Educators National Conference
Professor/University of Wisconsin-Milwaukee
Milwaukee, WI

Laurel Serleth
Drama Specialist
Evanston Schools District 65
Evanston, IL

Scott Shuler[*]
Arts Education Consultant
Connecticut Department of Education
Hartford, CT

Suzanne Shull
Music Teacher
Ridgeview Middle School
Atlanta, GA

Ruth Ann Teague
Music Teacher
Arthur P. Milton Elementary School

Gary, IN

Cheryl Tibbals[*]
Director of Assessment Administration
New Standards Project
Oakland, CA

Jorja Turnipseed
Professor of Music Education
Mississippi State University]
Mississippi State, MS

Willie Anthony Waters
Conductor
Miami, FL

Advisors to Planning and Steering Committees

Paul Lehman
Senior Associate Dean
University of Michigan
Ann Arbor, MI

Brent Wilson
Professor
Penn State University
University Park, PA

Management Team
  Project Staff

  Ramsay Selden
  Project Director
  Council of Chief State School Officers
  Washington, DC

  Frank Philip
  Consensus Coordinator
  Council of Chief State School Officers
  Washington, DC

  Jon Quam
  Project Advisor
  Council of Chief State School Officers
  Washington, DC

Ed Roeber
Project Advisor
Council of Chief State School Officers
Washington, DC

Bonnie Verrico
Administrative Assistant
Council of Chief State School Officers
Washington, DC

Project Officer

Mary Crovo
Assistant Director for Test Development
National Assessment Governing Board
Washington, DC

Subcontractors
Graham Down
President
Council for Basic Education
Washington, DC

Stephanie Soper
Program Manager
Council for Basic Education
Washington, DC

Ruth Mitchell
Assessment Consultant
Washington, DC

Robert Orrill
Executive Director, Academic Affairs
The College Board
New York, NY

Carol Myford
Research Scientist/ETS
Consultant/The College Board
Princeton, NJ

Joan Peterson
California Department of Education
Consultant/The College Board

Sacramento, CA

Dennis Palmer Wolf
Executive Director/PACE
Harvard University
Consultant/The College Board
Consultant/Council for Basic Education
Cambridge, MA

Liaisons for Funding Organizations
Doug Herbert
Director, Arts in Education Program
National Endowment for the Arts
Washington, DC

Mary Ann Stankiewicz
Consultant/The Getty Center for
Education in the Arts
Assistant Vice President for
Academic Affairs
Ringling School of Art and Design
Sarasota, FL

1. THE ARTS IN U.S. EDUCATION

The Importance of NAEP to Arts Education

This is an important moment for American culture. The arts are becoming part of the national vision of what all students should know and be able to do. The evidence is clear:

- National standards for student achievement have been developed in the arts in a process that paralleled the standards discussions being held in mathematics, language arts, science, history, and other areas.
- The standards process, while demanding, has generated important discussion and debate about which art forms, what kind of knowledge, and what skills in the arts are important for all students.
- The Governing Board—with funding from the National Endowment for the Arts, an independent federal agency, in collaboration with the Getty Center for Education in the Arts, a program of the J. Paul Getty Trust—commissioned the development of this framework for a planned national assessment of student performance in the arts in 1997. The present document, the framework, sets out for the educational community and the public the scope of what will be included and how the arts will be assessed.

- The framework process is a bold one. Pushing beyond the limits of the arts and music assessments of the 197 0s, this framework calls for the inclusion of theatre and dance as well. This work led to lively discussions of the importance of design and the media arts.

Such recognition brought not only long-awaited satisfaction, but responsibility. Faced with the significant opportunity to create an assessment solely about learning in the arts, the steering and planning committees met the challenge with a proposed assessment that is, at once, feasible, fair, and wise. The vision for the assessment—this framework—has two noticeable characteristics. First, the committees have wrestled with the difficult central issues of arts education. Second, they have proposed a plan that would recognize vision in the face of current practice.

The process for the NAEP arts education framework is founded on a vision of a society that believes the arts are essential to every child's complete development. Throughout their lives, they will draw from artistic experience and knowledge as a means of understanding what happens both inside and outside their own skin, just as they use mathematical, scientific, historical, and other frameworks for understanding. They are not expected to become talented artists. The expectation is that they will experience enough of the discipline, challenge, and joy of creating in different art forms to intimately understand the human significance of dance, music, theatre, and the visual arts.

The NAEP assessment will help to realize this vision. Assessment has the unique ability to fix attention in education. "What you test is what you get"—and its corollary, "you don't get what you don't test"—are well proved in our educational system. As the only national assessment in the United States, where our radically decentralized education system resists the comprehensive national examinations found in other countries, NAEP assessments are noticed when results are published biennially.

A group of art teachers once asked Alan Sandler, an architect long involved with education, "So why do we have to assess at all? We know our students' work. What's the point?" Sandler replied, "Good assessment is like good architecture. It directs people's attention and their activity in worthwhile ways."

NAEP does not assess students individually or report individual student results; instead, it reports on student achievement in general in a subject area. NAEP results show, for example, that students can handle the mechanics of writing fairly well, but do not express ideas persuasively; that they are reasonably proficient at routine computations, but do not perform well in applying mathematical concepts; and that their knowledge of history seems to leave them without a firm sense of chronology. The information provided by NAEP has had a discernible effect on the present educational reform: Being included in NAEP makes an important statement about the need for all children in our country to obtain the special benefits of learning that only the arts provide.

The Role of Arts Education

The standards, public attention, and this framework itself together make a statement about the role of the arts in U.S. education: They are as basic as literacy and numeracy.

They are basic because they bestow meaning on the world through movement, sound, color, and gesture—nonverbal systems of communication essential to understanding. We as human beings shape our world by transforming the activities of the physical body into meaning that defines human experience.

The arts are basic in a purely educational sense. They are essential to education reform because they give meaning to learning. They are an important vehicle for learning the skills so prized by reformers in both the education and business communities—problem solving, higher-order thinking, flexibility, persistence, and cooperation. The arts make schools better places to be, places where acceptance and encouragement foster growth. Students who learn to value the discipline of the arts equip themselves for challenges in work and in life.

However, to value the arts as basic and as instrumental to learning other things is to sell them short. Through music, dance, theatre, and visual arts, students become part of the human heritage of creativity. Through the arts, we touch transcendence and go beyond the mundane and the practical to the eternal and ideal. Participation itself expands the boundaries of the arts, so that every student—every person—who produces, performs, or responds is adding to the body of artistic wealth. This is the power of the arts: a sense of contributing to an eternal conversation reaching backward and forward beyond time.

No child in an American school should be deprived of the opportunity to see, hear, touch, and understand the accumulated wisdom of our artistic heritage, and to make his or her own contributions through productions and performances. Education can no longer be defined without the arts.

The Shape of the Arts Education NAEP

When the framework development process began in early 1993, an issues paper posed a series of questions. Answers that were forged out of a year of spirited discussion and thoughtful consideration are provided to the most important of those questions.

- *How can the NAEP arts assessment combine realism and vision? The task of designing an arts assessment is complicated by the fact that currently the arts are often a marginal experience for students at the elementary and middle school levels and are an elective subject in high school. In addition, many schools have cut arts education to the bone: It is occasional, rarely involves dance or theatre, and seldom combines in-school and out-of-school arts experiences. In some cases—arts magnet schools or schools that have elected to use the arts to motivate learning—arts education is abundant. Given this disparity of opportunity, how is it possible to design a national assessment for all students?*

This question was a point of concern and discussion for a year. Throughout the NAEP framework process, the committees struggled with the tension between "what is" and "what ought to be." Should only those programs that predominate in many schools be assessed? To do so would omit dance, theatre, and in some cases elementary arts instruction altogether. On the other hand, should we assess as if all children continually studied dance, music, theatre, and the visual arts beginning in kindergarten, and specialized in at least one art form in their high school years? To assess only on this assumption would risk frustration, since NAEP takes a representative sample of students from various types of schools and school populations across the country.

We need to know both kinds of information. Both are essential for understanding the "fit," or what is happening in the schools today, and the "gap," or how far students' abilities and knowledge are from the ideal. The information gained from the NAEP Arts Education Assessment will indicate where arts education needs to be strengthened and extended so future students can fully realize their potential.

- *What is the model of arts learning that will inform the kinds of exercises and examples developed for the assessment? Traditionally, only production and performance have been assessed, but many teachers, scholars, and artists would argue that there is an important place for aesthetics and for the social, cultural, and historical contexts of art. However, given this more diversified notion of artistic understanding, are these skills considered separable or integrated? Any assessment design will portray and broadcast an image of arts education.*

The NAEP framework process and the *National Standards* have framed a vision of arts education that integrates the aesthetic, social, cultural, and historical contexts of the arts with the knowledge and skills necessary to participate in the arts. Skills will not be considered as separable, and it has been decided to report the achievement of students as a whole according to the various artistic processes, not on separate scales for isolated knowledge or technical skills. The image of arts education portrayed by the NAEP Arts Education Assessment will be as close to a vision of the arts as basic, unified, and pervasive as practically possible.

- *What methods of assessment should be used? Portfolios, performances, written responses, interviews, and observations can and have been a part of assessment programs. But they are more costly and labor intensive than multiple-choice and short-answer questions. What kind of design decisions does this lead to?*

Many arts educators worry that an assessment of the arts will artificially quantify those essential aspects of the arts that seem unquantifiable—inspiration, imagination, and creativity. This framework has been designed to honor the essential aspects of the arts as much as is compatible with the constraints of funding and time available in schools for the NAEP assessment.

All advocates of arts education can take considerable comfort in the fact that longstanding assessments used by the arts—portfolios and performances—are now being adopted by other disciplines. Artists have always selected their works for portfolios and assessed their own work as they did so. Juries, panels, and audiences have always assessed performing artists. Therefore, the problem does not involve protecting the arts from inappropriate testing techniques, but extending the legitimate use of portfolios and performance measures beyond the theatre, the concert hall, the studio, and the individual classroom to the national level.

Performance assessments (the generic term for the class of assessments that is beginning to augment and, in some instances, replace conventional paper-and-pencil, machinescorable tests) have a long history in assessing the arts. It is entirely appropriate for the NAEP arts assessment to continue to move national assessments forward, much as they did by using many performance exercises in the 1970s NAEP visual arts and music assessments.

Consequently, the assessment will consist largely of multiple, related exercises organized around an activity. For example, in a theatre exercise, a group of students might assume characters and act out a scene from a story they have read or heard. This is a production exercise. Then they may respond individually in writing to open-ended questions about what they might change in their characters if they could do the scene again and why they would make those changes. The students might also respond to multiple-choice items asking them to identify elements of the scene. Questions and multiple-choice items should always be embedded in an exercise and not administered in isolation. The production exercise and the open-ended and multiple-choice items would all be scored separately.

The significant knowledge and skills unique to each domain should be embedded in an exercise in a way that clearly shows their application or use. Students might be asked to perform a movement typical of a traditional dance and thus to show by posture, alignment, and movement that the student knows and can apply the form and cultural context of the dance.

A special study was proposed to explore the use of portfolios. An existing successful national assessment using portfolios is the Advanced Placement Studio Art Portfolio Evaluation, which shows feasibility for such an assessment. However, the committees decided that the financial resources of the assessment would be better used in gathering information across the widest possible range of arts education than on an expensive and smaller portfolio project.

- *Should the definition be cut so sharply into four strands? What place, for instance, will be made for design and for media arts—courses that enroll many students and that link the arts to important fields like communication and industry? And what about the interdisciplinary nature of much artistic work: musical theatre; architecture; and the writing, design, and illustration of books?*

The inclusion of all four strands—dance, music, theatre, and visual arts—in the assessment is already a step forward. Design and media arts will be included as integral parts of these strands. A special study was proposed to explore the interdisciplinary nature of the arts by answering important questions about the problems interdisciplinary work poses: Where can you find truly interdisciplinary action (as opposed to layers of separate disciplines) and how can it be assessed?

- *Whose art? A Mark Morris performance folded country-western music and clog dancing into forms and sequences that owe much to George Balanchine and Martha Graham. An audience would understand the stark costumes and pale faces of a Paula Jossa Jones piece more fully if they had seen and thought about Asian performance forms like butto theater. These are only two of countless illustrations that contemporary American arts depend on to understand and borrow work that comes from world cultures and from all quadrants of American life. If this is to be a national assessment, how can its samples and requests reflect not only the diversity of children taking the assessment, but also the pluralism that American culture exhibits?*

The samples of possible stimulus materials will demonstrate the commitment of the NAEP arts framework process to embracing the pluralism that enriches our national arts. The largest possible range of the arts has been recommended as the field from which assessments can be designed.

- *Who will be sampled for the assessment? Will learning about the arts be assessed wherever it occurs, or only if students have had formal arts classes? How will students who play in garage bands or who attend dance academies outside of school be identified and assessed?*

A third special study (the two others were special studies of interdisciplinary learning in the arts and portfolios) was proposed to look at the accomplishments of students in special programs such as arts magnet schools and districts with exemplary regular arts education programs. The nature and extent of student learning in the arts will be gleaned from background questions that are factored into the information gained from the assessment itself when the NAEP results are reported.

- *Learning and production in the arts require time. Dancers and musicians must warm up before performing, visual artists may need to mix paints, actors must think themselves into character. How will it be possible to examine student performance in various aspects of an arts discipline (for example, performing, choreography, response to performance, or criticism) in ways that are safe and valid?*

The framework recommends to the designers of the NAEP assessments that the nature of the arts should be the guiding factor in specifying the shape and length of the assessments. It is expected that time for preparation and warmup will be allowed in addition to the time spent in production exercises and answering open-ended questions.

The task of constructing a NAEP assessment in arts education is both simple and complex. It is simple because there is apparent substantial agreement about the ends of an arts education as a result of the discussions and deliberations in the standards development and the NAEP framework process. On the other hand, it is complex because of the difficulty in constructing an assessment that accurately appraises student achievement on a national level with all the variables of experience and environment, and delivers it in a timely, cost-efficient manner.

For some, the NAEP assessment will be too soft; for others, it will be too hard. For some, it will go too far; for others, not far enough. Such is the nature of a process that strives for consensus (agreement at certain levels of acceptance) rather than absolute agreement (a process that builds from a broad base of national input).

As a large-scale national assessment, NAEP can accomplish certain goals in understanding what K–12 students know and can do that no other assessment can accomplish. It has a special role to play in its ability to define and refine an essence of knowledge and experience in the arts from the rich and diverse array of possibility. But NAEP cannot and should not be the sole assessment of arts education. Nor should it be thought of as the standard-by-standard measuring instrument for the voluntary *National Standards*. Many of the standards will have to be examined in other assessment formats over a longer duration than is possible with NAEP. However, it is one significant and unique measure that takes its place beside important work going on in many states, universities, private organizations, local districts, and classrooms.

During the course of framework development, the committees examined large-scale assessments from other countries, including Australia, Great Britain, the Netherlands, and Scotland. Much has been learned about the challenges in dealing with these complex subjects and the ways in which they might be assessed using authentic and valid means.

2. THE CONTENT AND PROCESSES OF THE ARTS

Because the assessment depends on a precise definition of what students should know and be able to do, this chapter first defines the processes and content of the arts in general and then lists the content and processes specific to each of the arts disciplines.

Definitions

As defined by both this assessment framework and the voluntary *National Standards,* arts education refers to dance, music, theatre, and the visual arts. The committees also felt it was important to include within these categories functional design areas such as architecture, industrial design, graphic design, and the media arts. In the discussion below, it is assumed that all four of the arts disciplines are included. It is also assumed that the processes and the content identified are applied in combination and are always integrated at various levels.

Processes

Creating refers to generating original art. This may include, but should not be limited to, the expression of a student's unique and personal ideas, feelings, and responses in the form of a visual image, a character, a written or improvised dramatic work, or the composition or improvisation of a piece of music or a dance.

Performing/interpreting means performing an existing work—a process that calls on the student's interpretive or re-creative skills. Typically, performing an existing work does not apply to the visual arts, where reproducing an artist's existing work is not central. However, it does suggest the engagement and motivation involved in creating a work of art.

Responding includes many varieties, including an audience member's response to a performance and the interactive response between a student and a particular medium. The response is usually a combination of affective, cognitive, and physical behavior. Responding involves a level of perceptual or observational skill; a description, analysis, or interpretation on the part of the respondent; and sometimes a judgment or evaluation based on criteria that may be self-constructed or commonly held by a group or culture. Responding calls on higher-order thinking and is central to the creative process. Although a response is usually thought of as verbal (oral or written), responses can and should also be conveyed nonverbally or in the art forms themselves. Major works of art in all traditions engage artists in a dialog that crosses generations.

Content

Two major components of learning are expected of students who study the arts. Students should gain knowledge and understanding about the arts, including the personal, historical, cultural, and social contexts for works; and should gain *perceptual, technical, expressive, and intellectual/reflective skills*. Both components are found in each arts discipline.

When students use the artistic processes of creating, performing, and responding, they draw from various kinds of knowledge and understanding about the arts to construct meaning. Students need to be able to place the arts in broader contexts to fully appreciate their significance. These contexts include a *personal* perspective, an understanding of how the arts fit into the students' immediate *society* and broader *culture*, and a *historical* perspective. Students need knowledge of *aesthetics* to understand varied concepts and philosophies of the nature, meaning, and intrinsic value of the arts that people from different cultures and periods have formulated and held. Students also need to know about and understand the different *forms* of expression, the *structure* of each, and the various technical processes by which art forms can be created.

The acquisition and application of skills determine the quality of the learning experience. Without the necessary skills, creating, performing, and responding cannot take place. *Perceptual skills* are needed to collect the sensory stimuli and discern nuance. *Technical skills* are needed to produce the work with quality. *Expressive skills* are needed to add a unique and personal nature to the work. *Intellectual/reflective skills* are needed to test different creative possibilities, solve artistic problems, refine one's work, and help each student consider the arts thoughtfully and beyond superficial qualities.

Throughout the processes of creating, performing, and responding in the arts, students are called on to apply knowledge and skills simultaneously. Knowledge and skills rarely function in isolation; one implies the other. Few important artistic behaviors are entirely based on knowledge, and arguably, none involve only skills. A skill cannot be mastered in the absence of relevant knowledge. Skills and techniques (knowing how) are infused with creating, performing, and responding. Students involved in these processes not only gain knowledge *about* the arts, but they also learn *through* and *within* the arts. Similarly, students use this knowledge of aesthetics and history as they create, perform, or respond in the arts. More knowledge is often gained as students engage in artistic processes.

The framework provides a general vision for the four arts disciplines and the flexibility to accommodate differences among them. Each discipline fits into the grand scheme of the framework, preserving the distinguishing characteristics of each medium.

For example, teachers and artists working in the visual arts place a high value on first-hand creative expression and response to visual media, but often give lower priority to the performance or duplication of existing art. Music education, on the other hand, has typically placed great emphasis on the performance of existing music and on students' responses to performance and through the performance. K–12 music education programs historically have minimized their emphasis on students' original musical compositions. Theatre views creating and performing as a combined act, and views the response of the audience, director, actors, and designers to the work as integral to the development of a performance. For dance, the processes of creation, performance, and critical evaluation of the work, while all present, often merge.

Exhibit 1 illustrates each art discipline's approach to the common framework. Each cell represents a subscale in which results may be reported. The columns will be summarized to report a comprehensive score for each arts area.

Content Specific to Each of the Four Arts

Dance

Dance incorporates creation, performance, and response. When actively involved in these processes, students not only learn *about* dance, but they also learn *through* and *within* dance. Dance skills and technique weave throughout the processes of creating, performing, and responding. Students use and apply knowledge of different dance forms and styles (aesthetics) along with personal, social, cultural, and historical contexts whether they are creating, performing, or responding.

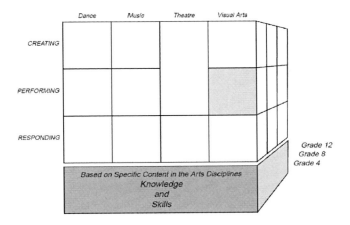

Exhibit 1. The framework matrix

Creating in Dance

Students must have the ability to create dance and to express their understanding through the language of movement. To convey ideas and feelings, students make use of movement and elements of choreography. They reveal in their dances insights into themselves, their social and cultural worlds, and their concepts of nature and the arts. Through a knowledge of vocabulary and compositional structures, students are able to collaborate with others in shared expression and the creation of dance.

The following framework depicts the expectations of dance education.

Dance Assessment Framework
Arts Processes in Dance
Creating—*When creating in dance, students:*
• *Invent solutions to movement problems, generating and selecting from alternatives.* • *Follow improvisational and compositional structures.* • *Collaborate to achieve solutions.*
Performing—*When performing in dance, students:*
• Accurately recall and reproduce movement. • Demonstrate physical technique. • Communicate through movement (expression).
Responding—*When perceiving, analyzing, interpreting, critiquing, and judging dance, students:*
• *Identify compositional elements and notice details.* • *Identify contexts (stylistic, cultural, social, historical) of the dance.* • *Make informed critical observations about the dance's and the dancer's technical and artistic components.*
Based on Specific Content From Dance
Knowledge—*Students apply knowledge of:* Skills—*Students apply cognitive, affective, and motor skills, including:*

Context: • *Personal* • *Social* • *Cultural* • *Historical* Aesthetics Form and Structure Processes	Perceptual Intellectual/Reflective Expressive Technical

Performing Dance

Dance uses the human body as both an instrument and a thinking medium. Students progressively develop dance knowledge, skills, techniques, and responses that allow them to use their bodies with confidence, success, and insight. Physical skills in dance include coordination, agility, flexibility, balance, strength, and control of movement. Through dance, students gain spatial awareness, bodily awareness, musicality, and an increased ability to observe and refine movement. Dance also fosters an awareness of historical, cultural, and stylistic elements involved in the creation and performance of movement. In dance, the cognitive, motor, and affective domains operate interdependently and simultaneously. Students apply intellectual skills throughout the process of creating and performing.

Responding to Dance

Responding to dance must include the vital dimension of experiencing, knowing, and thoughtfully interpreting dance. Whether responding to one's own dance or to the dance of others, students should develop new levels of understanding, insight, and perceptual acuity as a consequence of interacting with dance.

Knowledge and Skills

In dance, knowledge and skills are inextricably connected. Students combine both attributes to express themselves through movement and to create dance works that exist always within larger cultural contexts. Likewise, knowledge *about* dance is often learned *through* the act and skill of dancing.

The content for dance integrates knowledge and skills. It includes the use of a movement and verbal vocabulary to compose and describe dance. Students are expected to know and use dance forms and structures and to be able to apply effective criteria in the critique of dance.

Music

Music is a form of artistic expression communicated through the medium of sound. Music processes include creating (composing and improvising), performing (playing, singing, and conducting), and responding (listening, moving, analyzing, and critiquing).

Music uses a unique set of symbols. Performance of music demands the integrated development of intellectual/cognitive, feeling/affective, and psychomotor skills.

Creating

In music, performers are creative when interpreting a piece of music. However, for purposes of this assessment framework, creating refers specifically to improvising and composing new music. When improvising, musicians spontaneously create an original work or variation within certain limits or guidelines established by the particular style in which they are performing. For example, a person improvising in the blues operates creatively within the limits of the blues style. When composing music, students usually have the freedom to create what their imagination dictates, including the choice of any style or genre. Students should also have time to evaluate and revise their work before presenting it to the public.

Performing/Interpreting

All students should be able to sing and to perform on instruments. For purposes of the national assessment, performing refers to the process of singing and playing existing musical works (repertoire). The performing process involves a wide variety of critical judgments and sophisticated understanding of musical syntax to develop an interpretation and a performance of that interpretation. As with all the arts, students are constantly applying and exercising higher order thinking, such as analyzing, synthesizing, and evaluating, while creating and performing music.

Responding

Although composers and performers respond to the music they are creating and performing, for purposes of NAEP the response process focuses on the role of the audience. Composers, improvisers, and performers always seek to elicit a response from their audience. Students therefore must learn to understand and respond to music.

Individuals respond to music in three general ways: physically, intellectually, and emotionally. Physical responses to music involve movement, such as dance or other rhythmic movement. Intellectual responses to music include activities such as labeling, analyzing, classifying, placing a work within a particular context, and making critical judgments about a work or performance. Emotional responses are the wide range of affect. All three types of responses play an essential role in making individual judgments about music.

The student expectations for music are illustrated in the following framework.

Music Assessment Framework
Arts Processes for Music

Creating—*When improvising, composing, or arranging music, students:*
- Apply historical, cultural, and aesthetic understanding by creating stylistically appropriate alterations, variations, and improvisations.
- Use standard and/or nonstandard notation to express original ideas.
- Evaluate, refine, and revise successive versions of original work.
- Demonstrate skill and expressiveness in the choice and use of musical elements.
- Present the created work for others.

Performing—*When singing or playing music with musical instruments, students:*
- Select appropriate repertoire.
- Apply skill by performing with technical accuracy.
- Develop an appropriate and expressive interpretation by applying understanding of structure and cultural and historical contexts of music.
- Read musical notation accurately.
- Evaluate, refine, and revise the performance.
- Present the performance for others.

Responding—*When perceiving, analyzing, interpreting, critiquing, and judging music, students:*
- Select repertoire for listening.
- Analyze the elements and structure of music.
- Compare and contrast various musical styles.
- Identify formal and expressive qualities that distinguish a particular style of music.
- Place music within its cultural and historical context.
- Make critical judgments about technical and expressive qualities of musical performances and compositions.
- Use movement or words to interpret and describe personal responses to music.

Based on Specific Content in Music

Knowledge—*Students apply knowledge of:* **Skills**—*Students apply cognitive, affective, and motor skills, including:*

Context:	Perceptual
• *Personal*	Intellectual/Reflective
• *Social*	Expressive
• *Cultural*	Technical
• *Historical*	
Aesthetics	
Form and Structure	
Processes	

The Artistic Process of Music as a Whole

NAEP will assess students' ability to carry out the processes—creating, performing, and responding—each of which consists of several essential components or steps. For example, all three processes involve analyzing and evaluating. These three processes also require students to understand the syntax of music as well as cultural and historical contexts.

Knowledge and Skills

As with all the arts, knowledge and skills in music are so closely intertwined that it is nearly impossible to separate them.

Music knowledge includes the contexts of music, the form and structure of music, and the musical processes. Knowing musical context includes understanding the historical period, style, and culture in which a work is created; the performance traditions of that time or place; and the appropriate aesthetic criteria for judging the quality of the work and its performance.

Knowing form and structure includes understanding the building blocks of music: the materials, notations, elements, and forms of musical works. Knowing musical processes includes understanding the sequence and criteria for judgments involved in developing a new work, performing an existing work, or developing an opinion about a work or performance heard.

Music skills enable individuals to apply what they know by creating, performing, or responding to music. Technique is students' physical ability to transform their musical ideas into new creations or performances that accurately convey those ideas. Although technique is important to the processes of creating and performing, other skills are equally important. Perceptual skills enable the student to hear and interpret the details that make up music. These skills allow students to recall music in the mind even when it is not aurally present. Expressive skills give the work the meaning and feeling that moves the listener. Such skills also provide the basis for recognizing and responding to expression when it is present in a work or performance.

Creating and Performing

Different theatre processes call for different creative processes. All call for imaging, conceiving, and generating. In addition, playwriting requires the use of the first three processes to create character, story, and dialog. Acting calls for discovering and developing emotion and circumstances for a character. Designing calls for discovering, developing, and organizing an environment. To direct, students must analyze a script and develop an interpretation by organizing the time, place, spaces, and rhythms of a production. Creating in filmmaking and television demands the development and organization of the elements of theatre as well as the special elements of the medium.

Performing is central to theatre studies. Performing is the evidence of creating; it is the process viewed and heard by an audience. Performing is a highly complex collaborative activity in which the performer is aware of the audience and responds and adjusts the performance accordingly. The ways of learning demanded by performance are equally complex, requiring the interplay of all the processes noted in creating. Performing is impossible to assess through any means other than the processes themselves.

Theatre

Theatre is rooted in religious festival and the universal impulse of humans to play, imitate, create, and share ideas and feelings. Much of the joy of the theatre lies in bringing together diverse people, ideas, and artists in the interaction of production elements, performers, and the audience. A social art form, theatre reveals both the human condition and the human experience. It transports players and audiences through time and space.

In theatre, creating and performing are so closely related that the assessment will combine creating and performing as the framework below suggests.

Theatre Assessment Framework
Arts Processes for Theatre
Creating/Performing—*When creating and performing in theatre, students:*
• Develop scripts and scenarios. • Develop characters through an acting process. • Make design and technical choices to communicate locale and mood for dramatic material for theatre, film, and television. • Direct by interpreting dramatic texts and organizing time and people in planning and rehearsing improvised and scripted scenes.
Creating/Performing—*When creating and performing in theatre, students:*
• Develop scripts and scenarios. • Develop characters through an acting process. • Make design and technical choices to communicate locale and mood for dramatic material for theatre, film, and television. • Direct by interpreting dramatic texts and organizing time and people in planning and rehearsing improvised and scripted scenes.
Responding—*When perceiving, analyzing, interpreting, critiquing, and judging works in theatre, students:*
• Describe and analyze artistic choices in their own work and construct meaning. • Describe and compare elements, styles, genre, media, and dramatic literature. • Place work in context (personal, social, historical, and cultural). • Evaluate performances as audience and critic.
Based on Specific Content From Theatre
Knowledge—*Students apply knowledge of:* Skills—*Students apply cognitive, affective, and motor skills, including:*

Context: • *Personal* • *Social* • *Cultural* • *Historical* Aesthetics Form and Structure Processes	Perceptual Intellectual/Reflective Expressive Technical

Responding

Responding refers to students' reactions both as spectators to other's work and reflecting on their own work. They respond to outside artists and performers and those in their own school. They examine artistic choices in ideas, stories, scripts, designs, and actions by explaining, describing, clarifying, comparing, and evaluating. They apply their knowledge of the theatre and their analytical skills to determine which elements are successful in a performance. However, responding in theatre is more than analysis; it involves emotional and intuitive behaviors as well. Students become responsive audience members of theatrical performances, films, and television presentations. They recognize a variety of theatrical genres and styles and identify and compare them in theatre, film, and television. They reflect on how theatre creates meaning in their lives and in the lives of others now and in the past. Students describe the role and influence of theatre, film, and television in their lives and relate the impact of theatre and television in their locality, in their nation, and in the world.

Knowledge

Knowledge means knowing about the art of theatre—its historical, cultural, social, and personal contexts; its forms and structure; how it creates meaning; and its aesthetic qualities. Students understand the literary, visual, aural, oral, kinesthetic, and psychological aspects of a theatrical event. They are able to engage in self-criticism and consider form, structure, contexts, and aesthetic responses.

Skills

Skills are the abilities associated with the technical, perceptual, and expressive processes of theatre. This category includes activities such as creating a text, acting, staging, designing, and articulating a response. Abilities to create, perform, and respond in the theatre are predicated on the application of both knowledge and skills simultaneously.

Visual Arts

The visual arts are rightly described in the plural; at their broadest and most interesting, they include forms such as painting, drawing, printmaking, sculpture, folk art, and the decorative arts. They also embrace new media (film, photography, computer imaging, and video) and functional design areas such as architecture, industrial design, and graphic design. Under the influence of media, conceptual, and performance arts, the visual arts are increasingly about the realization of ideas in formats that are simultaneously visual, spatial, and temporal. The visual arts enable students to reflect on what they inherit from past and present world cultures.

In the NAEP Assessment Framework for Arts Education and related documents, the term "design" is often used in conjunction with "visual arts" because of an important distinction that has to do with functionality. The framework's particular use of the term "design" refers to ways of thinking, problem-solving strategies, and criteria for evaluation commonly applied by graphic designers, industrial designers, architects, and filmmakers in which concern for function and user/audience characteristics are as important as self- expression and aesthetic dimensions. This distinction adds emphasis to those aspects of visual arts that surround us but are often not considered products of legitimate artists. Rather than fragmenting the field, the emphasis can add to a full and robust understanding of the effects of visual arts in our everyday life.

This use of the term "design" should not be confused with the visual composition or organization of elements and "principles of design" in a work of art. In describing this latter concept, the document uses the terminology "principles of visual organization."

The framework below illustrates the vision for visual arts education.

Visual Arts Assessment Framework
Arts Processes for the Visual Arts

Creating—*When creating works of art and design, students define, invent, select, represent, create, and reflect:*

- Subjects, themes, problems, and ideas that reflect knowledge and understanding of context and values (personal, social, cultural, and historical) and aesthetics.
- Visual, spatial, and temporal concepts in planning works of art and design.
- Form, media, techniques, and processes to achieve "goodness of fit" with the intended meaning or function.
- Preliminary or formative ideas (sketches, models, etc.) before final execution.
- A product that reflects ongoing thoughts, actions, and new directions.
- Relationships between process and product, personal direction, and application of concepts learned to daily life.

Responding—*Students describe, analyze, interpret, evaluate, articulate, and apply:*

- Content, form, context, and aesthetics.
- Relationships between form and context, form and meaning or function, and critical/analytical models through understanding of the works of critics, historians, aestheticians, and artists and designers.
- Attitudes and prior knowledge.
- The development of a personal belief system and world view informed by experience in the arts.

Based on Specific Content From the Visual Arts

Knowledge—*Students apply knowledge of:* Skills—*Students apply cognitive, affective, and motor skills, including:*

Context:	Perceptual
• *Personal*	Intellectual/Reflective
• *Social*	Expressive
• *Cultural*	Technical
• *Historical*	
Aesthetics	
Form and Structure Processes	

Creating

Creating in the visual arts and areas of functional design involves students in the construction and communication of meaning through the making of a tangible object, visible performance, or environment. It involves feeling, thinking, and doing. The creative process fully integrates the artist's intuitive and emotional insights to the world with rational thought, critical judgment, and the physical and cognitive abilities required to make appropriate visual form.

Responding

Responding in the visual arts and design means interpreting works of art or design done by other students, other artists and designers, or the students themselves. Responding is an interpretive and evaluative behavior that reveals knowledge of how visual form communicates meaning. It includes the ability to articulate and formulate judgments. Interpretive abilities can be evaluated through oral, written, and visual presentations.

Knowledge and Skills

Knowledge in the visual arts relates to understanding the meaning of visual form and how it is conveyed. For example, students must be able to account for the influence of context (personal, social, cultural, and historical) on meaning in both creating and responding to works of art and design. They explore the content of visual form through examinations of subject matter, means of representation, media and processes, visual organization, composition, and theoretical frameworks (philosophical or aesthetic constructs) for creating and interpreting the visual arts. In areas of functional design, knowledge of user or audience characteristics is also critical to creating objects and environments that work—that is, meet performance criteria.

Skills in the visual arts relate to understanding how to construct or interpret meaning in visual form. Creating skills include gathering information; analyzing and synthesizing experience; generating many visual ideas or solutions; selecting from competing ideas, media, or processes; planning and organizing the visual execution of ideas; evaluating ideas and form; and applying technical proficiency in the making of visual objects. Responding includes many of these skills applied in interpretive contexts. Verbal skills, exhibited in oral and written presentations and the construction of convincing arguments, are also relevant.

3. Desired Attributes of the Assessment

Chapter two explained the content of the arts in general and of each art form as it is understood for purposes of the NAEP framework. The assessment will draw on that content for tasks or exercises that will take up about 60 minutes of students' time at grade 4 and 60 to 90 minutes at grades 8 and 12. The assessment exercises will consist mostly of constructed responses along with some multiple-choice items. The concept of matrix sampling implies that each student who participates in the assessment will do a limited number of exercises that contribute a piece of the puzzle. Aggregated together, the pieces will form the entire image of what all students know and can do in the arts.

Some constructed responses will ask students to perform using the language of the art form, such as dancing a dance, singing a song, acting out an improvised scene, or drawing a picture for visual arts. Others will employ some short or extended written responses. Typically, assessment exercises will be designed around stimulus materials where students will be responding to works of art and producing a work of their own.

All assessment exercises will be governed by the conditions described in the following sections.

Sample of Students

The sample of students assessed should reflect the general population in order to provide data on the achievements of the nation's students. In addition, at the middle and high school levels (and possibly at the elementary level), students who have pursued a specialized area of study, such as instrumental music, should be given the opportunity to demonstrate the extent to which they have mastered that area of study.

The Authenticity of Exercises

Assessment exercises should be as authentic as time and resources permit. In other words, if there are several ways to assess the same area of skill and knowledge, students should be asked to perform the exercises that most closely parallel the genuine artistic behaviors using the appropriate mode of response. For example, the most appropriate way to assess students' singing ability is to have them sing rather than answer written questions about singing.

Although the exercises will be as authentic as time and resources allow, it is also imperative that a national assessment such as NAEP be standardized. This does not suggest that it uses all multiple-choice questions, as the word "standardized" has sometimes come to mean. Instead, the exercises must offer the same opportunities and the same challenges, and should be available in the same circumstances, for all the students assessed. No comparison of students is possible without standardization. Exercises should be both as faithful as possible to artistic learning and standardized in form, content, and context for a large number of students.

Characteristics of the Assessment Exercises

Tasks should be designed to elicit higher order thinking, which may be expressed in words but often is best expressed in purely artistic behaviors. Some students whose creative achievement is greater than their verbal abilities may score poorly on an arts assessment when asked to articulate their artistic understanding in words. Tasks should therefore elicit the response in the most appropriate form for determining actual learning.

Tasks should be designed to differentiate between students at both the low and high ends of the achievement spectrum. At the low end, it must be possible to measure the difference between students with no training and those with some training. At the high end, the exercises must provide sufficient richness and depth so that exceptionally talented students and those who have pursued indepth study can demonstrate the extent of their accomplishments.

Forms of Student Response Used in Exercises

It is impossible to adequately describe many artistic behaviors in words. Appropriate aural, visual, and kinesthetic responses to student performance must therefore be developed. However, some components of the artistic process can be expressed in words. Obviously, students' ability to use appropriate dance, musical, dramatic, or visual arts vocabulary can only be assessed by asking students to use that vocabulary. Evaluating products, performances, and compositions often requires speaking or writing.

Exercise Formats

The following issues must be considered carefully:

- *Performance exercises should be demanding, rigorous, and authentic.* They should require students to engage in activities typical of the artistic process. Assessment exercises should actively involve students as both participants and audience members with attention to the integration of the artistic processes—creating, performing, and responding. Students' knowledge of the arts, the skills and techniques they are able to employ, and their understanding of the historical, personal, social, and cultural contexts in which the arts exist should be embedded and assessed within the framework of the three processes.

- *Performance exercises should require students to apply and demonstrate what they know and are able to do.* These performance exercises will include multiple tasks. In theatre, for example, different students might plan, write, develop dialog, act, design sets, create dramatic material, interpret, and critique performances and productions, and also demonstrate an understanding of the role and influence of theatre, film, and electronic media in their lives and in other historical, cultural, and social contexts. Open-ended questions, requiring students to respond in writing to prompts, should be part of the exercises rather than administered in isolation.

Student Responses

Student responses will vary from written explanations and analyses to individual performances and group productions, with the latter two dependent on the availability of videotape or onsite trained observers. Students will perform exercises in groups and individually. Groups will vary in size depending on the demands of the exercise.

The guideline for selecting a mode of response should be the authenticity of the task. Does it match what is expected of a performer or respondent in that art form? Are the students given an opportunity to show that they can critically appraise a complete piece of music, an exhibition of drawings, a dance, or a play?

Length of Performance Exercises

Authenticity should be the guideline for this category. Dancers and musicians must warm up; painters and designers must think and brainstorm before producing their work; actors must set a scene both physically and mentally. NAEP assessment exercises have traditionally been designed to intrude only minimally on a school's schedule; however, intrusiveness can be mitigated by the value of the assessment exercises so that the school, the teachers, or the students will not resent the time spent on them.

Physical Environment for the Assessment

If arts creation and performance are to be properly assessed, appropriate and adequate rooms must be provided. When possible, designated school space (art rooms, music rooms, dance studios, or areas suitable for theatre) should be used to provide an authentic environment. If such space is not available, multipurpose areas with room to carry out the exercises should be used.

Resources

Resources will be needed to maintain an authentic environment for assessment. Assessments may use audio and video clips to which students could be asked to respond. They may need audio and video capacity (tape recorders and video recorders) if performances are to be scored offsite. Paper and pencil, art materials, costumes, storyboard formats, and microphones may also be required.

Attributes of Assessment Facilitators

Training of facilitators will be important in this NAEP assessment. Facilitators who will conduct this assessment in the schools must be sensitive to the creative process and must possess some understanding of the arts discipline being assessed.

In addition, some representatives of the arts disciplines have requested specific attention to the attributes of the facilitators. For dance, a substantial part of learning involves understanding and learning movement from live demonstrations. To assess students' knowledge and skills, they must be placed in an authentic dance situation. Videotape stimulus materials may not provide enough three-dimensional information for students to fully grasp the movement requested of them. It may be important to have a person with special dance training administer the assessment.

For theatre, an arts-trained facilitator would provide a cooperative, comfortable atmosphere so that students do not feel inhibited or hampered in their efforts to create and perform.

In the visual arts, onsite facilitators should be knowledgeable about students, classrooms, and the visual arts. Although the administration of the exercises will strive for the greatest reliability through video, written, photographic, or actual object prompts and stimulus presentations, unanticipated situations can best be handled by experienced facilitators. A working knowledge of art materials and techniques is desired as well as familiarity with a broad approach to art education, including production, critical thinking and writing about art, historical and social context of art, and the philosophy of art.

Special Studies

The planning and steering committees recommended three special studies to accompany the large-scale assessment.

An Exploration of Interdisciplinary Assessment

This study would have two major objectives: (1) to identify interdisciplinary content in the arts that could be a suitable target of the assessment and (2) to see how assessments of this interdisciplinary content could be planned, developed, and scored. The study could have very useful implications for developing assessments that address interdisciplinary connections across disciplines in education and for resolving some problems and questions involved in such assessments.

First, three kinds of interdisciplinary work must be defined and considered as suitable for the NAEP assessment. Interdisciplinary can mean combining the parts of a single arts discipline; for example, combining jazz and classical music or painting and ceramics. Interdisciplinary can involve combining disciplines among the arts themselves; for example, the production of a music video, which includes all four arts. Finally, interdisciplinary can mean a combination of the arts and other subjects, such as studying the physics of musical sounds or understanding the importance of art in the social structure of Colonial America.

Assessing both the first and third types of interdisciplinary learning requires more resources than we can expect for the NAEP Arts Education Assessment (although in the future it might be possible to connect or relate portions of two NAEP assessments; for example, the arts and history). We concentrate this special study on the second definition, a combination of two or more of the arts disciplines—dance, music, theatre, and visual arts.

The first step of this special study would be to analyze the content of the arts assessment (as specified in the framework, content outlines, and standards) to identify those aspects of the content that are truly, inherently, and significantly interdisciplinary. It is important for interdisciplinary assessments (as well as instruction) to address legitimately interdisciplinary topics or issues. Interdisciplinary activities can be conceived specifically, but that must be avoided; we must attend to aspects of learning that are truly and impartially interdisciplinary. This first step would identify such topics or issues to determine and describe the kinds of interdisciplinary work that are present, are important, and that must be assessed.

Next, a small number of those topics or issues should be selected and plans should be developed for how to assess them. A premium should be placed on adherence to the intent of the topic, issue, or goal. Given its nature, what assessment techniques would be useful and appropriate? This will help reveal the kinds of responses that are needed or appropriate to measure these areas, which is the main purpose of the study. For this reason, a range of interdisciplinary topics or issues, and their appropriate assessment responses, should be explored.

These plans should then lead to a series of practical trials and considerations. What exercises should be administered? How should they be administered? How should they be scored? How should scores be attributed to the structural parts of the assessment?

An exercise could be as simple as asking students to assess a piece of music for its qualities as music and as stimulus for dance, with sketches of proposed moves for the dance. Alternatively, the exercise might be to take a scene from a musical and evaluate the contributions of music, dance (or choreographed motion), acting, scene, and costume design to the effect.

Such exercises would elicit information of a different order than that focused on a single art form. We would be able to judge how evenly the students' knowledge was spread across the art forms (if that is the objective); whether they could apply knowledge and skills across the board; and how they perceived meaning expressed in the facets of the scene.

There is little doubt of the potential need and value of such interdisciplinary exercises. Developing and scoring them, however, presents unresolved problems. Is it possible to write scoring rubrics that are themselves interdisciplinary, or should we use multiple, discipline-specific rubrics? Can we do both, thereby leaving open the option to use one exercise as the origin of multiple scores? Can we score interdisciplinary exercises with any degree of reliability, once we know what the goal is? Do we need to use raters from each of the disciplines involved (i.e., four different raters in the case of the opera excerpt)?

It is fortunate that difficulties do not imply impossibilities. The findings of a special exploratory study on the assessment of interdisciplinary arts learning could yield information about how students understand the interdisciplinary aspects of the arts in real-life settings. The findings should also inform interdisciplinary assessment and encourage cross-disciplinary teaching. This "connecting" technique could also lead to economical uses of assessment resources by providing multiple information from a single stimulus.

A Portfolio Study

In a sense, portfolio assessment is coming home for arts educators. It is fitting that large-scale use of portfolio procedures and principles be tested with the arts. A portfolio is a collection of work produced over time and unified by a theme or purpose. For a NAEPlike assessment, the time element causes problems. How are the conditions of collecting and maintaining a portfolio to be maintained and, for some period of time, to be standardized sufficiently to allow for valid comparison?

Nevertheless, portfolios are being used and these problems are being addressed in large-scale assessments in writing and mathematics. NAEP, in its writing and reading assessments, is experimenting with portfolios of students' work. In the arts, the Advanced Placement (AP) Studio Art Portfolio Evaluation asks students to submit collections of original works that are then assessed holistically by groups of raters.

One basic form of special study would be a portfolio of drawings or paintings, much like the AP Studio Art Portfolio. Size, theme, and deadline specifications would have to be determined, and raters would be trained to look for age-appropriate abilities across several works as opposed to isolated examples. The key issue for NAEP is how and whether portfolio methods can be incorporated as a data collection approach at the national level.

Many other kinds of portfolios in the arts are possible; for example, a dancer could record the development of a suite of dances, a theatre director could keep a portfolio of developments during the production of a play, or a singer could keep an audiotape portfolio of his or her performance.

The focus of a portfolio special study would be to explore the feasibility of the assessment format for NAEP. Its success would depend on maintaining a delicate balance between the demands of a standardized assessment and a student's need for unhampered development of ideas.

Comparing Arts Education Programs

The United States is not without exemplary arts education programs. There are excellent high schools for the performing arts and also elementary schools whose entire instructional program is built around the arts. There are also school districts in which all students receive regular, sequential arts education taught by qualified arts educators in grades K–12. What qualities do these programs have that may or may not be present in other schools or districts? A special study is proposed to examine and compare student performance on the NAEP Arts Education Assessment when students are involved in programs with these different levels of resources and implementation.

A special study would select schools and districts that reflect variety in program breadth and depth. Students would be given the same assessments as students in matched schools that are already part of the national sample. In that way it would be possible to determine the effects of special training. Do students know more? Can they apply what they know more effectively? By looking at background variables, we will also obtain information about the effects of different intensities of arts study. All special studies proposed were not conducted due to budget constraints.

Background Information

Background information requested at the time of the assessment will be essential to understanding the results of the national assessment. The planning committee has prepared a set of general and specific questions to help profile the school's educational environment and culture. Questions will be asked about instructional content, instructional practices and experiences, teacher characteristics, school conditions and context, conditions beyond school, and reporting groups. Typically, NAEP uses three questionnaires: one for the student, one for the teacher, and one for the principal.

Ethical Responsibilities to Students

These responsibilities include ensuring the physical safety of students—for example, not asking them to perform dance movements before being properly warmed up or to undertake theatrical improvisations involving potentially dangerous props or scenery. Ethical responsibility also means respecting the ethnic and cultural sensibilities of students by choosing topics for assessments that would not be construed as insulting or biased against any ethnic, racial, religious, geographic, or cultural group.

The assessment must be sensitive to students' privacy and not ask them to reveal personal information. The assessment should provide guidelines for the protection of any student videotapes or audiotapes.

Issues and Strategies Specific to Each Art Form

In addition to this framework, the NAEP arts project has developed a series of documents that recommend design parameters to the Governing Board. As discussed in the introduction, this framework is intended to be a broad description of the proposed NAEP Arts Education Assessment, much like an artist's color rendering of a new building helps the casual observer visualize the end product.

Similarly, the specifications document is similar to specific blueprints or working drawings for the test development contractor. This higher level of specificity and clarity was needed to construct the assessment in the second phase of the project in 1994. Thus, the following descriptions are broad suggestions about what the assessment looks like in the various arts areas. Practitioners seeking more specific and detailed prescriptions as a guide in building their own assessments should refer to the specifications document.

Dance

Standardized assessment of dance provides a unique challenge. First, the art form itself is temporal; it leaves few lasting traces and no permanent objects to assess. Second, evidence of learning in dance can be particularly difficult to separate from innate ability because all children are constantly developing and practicing their instrument—the body. Because the child's body is both an instrument of creating in dance and an everyday functional body, a dance assessment must be careful to distinguish between growth and learning that is the result of dance training and that which comes from another source. Typical physical activities such as sports, self-directed movement improvisation, playing, and watching and imitating are sources of dancelike behavior that are distinct from formal education in creative movement.

Repertoire

Dance has no universally accepted pedagogies or methods for dance education. Because so little dance instruction exists in schools, the assessment must be extremely careful to avoid limiting the exercises to a narrow range of styles.

Use of Videotape

There are two possible applications of video technology in dance. First, videotape may be a reliable and cost-effective means of recording student responses. Second, videotape may be a way to provide a stimulus for the response. However, the use of video presents problems that must be addressed. In the collection of data:

- The presence of the camera may change student responses.
- Subtlety and nuance of behavior may be lost in the translation from three to two dimensions.

- It is difficult to position video cameras properly to see and record every student during the entire exercise.

As a stimulus for student response, video prompts must be of good quality and the playback equipment must project an image that can be seen clearly by the students. If slides or color reproductions of various dance styles can be used, they would likewise need to be of appropriate size to allow individual examination.

Space
The dance assessment will require a quiet space for watching and responding to videotapes and a gym or other spacious, well-lighted room free of obstructions for the movement exercises.

Time
A substantial period of time is needed to extract a meaningful sample of what students know and can do. Two types of assessment exercises combine to present an appropriate overview of dance: performance exercise and open-ended, paper-and-pencil tests. A test time of 60 minutes for grade 4 and 90 minutes for grades 8 and 12 is preferred. The test could combine one performance exercise for creating/performing with open-ended verbal or response exercises for responding.

Class Design
To put students at ease, the size of the group for movement activities should be no fewer than 4 students and no more than 12. Each student should have adequate space to fully perform the exercises. The arrangement of students should be changed frequently to allow everyone to be observed and to assess student performance independently.

Music

Repertoire
Assessments in music should include activities that give the students opportunities to perform, compose, explain, and express their responses to music. Assessing students' ability to create, perform, and respond to music requires making choices about which music to use. Singing, playing, and listening are processes that necessarily involve repertoire. One of the great challenges to the developers of a national assessment is to select appropriate repertoire.

There is no "canon," or universal body of musical literature, studied by all students in the United States. Developers of NAEP, therefore, cannot assume that all students have studied particular musical works. Examples used in the assessment must be drawn from the rich musical diversity of the United States and the world.

Because students do not have a common singing or playing repertoire, they must either learn a work during the assessment through sight-reading and/or rote imitation or they must be allowed to perform a work they already know.

Stimulus Materials

Stimuli for music exercises will be both aural and visual. These stimuli should be provided through videotapes, audiotapes, notated music, and other visual formats.

Sources for stimuli include:

- High-quality recordings of the suggested repertoire, including commercial recordings of a variety of music from across America and around the world, and recordings and notated examples in standard general music text series.
- Visual materials, including still images and video recordings.
- Specially recorded examples for the assessment.
- Collections of notated repertoire for performance and selective music lists developed by professional music educators.

Theatre

Like dance, theatre is temporal, and the acts of creation and performance are central to any assessment in theatre. Therefore, ways must be found either to rate student responses as they occur or to record students' acts of creating and performing so they can be rated fairly later.

Videotaping

To adequately assess the creating and performing exercises, students will need to be videotaped under the best conditions possible. There must be enough light so that all actions and facial expressions can be captured by the camera. Microphones must be placed in ways to pick up all of the sounds. Because many schools do not have complete stages or auditoriums, the space required for the exercises should be large and open so students can move unhampered by furniture or architectural barriers. Unless the quality of the information and data collected can be otherwise assured, raters with theatre education expertise will have to be onsite.

Facilitators

The assessment facilitators must provide a cooperative, comfortable atmosphere so that students do not feel inhibited or hampered in their efforts to create and perform. This can best be done by a theatre educator. At the same time, due to the nature of the assessment and the need for reliability, facilitators may not coach the students.

Group Work

Because theatre is a collaborative art form, many of the creating and performing exercises should be done by groups of students. The size of the group will vary depending on the specific exercise.

Stimulus Materials

The choice of stimulus material is especially sensitive in theatre. Some exercises need to be culturally neutral so that student responses are not restricted by unfamiliarity with a particular style or period of theatre. On the other hand, it will be important to provide some scripts or videos of scenes that are from easily recognizable works.

Electronic Media

In this century, live theatre has been transformed to reach broader audiences through film and television productions. Any assessment in theatre should include a strong film and electronic media component, recognizing that there are significant differences among live theatre, film, and electronic media. The assessment exercises in this area should involve students in both the similarities and the differences.

Visual Arts

It is important for the physical design of the assessment to reflect the creative process and the nature of the exercises that students are asked to perform. For example, art and design activities should encourage students to study the train of thinking (as revealed in notes and sketches) for insight, which may alter the direction of their creative solution. If the test design does not foster such a review, it is not authentic. A test form that allows students to keep the whole process in view is better than a booklet format in which previous responses are covered by turning the page. Likewise, formats must allow for sufficient drawing space to encourage detail. In addition, careful decisions must be made regarding the proportions of the space in which students will draw or paint, the diagrams or visuals chosen to encourage thinking, and the design of typographic prompts that move students through the activity.

Because art and design activities carried out in the classroom rely heavily on discussion with teachers, the assessment itself must encourage students in the absence of teachers. The infusion of prompt questions, visuals, and videotaped demonstrations may simulate the role of the teacher in arts instruction. They also could encourage the redesign of solutions by staging the introduction of new concepts throughout the design process, thus assessing students' abilities to analyze and evaluate during the creative process.

Assessment exercises for the visual arts can emanate from many sources, such as the work of art or design, a problem/theme/issue, cultural/historical contexts, and artists' self-expression. Although exercises may begin their focus from one of these orientations, all four approaches can assess the same content (subject matter, form, content, media and processes, criticism, and aesthetics). Some approaches will be more effective than others for certain age groups.

If technically feasible, some of the exercises should be designed as sequential, interconnected units that cross grade levels, with some units displaying levels of complexity appropriate for more advanced students. Exercises should include a mix and a balance of creating and responding experiences that engage a wide variety of knowledge and skills in studio production, art criticism, art history, and aesthetics. Exercise content should be sensitive to equitable representation both in production (i.e., two- and three-dimensional work, conventional and nonconventional or inventive media) and in style or context (i.e., classical and folk art of all cultures, gender-equitable selections).

Inferring Understanding from Student Responses in the Visual Arts

Students complete exercises that require a range of intellectual, technical, perceptual, and expressive skills. The analysis of the evidence that results from the performance of those skills (i.e., art works, journals, critical writing, process review) enables experts in the field to make inferences about the students' mastery and understanding of the visual arts. The content may include personal, social, cultural, historical, and aesthetic contexts; art forms and structures; and critical and creative art processes. Because the nature of how the data are gathered will be a departure from past NAEP approaches, the validity of these inferences is a central issue in assessment. The richness of the data is extremely important for an accurate characterization of learning in the visual arts.

Time

Art is a process during which many different kinds of sophisticated and complex perceptual, expressive, creative, and technical actions take place. The student needs time to work through these processes. The idea of small-, medium-, and large-sized assessment blocks works well for the processing needs of visual arts and design.

Raters or Scorers

Scorers will need more advanced levels of experience and understanding than facilitators. They need to be aware of and have experience in the subtle visual and contextual discrimination necessary to rate a creating or responding product. Substantial training in and experience with scoring of portfolio-type process materials are essential.

Desired Emphasis for Each Arts Area

Following are recommendations concerning the grade-level distribution of the assessment exercises across the three artistic processes for each arts discipline. The distribution of exercises across the artistic processes will be described in terms of "proportion of the exercise pool," but such proportions are not intended to refer simply to the proportions of the total number of exercises in a given category. Simple proportions of exercises are problematic because single exercises may vary widely in the amount of time they require and the amount of information they yield (especially across, but also within, formats). In this document, specifications of "proportion of the exercise pool" correspond to proportion of total student time at a particular grade level that would be required if the entire grade-level pool could be administered to a single individual, tempered by the understanding that the statistical efficiency of different exercise formats may vary. It should not be taken to refer strictly to numbers of exercises in different categories.

Dance

Dance is first and foremost a physical art form. The assessment of dance education should include a distribution of content that reflects a major emphasis on dance at all grade levels. At grade 4, creating receives more emphasis than performing and responding. The proportion of student time spent on creating at grade 8 should be less than at grades 4 and 12 because middle school students have special needs in overcoming "being alike" rather than "being original." At grade 12, responding receives increased emphasis over creating and performing.

Recommended Percentages for Dance			
	Grade 4	Grade 8	Grade 12
Creating	40%	20%	30%
Performing	30%	40%	30%
Responding	30%	40%	40%
When computing total scores for the dance assessment, the relative weights for creating, performing, and responding should reflect the proportion of time spent on each process at each grade level.			

Music

The nature of music requires a unique allocation of assessment priorities. Some parts of the musical process require more time to complete than others. Creating a composition may take months or years, but listening and responding to the composition may require only minutes.

Most music students at the fourth-grade level spend more time on performance, such as singing and playing instruments. Older students spend more time in responding activities, such as analyzing and critiquing. The *National Standards* establish the expectation that musically educated individuals should create (improvise, compose, and arrange) music. All students should spend a substantial percentage of their instructional time engaging in creating activities. The recommended percentages for the three processes in this assessment are as follows:

Recommended Percentages for Music			
	Grade 4	Grade 8	Grade 12
Creating	20–30%	20–30%	20–30%
Performing	40–50%	35–45%	30–40%
Responding	25–35%	30–40%	35–45%
When computing total scores for the music assessment, the relative weights for creating, performing, and responding should reflect the proportion of time spent on each process at each grade level (for example, at grade 4, 25% for creating, 45% for performing, and 30% for responding; at grade 8, 25% for creating, 40% for performing, and 35% for responding; at grade 12, 25% for creating, 35% for performing, and 40% for responding).			

Theatre

At grade 4, the emphasis in theatre curriculum is on students doing, not on their responding skills, recognizing that some analysis is required when creating and performing. For this reason, it is recommended that the assessment emphasis in fourth grade be weighted so that 70 percent of the subscores are collected in the area of creating and performing, with 30 percent collected in responding. To achieve this weighting, it is estimated that 70 percent of the student assessment time will need to be focused on creating and performing, with 30 percent devoted to responding exercises.

At grades 8 and 12, it is recommended that 60 percent of subscores be collected in creating and performing, with 40 percent collected in responding. To achieve this emphasis, it is estimated that 60 percent of student assessment time be devoted to creating and performing, with 40 percent allocated to responding. It is further recommended that responding exercises include an evaluation of students' reactions as practitioners as well as critics. In this way, the assessment will reflect the collaborative nature of theatre.

Recommended Percentages for Theatre			
	Grade 4	Grade 8	Grade 12
Creating/Performing	70%	60%	60%
Responding	30%	40%	40%
When computing total scores for the theatre assessment, the relative weights for creating/performing and responding should reflect the proportion of time spent on each process at each grade level.			

Visual Arts

At all three grade levels, students should spend a greater proportion of time working on creating exercises (50–70 percent) than on responding exercises (30–50 percent):

Recommended Percentages for Visual Arts			
	Grade 4	Grade 8	Grade 12
Creating	50–70%	50–70%	50–70%
Responding	30–50%	30–50%	30–50%
When computing total scores for the visual arts assessment, creating and responding should be equally weighted at each grade level (for example, at grades 4, 8, and 12, 50% for creating and 50% for			

4. PRELIMINARY ACHIEVEMENT LEVEL DESCRIPTIONS

The attention now turns from the design of the assessment and its exercises to interpreting the results. For the information to be useful as a basis for policy decisions, it is important to report how many students achieve at certain levels. Governing Board policy defines three levels of achievement—basic, proficient, and advanced—to be used in reporting the results of the NAEP Arts Education Assessment at grades 4, 8, and 12. These achievement levels describe how well students should perform on the assessment.

According to NAEP, **Basic** denotes partial mastery of the content but performance that is only adequate for work at the three grade levels. **Proficient** represents solid academic achievement and competency over challenging subject matter. **Advanced** performance on this assessment represents achievement that is equal to that expected of top students.

Because the assessment is based on the new *National Standards,* which sets high expectations for student learning, the results will describe the range of scores from the lowest level, proceeding through (or beyond) the areas of expected achievement. The NAEP proficient level is set as the target for students and represents the achievement levels described in the *National Standards.* The planning committee recognizes that due to inadequate opportunities for arts study in many schools, a number of students may score below the basic level. Although this may be cause for concern, it will also demonstrate the deficiencies in arts education instruction or indicate where additional study opportunities must be provided if all students are expected to achieve the world-class standards.

These preliminary achievement level descriptions will be used by the test development panel to guide test and item construction. This will ensure that exercises in the Arts Education Assessment will provide information on the various types of knowledge and skills included in the achievement level descriptions for each grade level. After the assessment is field tested, refined, and administered to the national sample of students, the preliminary achievement level descriptions will inform the final achievement level-setting process. In this stage, panelists examine the assessment exercises and the student performance data to recommend to the Governing Board the achievement levels to be used in reporting the NAEP arts education results.

The achievement levels portrayed here in the NAEP framework are general in nature and only describe the broad expectations. They are framed by the three major arts education processes—creating, performing, and responding—and are set at the three grade levels examined. For additional detail in each of the four arts areas at grades 4, 8, and 12, refer to the specifications document.

Preliminary Achievement Level Descriptions for Dance

NAEP uses the following descriptors as expectations for student achievement:

- **Basic** denotes partial mastery of the content but performance that is only adequate for work at the three grade levels.
- **Proficient** represents solid academic achievement and competency over challenging subject matter, as suggested in the National Standards for Arts Education.
- **Advanced** performance on this assessment represents achievement that is equal to that expected of top students.

Grade 4

Dance Process	Fourth-grade students at the basic level in dance:	Fourth-grade students at the proficient level in dance:	Fourth-grade students at the advanced level in dance:
Creating	• Stop after finding a single solution to a movement challenge and rely on imitation of others rather than generating their own ideas.	• Find multiple ways to solve a movement challenge but may rely on only one movement element.	• Find multiple ways to solve a movement challenge incorporating a variety of movement elements (time, space, and force).
	• Create a movement sequence that has a clear beginning, middle, and end but may be unable to repeat it accurately.	• Create a movement sequence that has a clear beginning, middle, and end and make effective use of time, space, and force; accurately repeat it.	• Create, repeat, and perform a dance that has a clear beginning, middle, and end; make effective use of time, space, and force; and communicate an idea.
	• Participate as observers or performers but will not offer any ideas to the group or partner in the process of creating a movement sequence.	• Contribute and work cooperatively with a partner or a group of students in creating a movement sequence.	• Contribute and work cooperatively with a partner or group of students in the process of creating a dance that successfully communicates a shared idea.
Performing	• Accurately reproduce and perform locomotor and nonlocomotor movement.	• Accurately reproduce and perform locomotor and nonlocomotor movement using time, space, and force.	• Accurately reproduce and perform locomotor and nonlocomotor movement using time, space, and force; perform with confidence and use the entire body.

(Continued)

Dance Process	Fourth-grade students at the basic level in dance:	Fourth-grade students at the proficient level in dance:	Fourth-grade students at the advanced level in dance:
	• Have difficulty maintaining balance, isolating various body parts, and controlling their movement while performing basic movement sequences.	• Maintain balance and alignment, and control all of the body parts while performing basic movement sequences.	• Maintain body alignment while performing basic movement sequences; possess strength, flexibility, balance, and coordination.
	• Perform without commitment or expressive qualities.	• Perform movement phrases with full physical commitment.	• Perform movement sequences expressively through both literal and abstract gestures and movements.
Responding	• Discuss dance using general vocabulary.	• Recognize and label some movement elements.	• Use appropriate dance vocabulary to describe movement elements and details.
	• Speculate about the culture and/or time period of a dance.	• Accurately place a dance in a culture and time period.	• Accurately describe dances from a variety of cultures and time periods.
	• Give personal opinions about a dance, offering no supportive rationale.	• Give personal opinions about a dance, providing supporting rationale.	• Give personal opinions about a dance, providing supportive rationale; identify individual elements of the dance, including but not limited to the quality of the performance and production elements (for example, sound, costumes, lighting, set).

Grade 8

Dance Process	Eighth-grade students at the basic level in dance:	Eighth-grade students at the proficient level in dance:	Eighth-grade students at the advanced level in dance:
Creating	• Stop after finding a single solution to a movement challenge and rely on imitation of others rather than generating their own ideas.	• Find multiple ways to solve a brief movement challenge.	• Find multiple ways to solve a brief movement challenge, choosing the most effective solution and articulating the reasons for the selection.

(Continued)

Dance Process	Eighth-grade students at the basic level in dance:	Eighth-grade students at the proficient level in dance:	Eighth-grade students at the advanced level in dance:
	• Create and accurately repeat a movement sequence that demonstrates a clear beginning, middle, and end.	• Create, repeat, and perform dance that demonstrates effective use of time, space, force, body shapes, dynamics, and rhythm; has a beginning, middle, and end.	• Create, repeat, and perform dance that demonstrates effective use of time, space, force, body shapes, dynamics, and rhythm; has a beginning, middle, and end; deals with an issue of personal significance.
	• Participate as observers or performers but will not offer any ideas to the group or partner.	• Contribute and work cooperatively with a partner or a group of students in creating a movement sequence.	• Contribute and work cooperatively with a partner or group of students in creating a dance that successfully communicates a shared idea.
Performing	• Perform locomotor and nonlocomotor movements using accurate time, space, and force in a variety of ways.	• Accurately demonstrate basic dance steps, positions, and patterns from a variety of dance styles and traditions.	• Accurately perform dances from a variety of styles and traditions.
	• Have difficulty maintaining proper alignment of the body and lack clarity in movement while performing basic movement sequences.	• Maintain body alignment while performing basic movement sequences; possess strength, flexibility, balance, and coordination.	• Maintain body alignment appropriate to the dance form while performing a variety of dances; possess strength, flexibility, balance, and coordination.
	• Perform without commitment or expressive qualities.	• Perform dance sequences, communicating expressively through both literal and abstract gesture and movement.	• Perform a dance expressively through both literal and abstract gesture and movement to communicate an idea or feeling.
Responding	• Label some elements of dance using general vocabulary.	• Use appropriate dance vocabulary to describe movement elements and choreographic principles viewed in a dance.	• Use appropriate dance vocabulary to describe and analyze the use and effect of movement elements and choreographic principles in a variety of dances

(Continued)

Dance Process	Eighth-grade students at the basic level in dance:	Eighth-grade students at the proficient level in dance:	Eighth-grade students at the advanced level in dance:
	• Speculate about the culture and/or time period of a dance.	• Accurately describe dances from a variety of cultures and time periods.	• Explain how a dance reflects and impacts a society politically, culturally, and socially.
	• Give opinions about a dance, offering some supporting rationale.	• Give opinions with supporting rationale about works of dance; identify individual elements of the dance, including but not limited to the quality of the dancers' and production elements (for example, sound, costumes, lighting, set).	• Give opinions with supportive rationale about dances; make critical judgments about the form, content, and meaning of dance.

Grade 12

Dance Process	Twelfth-grade students at the basic level in dance:	Twelfth-grade students at the proficient level in dance:	Twelfth-grade students at the advanced level in dance:
Creating	• Stop after finding a single solution to a brief movement challenge and rely on imitation of others rather than generating their own ideas.	• Use improvisation to find multiple ways to solve a brief movement challenge, choosing the most effective solution and articulating reasons for the selection.	• Select and manipulate improvised movement material to make a complete dance.
	• Create and accurately repeat a dance that demonstrates a clear beginning, middle, and end.	• Create, repeat, and perform dance that demonstrates effective use of time, space, force, body shapes, dynamics, and rhythm; has a beginning, middle, and end; and deals	• Create, repeat, and perform dance that demonstrates effective use of time, space, force, body shapes, dynamics, and rhythm; has a beginning, middle, and end; includes choreographic principles such as theme and variation, canon, call, and response; and deals with a contemporary social issue.

(Continued)

Dance Process	Twelfth-grade students at the basic level in dance:	Twelfth-grade students at the proficient level in dance:	Twelfth-grade students at the advanced level in dance:
		with an issue of personal significance.	
	• Participate as observers or performers but will not offer ideas to the group or to partners in the process of creating a movement sequence.	• Contribute and work cooperatively with partners or a group of students in the process of creating a movement sequence.	• Contribute and work cooperatively with partners or a group of students in the process of creating a dance that successfully communicates a shared idea.
Performing	• Accurately recall and perform movement sequences using time, space, and force.	• Accurately recall and perform dances from a variety of dance styles and traditions; demonstrate time, space, and force; perform accurate dance steps, positions, and patterns from a variety of dance styles and traditions.	• Accurately recall and perform from a variety of dance styles and traditions; demonstrate time, space, and energy; perform accurate dance steps, positions, and patterns; perform with confidence using the entire body and demonstrating full commitment and involvement.
	• Have difficulty maintaining proper alignment of the body and lack clarity in movement while performing basic movement sequences.	• Maintain body alignment appropriate to the dance form while performing complex movement sequences.	• Maintain body alignment appropriate to the dance form, demonstrate clear articulation with all parts of the body while performing complex movement sequences, will self-correct during and after each performance of the complex movement sequence.
	• Perform a dance without commitment or expressive qualities.	• Perform a dance expressively through both literal and abstract gesture and movement to communicate an idea.	• Perform a dance expressively through both literal and abstract gesture and movement to communicate an idea; vary the choreography to communicate a different idea.

(Continued)

Dance Process	Twelfth-grade students at the basic level in dance:	Twelfth-grade students at the proficient level in dance:	Twelfth-grade students at the advanced level in dance:
Responding	• Use appropriate dance vocabulary to describe movement elements and choreographic principles viewed in a dance.	• Use appropriate dance vocabulary to describe and analyze the use and effect of movement elements and choreographic principles viewed in a variety of dances.	• Use appropriate dance vocabulary to describe, analyze, compare, and contrast how different choreographers manipulate the movement elements and choreographic principles to communicate meaning.
	• Identify the cultural context and historical period of various dances.	• Explain how a dance reflects and impacts a society politically, culturally, and socially.	• Compare and contrast the ways in which different dances reflect and impact societies politically, culturally, and socially; use historical and cultural information to enhance their own work in dance performance, choreography, and criticism.
	• Give opinions with supporting rationale about works of dance; identify individual elements of the dance, including but not limited to the quality of performance and production elements (for example, sound, costumes, lighting, set).	• Give opinions with supporting rationale about works of dance; make critical judgments about the form, content, and meaning of dance.	• Give opinions with supporting rationale about works of dance; use a set of aesthetic criteria to make and support critical judgments about the form, content, and meaning of dance; use cultural references to reflect sensitively upon the intent and meaning of the choreography of others.

Preliminary Achievement Level Descriptions for Music

NAEP uses the following descriptions as expectations for student achievement:

- **Basic** denotes partial mastery of the content but performance that is only adequate for work at the three grade levels.
- **Proficient** represents solid academic achievement and competency over challenging subject matter, as suggested in the *National Standards for Arts Education*.
- **Advanced** performance on this assessment represents achievement that is equal to that expected of top students.

	Grade 4		
Musical Process	Fourth-grade students at the basic level in music:	Fourth-grade students at the proficient level in music:	Fourth-grade students at the advanced level in music:
Creating	• Compose short pieces that are inconsistent in the manipulation of dimensions such as instrumentation, form, loudness, tempo, meter, tonality, and mood.	• Compose short pieces or accompaniments that are consistent* in the manipulation of dimensions such as instrumentation, form, loudness, tempo, meter, tonality, and mood.	• Compose longer pieces and accompaniments and may be able to imitate various styles when creating original music.
	• Improvise repetitious "answers" to given rhythmic and melodic phrases, demonstrate little understanding of style and form when creating simple melodic or rhythmic accompaniments or embellishments.	• Improvise varied "answers" to given rhythmic and melodic phrases and create simple melodic or rhythmic ostinato accompaniments or embellishments on familiar melodies using appropriate matching styles and forms.	• Improvise varied "answers" to given rhythmic and melodic phrases; improvise melodies and rhythms using matching styles and forms; demonstrate a high level of independence and creativity, going beyond the demands of the task.
Performing	• Sing in unison with others but have difficulty singing independently. The performance may contain inaccurate pitches and rhythms or may lack expression.	• Sing independently and can sing partner songs, rounds, and ostinatos as a member of an ensemble, responding appropriately to the cues of a conductor. The performance is	• Sing independently and can sustain their own part in an ensemble. The performance is technically accurate and expressive. While the students will be able to follow a conductor's cue,

(Continued)

Musical Process	Fourth-grade students at the basic level in music:	Fourth-grade students at the proficient level in music:	Fourth-grade students at the advanced level in music:
		technically accurate (correct pitches and rhythms) and expressive (attention to dynamics, phrasing, and style).	they will also be able to make independent decisions about expressive qualities to enhance the performance. Advanced students may be able to sing a range of more than a 10th, use a strong and focused tone quality, and sing a solo part on an ostinato or in a round or partner song.
	• Play easy, rhythmic, melodic, and chordal patterns on classroom instruments such as the recorder, xylophone, keyboard, or autoharp. The performance may be inconsistent, containing technical and expressive inaccuracies. Basic students may have difficulty keeping up with an ensemble.	• Play easy, rhythmic, melodic, and chordal patterns on classroom instruments such as the recorder, xylophone, keyboard, or autoharp. The performance is technically accurate (correct pitches and rhythms) and expressive (attention to phrasing and dynamic). Proficient students should be able to play independently and in unison with others as members of an ensemble.	• Play an instrument with technical accuracy and expression. The repertoire is more difficult than that performed in a music class or beginning ensemble class. Advanced students can play independently as a soloist and as a member of an ensemble, demonstrating knowledge of tone production and expression that goes beyond the demands of the task.
	• Read notation with difficulty and require practice to produce a performance that may contain technical and expressive inaccuracies.	• Read notation sufficiently to perform simple melodic or rhythmic phrases accurately after practice. The repertoire difficulty is at the level recommended by the *National Standards* and should include whole, half, quarter, and eighth notes; corresponding rests; and pitch notation in the treble clef. Proficient and articulation, and expressive	• Read notation sufficiently to perform melodic or rhythmic phrases accurately at sight. The difficulty of the repertoire may exceed that recommended by the *National Standards*. The performance indicates use of basic symbols for dynamics, meter, tempo, and articulation, and expressive symbols (for example, p, f, cresc.).

(Continued)

Musical Process	Fourth-grade students at the basic level in music:	Fourth-grade students at the proficient level in music:	Fourth-grade students at the advanced level in music:
		students should be familiar with basic symbols for dynamics, meter, tempo, symbols (for example, p, f, cresc.).	
Responding	• When listening to music, recognize when music changes from one section to another, but may not be able to identify simple forms. Basic students may be able to identify various genres of Western music as being the same or different, but lack sufficient knowledge of musical terminology to support responses; distinguish being non-Western music from Western music without being able to make distinctions about geographical origins; and recognize a limited number of musical instruments by sight, sound, and name.	• When listening to music, identify elements and simple forms through movement and verbal response (for example, ABA and call and response); identify various genres of Western music and have sufficient knowledge of musical terminology to support responses; identify non-Western music and make distinctions about geographical origins; recognize voices and most band and orchestra instruments by sight, sound, and name; and recognize instruments that are unique to folk, popular, and non-Western styles.	• When listening to music, identify selected extended musical forms (for example, theme and variations, fugues); predict events in the music such as cadences; identify various genres of Western music and use an extensive vocabulary of musical terminology to support responses; identify non-Western music by origin and genre; recognize, name, and classify instruments of the symphony orchestra; and recognize and name some instruments unique to folk, popular, and non-Western styles. Advanced students are able to defend preferences based on musical understanding.
	• Evaluate the quality of a performance or composition with limited insight and by using general, nonmusical terminology.	• Accurately evaluate the quality of a performance or composition and use appropriate musical terminology to support a response.	• Accurately evaluate the quality of a composition or performance and use appropriate musical terminology to support responses, improve their own performance or composition through self-evaluation and practice.

(Continued)

Grade 8

Musical Process	Eighth-grade students at the basic level in music:	Eighth-grade students at the proficient level in music:	Eighth-grade students at the advanced level in music:
Creating	• Compose short pieces (melodies, rhythms, or accompaniments) that are inconsistent in the use of musical elements.	• Compose short pieces (melodies, rhythms, or accompaniments) that are consistent in the use of musical elements to achieve unity, variety, tension/release, and balance. Proficient students can use traditional (acoustic instruments, voice) or nontraditional (synthesized sounds, MIDI) sound sources. The composition may be recorded using traditional or nontraditional methods or notation (analog recording, digital sequencing, conventional notation, or notation created for the piece).	• Compose music in familiar styles that are consistent in the use of musical elements and creative using traditional or nontraditional sound sources and notation, able to generate many ideas from which to choose and evaluate and refine work in progress.
	• Improvise (vocally or instrumentally) with uncertainty short melodies or rhythms that are inconsistent with the style and guidelines given for the task.	• Improvise (vocally or instrumentally) melodic or rhythmic variations or simple harmonic accompaniments that are consistent with the style of music being used for the task.	• Improvise (vocally or instrumentally) extended melodies, rhythms, or accompaniments in familiar styles; demonstrate a high level of independence and creativity in approaching and completing the task and may go beyond the demands of the task.
Performing	• Sing independently, but the performance may contain inaccurate pitches and rhythms or lack expression. (At the basic level, the young male whose voice is changing may be able to sing cambiata parts written for a narrow	• Sing independently and can sustain a part in an ensemble section. The performance is technically accurate and expressive. Repertoire difficulty is at the level recommended by the *National Standards* and includes	• Sing independently and can sustain a part in an ensemble. The performance is technically accurate and expressive. Advanced students may be able to sing repertoire more difficult than the level recommended by the *National*

(Continued)

Musical Process	Eighth-grade students at the basic level in music:	Eighth-grade students at the proficient level in music:	Eighth-grade students at the advanced level in music:
	range, but a general lack of understanding about his own voice causes technical errors (for example, attempts at matching pitch may result in one- or two-octave leaps)).	two- and three-part ensemble singing. (At the proficient level, the young male whose voice is changing should be able to sing songs or cambiata parts written specifically for his range.)	*Standards*, use a tone quality that is well supported and focused with possible vibrato, sing a solo part in chamber ensemble of three or four parts, sing with a range of more than a 12th, and/or create an expressive and stylistically correct performance without the aid of instruction. (At the advanced level, the young male who is in the process of a voice change can control the flow of breath and placement so that he can avoid accidents. He understands his limitations and can make adjustments by deliberately changing octaves or by requesting appropriate keys so that he can create a successful singing experience for himself.)
	• Play an instrument as a soloist, accompanist, and/or member of an ensemble. The performance is inconsistent, containing technical and expressive inaccuracies, and the repertoire difficulty is below the level recommended by the *National Standards*.	• Play an instrument with technical accuracy and expression as a soloist, accompanist, and/or member of an ensemble. Repertoire difficulty is at the level recommended by the *National Standards*.	• Play an instrument with technical accuracy as a soloist, accompanist, and/or member of an ensemble (including chamber ensemble). The performances are expressive and stylistically correct. Repertoire difficulty exceeds the level recommended by the *National Standards*, requiring technical facility and knowledge of production and style that go beyond the proficient level of playing.

(Continued)

Musical Process	Eighth-grade students at the basic level in music:	Eighth-grade students at the proficient level in music:	Eighth-grade students at the advanced level in music:
Responding	• Read notation with difficulty and require practice to be able to perform simple melodies or rhythms that may contain technical and expressive inaccuracies.	• Read notation sufficiently to perform simple melodies or rhythms accurately after practice. The repertoire at the level recommended by the *National Standards* and should include whole, half, quarter, eighth, sixteenth, and dotted notes; corresponding rests; pitch notation in both treble and bass clef. Proficient students should be familiar with basic symbols for dynamics, meter, tempo, and articulation, and expressive symbols (for example, p, f, cresc.) and should be able to use standard notation to record musical ideas.	• Read notation quickly, sufficiently, and accurately to be able to perform simple melodies at sight; read music accurately and expressively after practice that is more difficult than the level recommended by the *National Standards*. Students can record musical ideas correctly using notation.
	• When listening to music, can identify simple forms (for example, ABA and rondo) and can identify some Western music by historical periods and genre, but have insufficient knowledge of musical terminology to discuss style. Basic students can identify some styles of folk, popular, and non-Western music; make "same" and "different" distinctions about the geographic origins of non-Western music; and recognize and name some instruments used in Western and non-Western music.	• When listening to music, can identify and discuss commonly used musical forms (for example, theme and variations, fugues) and can identify some Western music by historical periods with sufficient knowledge of musical terminology to support responses. Proficient students identify and describe stylistic elements heard in folk, popular, and non-Western music; identify some non-Western music by country; recognize most instruments of the band and	• When listening to music, can identify, compare, and contrast elements of complex musical forms (for example, sonata-allegro, fugue); able to predict certain events in music such as phrase lengths or direction of resolutions in cadences, as well as genre and style of unfamiliar music; and have a working vocabulary of musical terminology for discussing the expressive qualities of various styles of Western music, from Renaissance to contemporary. Advanced students identify and describe

(Continued)

Musical Process	Fourth-grade students at the basic level in music:	Fourth-grade students at the proficient level in music:	Fourth-grade students at the advanced level in music:
		orchestra; and identify other instruments unique to folk, popular, and non-Western styles.	musical elements heard in a wide variety of folk, popular, and non-Western music styles; classify some non-Western music by country and genre; recognize and classify instruments of the band and orchestra; and identify instruments unique to folk, popular, and non-Western styles.
	• Evaluate compositions or performances with limited insight or use of musical vocabulary. Basic students can identify technical problems in performances, but responses are limited to common musical terms (for example, fast, slow, loud, soft).	• Evaluate the quality of compositions or performances and use a basic musical vocabulary to defend response, use self-evaluation to improve successive performances.	• Can compare and contrast the quality of compositions and performances using specific musical terms to describe technical and expressive elements of music and their relationship to the style of music being played. As performers, advanced students use critical analysis and independent study to improve successive performances.

Grade 12

Musical Process	Twelfth-grade students at the basic level in music:	Twelfth-grade students at the proficient level in music:	Twelfth-grade students at the advanced level in music:
Creating	• Compose original pieces, but the results are fragmented and lack unity. Basic students can compose only for media close to their own performing instrument or voice.	• Compose original pieces that are consistent in the use of musical elements using traditional or nontraditional media and/or notation, arrange simple pieces with or without accompaniment based on knowledge of vocal and/or instrumental ranges and style,	• Compose complex works that show consistency, creativity, expression, and a high level of technical skill; generate many original ideas, selecting and refining as they work; and may be able to orchestrate pieces for several instruments or arrange for several voices.

(Continued)

Musical Process	Twelfth-grade students at the basic level in music:	Twelfth-grade students at the proficient level in music:	Twelfth-grade students at the advanced level in music:
		demonstrate creative use of expressive elements.	
	• Improvise (vocally or instrumentally) melodies or rhythms within limited sets of pitches, rhythms, and styles.	• Improvise original pieces, variations, and harmonic accompaniments that are consistent with the style used for the task.	• Improvise stylistically and expressively in a variety of styles; improvise in one or more favored styles with a high level of creativity, expression, and confidence.
Performing	• Sing independently, but the performance may be technically or expressively inconsistent.	• Sing independently and can sustain their own part in an ensemble section. The performance is technically accurate and expressive. Repertoire difficulty is at the level recommended by the *National Standards* and includes four-part harmony with or without accompaniment.	• Sing independently and can sustain a solo part in a chamber ensemble of four or more parts. The performance is technically and stylistically accurate and expressive. Advanced singers should be able to sing repertoire that exceeds the difficulty level recommended by the *National Standards* and produce a tone quality that is strong, vibrant, and stylistically correct.
	• Play an instrument as a soloist, accompanist, and/or member of an ensemble. The performance may be inconsistent, containing technical and expressive inaccuracies, and the repertoire difficulty may be below the level recommended by the *National Standards*.	• Play an instrument with technical accuracy as a soloist, accompanist, and/or member of an ensemble (including chamber ensemble). Performances are expressive and stylistically correct. Repertoire difficulty is at the level recommended by the *National Standards* and includes four-part	• Play an instrument with technical accuracy as a soloist, accompanist, and/or member of an ensemble (including chamber ensemble). Advanced students play with technical facility, expression, range, and tone quality needed to accurately perform musical works that exceed the level of difficulty recommended by the *National Standards*.

(Continued)

Musical Process	Twelfth-grade students at the basic level in music:	Twelfth-grade students at the proficient level in music:	Twelfth-grade students at the advanced level in music:
	harmony with or without accompaniment.		
	• Read notation sufficiently to perform easy selections somewhat accurately after practice and describe how musical elements are used in a given score of one or two staves, use standard notation to read simple melodies and rhythms.	• Sight-read music accurately and expressively at the level of difficulty recommended by the *National Standards*. Proficient students read notation sufficiently to describe how the elements of music are used in a given score of up to four staves. Students use standard notation to record musical ideas.	• Read notation of technically difficult literature and accurately incorporate expressive symbols and stylistic qualities in performance and can sight read music at a difficulty level recommended by the *National Standards*, read a full instrumental or vocal score and accurately describe how the elements of music are used, use standard notation to record musical ideas, and interpret nonstandard notation used by some 20th-century composers.
Responding	• When listening to music, can identify musical forms (for example, theme and variations, symphony), can identify some Western music by historical periods, and have some knowledge of musical terminology to support responses. Basic students can identify some styles of folk, popular, and non-Western music, making some distinctions about the geographical origins of non-Western examples, and can recognize most instruments of the symphony orchestra. Basic students	• When listening to music, can identify and discuss elements of extended musical forms (for example, concerto, opera), can identify Western music by historical periods and have sufficient knowledge of musical terminology to support responses, can accurately predict styles or genres of unfamiliar music. Proficient students are able to describe stylistic elements heard in folk, popular, and non-Western music; identify some non-Western	• When listening to music, can identify, compare, and contrast elements of complex musical forms (for example, oratorio, sonata-allegro form); have an extensive vocabulary for identifying and discussing the elements and the expressive qualities of various styles and periods of Western music, from Medieval through contemporary; can make predictions about genre, style, and composers of music that is being heard for the first time; can identify and describe musical elements heard in

(Continued)

Musical Process	Twelfth-grade students at the basic level in music:	Twelfth-grade students at the proficient level in music:	Twelfth-grade students at the advanced level in music:
	may be able to identify other instruments unique to Western, folk, popular, and non-Western styles.	music by country; recognize instruments of the band and orchestra; and identify many other instruments unique to folk, popular, and non-Western styles. Students can discuss acoustical characteristics of different classes of instruments.	a wide variety of folk, popular, and non-Western music styles; can classify non-Western music by country and genre and may know one or more of these styles indepth; are able to recognize, name, and classify instruments of the symphony orchestra; identify a wide variety of instruments unique to folk, popular, and non-Western styles; and discuss acoustical characteristics of different classes of instruments as well as synthesized sound. Advanced students can evaluate the aesthetic qualities of music and can explain the musical processes that the composer uses to evoke feeling.
	• Evaluate compositions or performances and use a basic musical vocabulary. Basic students can evaluate technical aspects of performances, but may lack sufficient knowledge to judge stylistic qualities.	• Compare and contrast the quality of compositions or performances, use a basic musical vocabulary to describe the elements of music (pitch, rhythm, tempo, instrumentation, ensemble). Proficient students use a process of self-evaluation to improve successive performances.	• Compare and contrast the quality of compositions and performances using specific musical terms to describe technical and expressive elements of music and their relationship to the style of music being played; can offer suggestions to improve performances; and as performers, use critical analysis and research to improve successive performances.

* For the purpose of this assessment, the term "consistent" has been chosen to define the quality of a created work. Consistency is the logical use of musical elements (pitch, meter, rhythm, form, timbre, dynamics, and other expressive qualities) to achieve style and balance.

Preliminary Achievement Level Descriptions for Theater

NAEP uses the following descriptions as expectations for student achievement:

- **Basic** denotes partial mastery of the content but performance that is only adequate for work at the three grade levels.
- **Proficient** represents solid academic achievement and competency over challenging subject matter, as suggested in the *National Standards for Arts Education*.
- **Advanced** performance on this assessment represents achievement that is equal to that expected of top students.

At the fourth grade, students are not as willing to "fall into dramatic play" as they are up to age 8. Students need to be motivated and challenged to participate. They are interested in dealing with adult problems and often insist on bringing realistic details to their work. They prefer to work in groups of their own gender. Most performance work at this level is informal production. Students are making critical and creative choices in all aspects of the creating and performing processes.

Theatre Processes	Fourth-grade students at the basic level in theatre:	Fourth-grade students at the proficient level in theatre:	Fourth-grade students at the advanced level in theatre:
		Grade 4	
Creating/ Performing	• Collaborate to develop scripts and scenarios and to improvise dialog in which they describe one of the following: characters, environments, or situations. • Develop characters and assume roles using some movement and vocal expression.	• Collaborate to develop scripts and scenarios in which they describe characters, environments, and situations; and improvise dialog to tell a story. • Develop characters using variations of movement and vocal expression, assume roles that exhibit concentration, and contribute to the action of the dramatization.	• Collaborate to develop scripts and scenarios in which they describe characters, environments and situations; improvise dialog to tell a story with a clear beginning, middle, and end. • Develop characters using variations of movement and vocal expression; assume roles that exhibit concentration, focus, and commitment; and contribute to the action of the dramatization.

(Continued)

Theatre Processes	Fourth-grade students at the basic level in theatre:	Fourth-grade students at the proficient level in theatre:	Fourth-grade students at the advanced level in theatre:
	• Use some of the design choices the group has made, and remain within the playing space during the dramatic play.	• Make design choices that reflect environments that communicate locale and mood using visual and aural elements, and collaborate to establish playing spaces by safely organizing available materials to suggest some the following: scenery, properties, lighting, sound, costumes, and makeup.	• Make design choices that reflect environments that communicate locale and mood using visual and aural elements, and collaborate to establish playing spaces by safely organizing available and imagined materials to suggest scenery, properties, lighting, sound, costumes, and makeup.
	• Participate in the improvisations as a way of organizing their classroom dramatizations.	• Collaboratively plan improvisations as a way of organizing their classroom dramatizations.	• Collaboratively plan improvisations as a way of organizing their classroom dramatizations, taking a leadership role.
Responding	• Describe artistic choices in their own dramatic work, identifying elements of classroom dramatizations they chose in their creative and performing work.	• Describe and analyze artistic choices in their own dramatic work, identifying and describing elements of classroom dramatizations; provide rationales for personal choices in their creative and performing work; and constructively suggest alternatives.	• Describe and analyze artistic choices in their own dramatic work, identifying and describing elements of classroom dramatizations; provide rationales for personal choices in their creative and performing work; and constructively suggest alternatives for dramatizing roles, arranging environments, and developing situations along with means of improving the collaborative process.
	• Describe some elements and effects of theatre, film, and television.	• Describe and compare various elements and effects of theatre to film and television.	• Describe and compare various elements and effects of theatre to film and television, and provide

(Continued)

Theatre Processes	Fourth-grade students at the basic level in theatre:	Fourth-grade students at the proficient level in theatre:	Fourth-grade students at the advanced level in theatre:
			rationale for those they felt were most effective.
	• Place work in personal and social contexts by identifying similar characters and situations in theatre, film, and television.	• Place work in personal, social, and cultural contexts by identifying and comparing similar characters and situations in theatre, film, and television.	• Place work in personal, social, historical, and cultural contexts by identifying and comparing similar characters, situations, and themes in theatre, film, and television.
	• State personal preferences, as an audience, for entire performances and for certain parts of them.	• Evaluate performances as an audience, articulating emotional responses to dramatic performances; state personal preferences and for certain parts of them.	• Evaluate performances as an audience, articulating emotional responses to dramatic performances; state personal preferences for entire performances and for certain parts of them; and provide reasons for their preferences.

Eighth graders are sometimes inhibited by their physical growth and development. They may hide or flaunt their changing voices or bodies. A shyness may develop when there was none before. They may be very interested in the opposite sex but refuse to play or have any relationship with someone they either admire or do not like. These changes may make it seem as though students are taking a step backward from where they were at earlier stages; however, the stage is natural and the students must not be judged negatively in assessing achievement relating to these aspects.

Grade 8

Theatre Processes	Eighth-grade students at the basic level in theatre:	Eighth-grade students at the proficient level in theatre:	Eighth-grade students at the advanced level in theatre:
Creating/ Performing	• Individually and in groups, develop scripts and scenarios from adaptations of storylines or create original work that includes simple characters, environments, and actions.	• Individually and in groups, develop scripts and scenarios from adaptations of storylines or create original work that includes characters, environments, and actions that create tension and suspense.	• Individually and in groups, develop scripts and scenarios from adaptations of storylines or create original work that includes characters, environments, and actions that create tension, suspense, and resolution in a

(Continued)

Theatre Processes	Eighth-grade students at the basic level in theatre:	Eighth-grade students at the proficient level in theatre:	Eighth-grade students at the advanced level in theatre:
			coherent and wellformed scene that is compelling, focused, and unique.
	• Develop characters that suggest artistic choices through limited script analysis and the rehearsal process, demonstrating some acting skills.	• Develop characters that suggest artistic choices through script analysis and the rehearsal process, demonstrating acting skills, working in an ensemble, and interacting as invented characters.	• Develop characters that suggest artistic choices through script analysis and the rehearsal process, demonstrating acting skills, working in an ensemble, and interacting as invented characters; and demonstrate and maintain believability and emotional authenticity of invented characters.
	• Make designs to communicate locale, understand the use of a few technical theatre elements, and work collaboratively to select and create some elements of scenery and properties to signify environment and costumes to suggest character.	• Make designs to communicate locale and mood; understand the use of the most technical theatre elements; and work collaboratively and safely to select and create some elements of scenery, properties, lighting, and sound to signify environment and costumes and makeup to suggest character.	• Make designs to communicate locale, mood, and theme; understand the use of technical theatre elements; and work collaboratively and safely to select and create some elements of scenery, properties, lighting, and sound to signify environment and costumes and makeup to suggest character.
	• Direct by interpreting dramatic texts and rehearsing improvised and scripted scenes.	• Direct by interpreting dramatic texts and rehearsing improvised and scripted scenes demonstrating social and consensus skills.	• Direct by interpreting dramatic texts and leading groups in planning and rehearsing improvised and scripted scenes demonstrating social and consensus skills.

(Continued)

Theatre Processes	Eighth-grade students at the basic level in theatre:	Eighth-grade students at the proficient level in theatre:	Eighth-grade students at the advanced level in theatre:
Responding	• Describe their artistic choices and construct meaning, describing the perceived effectiveness of their contributions to developing improvised and scripted scenes.	• Describe and analyze their artistic choices and construct meaning, articulating those meanings and describing the perceived effectiveness of their contributions to developing improvised and scripted scenes.	• Describe and analyze their artistic choices and construct meaning, articulating those meanings and describing the perceived effectiveness of their contributions to the collaborative process of developing improvised and scripted scenes.
	• Describe archetypal characters and situations in dramas from and about various historical periods; define the elements of film (composition, movement, sound, and editing); and describe characteristics of characters, environments, and actions in theatre, musical theatre, film, and television.	• Describe and compare archetypal characters and situations in dramas from and about various genres and historical periods; identify the elements of film (composition, movement, sound, and editing); and describe characteristics and compare the presentations of characters, environments, and actions in theatre, musical theatre, film, and television.	• Describe and compare archetypal characters and situations in dramas from and about various artistic styles, genres, and historical periods; identify the elements of film (composition, movement, sound, and editing) and explain how these elements are integral to the content of the work; and describe characteristics and compare the presentations of characters, environments, and actions in theatre, musical theatre, film, and television, recognizing the special relationship between audience and performers.
	• Place work in personal and social contexts by analyzing the social impact of dramatic events in their lives, in the community, and in other cultures; and	• Place work in personal, social, and cultural contexts by analyzing the emotional and social impacts of dramatic events in their lives, in the	• Place work in personal, social, historical, and cultural contexts by analyzing the emotional and social impacts of dramatic events in their

(Continued)

	Eighth-grade students at the basic level in theatre:	Eighth-grade students at the proficient level in theatre:	Eighth-grade students at the advanced level in theatre:
Theatre Processes	explain how culture affects the content of dramatic performances and how social concepts such as cooperation, communication, self-esteem, risk taking, and sympathy apply in theatre and daily life.	community, and in other cultures; and explain how culture affects the content of dramatic performances and how social concepts such as cooperation, communication, collaboration, self-esteem, risk taking, sympathy, and empathy apply in theatre and daily life.	lives, in the community, and in other cultures; and explain how culture affects the content and production values of dramatic performances and how social concepts such as cooperation, comm-unication, collaboration, self-esteem, risk taking, sympathy, and empathy apply in theatre and daily life.
	• Evaluate performances as audience by using articulated criteria to describe the perceived effectiveness of artistic choices found in dramatic performances.	• Evaluate performances as audience by using articulated criteria to describe and analyze the perceived effectiveness of artistic choices found in dramatic performances.	• Evaluate performances as audience by using articulated criteria to describe, analyze, and constructively evaluate the perceived effectiveness of artistic choices found in dramatic performances.
	• Identify a few exemplary artists and works of theatre, film, and television.	• Identify some exemplary artists and works of theatre, film, and television.	• Identify some exemplary artists and works of theatre, film, and television; explain why they are considered exemplary.
	• Describe the effect of publicity on audience response to dramatic performances.	• Describe and analyze the effect of publicity, study guides, and programs on audience response to dramatic performances.	• Describe and analyze the effect of publicity, study guides, programs, and physical environments on audience response to dramatic performances.

(Continued)

Twelfth-grade students are young adults. Connected to a real and often confusing world, they struggle to make sense of their environment and the world around them. They are more willing to role-play someone else than play themselves. They rely on peer groups and the media for their identity and their information. They are open to new ideas.

Grade 12

Theatre Processes	Twelfth-grade students at the basic level in theatre:	Twelfth-grade students at the proficient level in theatre:	Twelfth-grade students at the advanced level in theatre:
Creating/ Performing	• Develop scripts and scenarios with character, conflict, and resolution.	• Develop imaginative scripts and scenarios so that story and meaning are conveyed to an audience.	• Develop imaginative scripts and scenarios for theatre, film, and television that include original characters with unique dialog that motivates action so that the story and meaning are conveyed to an audience.
	• Develop characters through the acting process, including analyzing the physical and social dimensions of characters; and in a group, present the characters.	• Develop characters through the acting process, including analyzing the physical, emotional, and social dimensions of characters, and in an ensemble, create and sustain characters that communicate with audiences.	• Develop characters through the acting process, including analyzing the physical, emotional, and social dimensions of characters, and in an ensemble, create and sustain characters from classical, contemporary, realistic, and nonrealistic dramatic texts that communicate with audiences.
	• Make design and technical theatre choices to communicate locale and mood by sketching designs for a set, lighting, props, costumes, or makeup appropriate for a scene or scenario; select sound effects to convey environment; and demonstrate knowledge of production elements	• Make design and technical theatre choices to communicate locale and mood by sketching designs for a set, lighting, props, costumes, or makeup appropriate for a scene or scenario, considering some cultural and historical perspectives; select music and sound effects to convey environments that	• Collaborate with a director to develop a unified production concept and make design and technical theatre choices that communicate this as well as locale and mood by sketching a design for a set, lighting, props, costumes, or makeup appropriate for a scene

(Continued)

Theatre Processes	Twelfth-grade students at the basic level in theatre:	Twelfth-grade students at the proficient level in theatre:	Twelfth-grade students at the advanced level in theatre:
	(stage management, promotional or business plans) for a production.	clearly support the text; and design some production elements (stage management, promotional or business plans) for a production.	or scenario, considering the cultural and historical perspectives as well; select music and sound effects to convey environments that clearly support the text and reflect a unified production concept; design coherent stage management, promotional, or business plans for a production; and explain how scientific and technological advances have impacted set, lights, sound, costume design, and implementation for theatre, film, and television productions.
	• Direct by interpreting dramatic texts and organizing time and people in planning and rehearsing improvised and scripted scenes.	• Direct by interpreting dramatic texts and organizing time and people in planning and rehearsing improvised and scripted scenes, effectively communicating directorial choices to an ensemble.	• Direct by interpreting dramatic texts and organizing time and people in planning and rehearsing improvised and scripted scenes, effectively communicating directorial choices, including a unifying concept to an ensemble; and explain and compare the roles and interrelated responsibilities of the various personnel involved in theatre, film, and television productions.
Responding	• Describe artistic choices and construct meaning by evaluating their own	• Describe and analyze artistic choices and construct meaning by evaluating their own collaborative efforts and	• Describe and analyze artistic choices and construct meaning by

(Continued)

Theatre Processes	Twelfth-grade students at the basic level in theatre:	Twelfth-grade students at the proficient level in theatre:	Twelfth-grade students at the advanced level in theatre:
	collaborative efforts and artistic choices.	artistic choices, and analyze the effect of their own cultural experiences on their dramatic work.	evaluating their own collaborative efforts and artistic choices, analyze the effect of their own cultural experiences on their dramatic work, and articulate and justify personal aesthetic criteria that compare perceived artistic intent with the final aesthetic achievement.
	• Describe some elements, genres, media, and dramatic literature from various cultures and historical periods.	• Describe and compare elements, styles, genres, media, and dramatic literature, focusing on comparing how similar themes are treated in drama from various cultures and historical periods.	• Describe and compare elements, styles, genres, media, and dramatic literature, focusing on comparing how similar themes are treated in drama from various cultures and historical periods and discussing how theatre can reveal universal concepts.
	• Place work in personal, social, historical, and cultural contexts by identifying some of the lives and works of representative theatre artists in some cultures and historical periods.	• Place work in personal, social, historical, and cultural contexts by identifying and comparing the lives, works, and influence of representative theatre artists in various cultures and historical periods.	• Place work in personal, social, historical, and cultural contexts by identifying and comparing the lives, works, and influence of representative theatre artists in various cultures and historical periods and identifying cultural and historical influences on American theatre; and analyze the social impact of underrepresented theatre and film artists

(Continued)

Theatre Processes	Fourth-grade students at the basic level in theatre:	Fourth-grade students at the proficient level in theatre:	Fourth-grade students at the advanced level in theatre:
	• Evaluate performances as audience and critic, analyzing and critiquing parts of dramatic performances.	• Evaluate performances as audience and critic, analyzing and critiquing parts of dramatic performances, taking into account context.	(for example, Native American, Chicano). • Evaluate performances as audience and critic, analyzing and critiquing parts of dramatic performances, taking into account context and constructively suggesting alternative artistic choices; analyze and evaluate critical comments about dramatic work, explaining which points are most appropriate to inform further development of the work; and analyze how dramatic forms, production practices, and theatrical traditions influence contemporary theatre, film, and television productions.

Preliminary Achievement Level Descriptions for the Visual Arts

NAEP uses the following descriptions as expectations for student achievement:

- **Basic** denotes partial mastery of the content but performance that is only adequate for work at the three grade levels.
- **Proficient** represents solid academic achievement and competency over challenging subject matter, as suggested in the *National Standards for Arts Education*.
- **Advanced** performance on this assessment represents achievement that is equal to that expected of top students.

In creating and responding to works of art and design, fourth-grade students are involved in exploratory, trial-and-error experiences.

Visual Arts Processes	Fourth-grade students at the basic level in visual arts:	Fourth-grade students at the proficient level in visual arts:	Fourth-grade students at the advanced level in visual arts:
Creating/ Performing	• Develop one or two ideas/ approaches to a problem, with little originality in content or form, reflecting no awareness of the relationship between the art/design work and the context.	• Develop several ideas/approaches to a problem, some of which are original in their content and form, and reflect some awareness of the relationship between the art/design work and the context.	• Develop many ideas/approaches to a problem, most of which are original in content and form, and reflect awareness and understanding of the relationship between the art/design work and the context.
	• Visually and in written form demonstrate a limited understanding of the relationship between principles of visual organization and the construction of meaning or function.	• Visually and in written form demonstrate a general understanding of the relationship between principles of visual organization and the construction of meaning or function.	• Visually and in written form demonstrate a high level of understanding of the relationship between principles of visual organization and the construction of meaning or function.
	• Explore ideas, media, and tools in a limited way.	• Explore a variety of ideas, media, and tools.	• Experiment creatively with a variety of ideas, media, and tools.

(Continued)

Visual Arts Processes	Fourth-grade students at the basic level in visual arts:	Fourth-grade students at the proficient level in visual arts:	Fourth-grade students at the advanced level in visual arts:
	• Demonstrate a limited understanding of the relationship of design-related problems and processes to real-life situations, using a random process to develop a singular solution to a problem.	• Demonstrate an understanding of the relationship of design-related problems and processes to real-life situations, using a linear process to develop a singular solution to a problem.	• Demonstrate a high level of understanding of the relationship of design-related problems and processes to real-life situations, understand the relationships between the process and its solution, and use a clear planning process (models, sketches, diagrams) to generate multiple solutions to each problem.
	• Seek the most obvious answer to a question about process or content rather than integrate information from a variety of sources.	• Integrate information from a variety of sources, take an idea and expand upon it, and find answers to questions about process or content.	• Integrate information from a variety of sources, take an idea and expand upon it, and invent answers to questions about process or content.
	• Find, select, and integrate information from a few sources, precluding much extension or elaboration of ideas.	• Find, select, and integrate information from a variety of sources, enabling some extension and elaboration of ideas and selection of methods and processes from several approaches to solving problems.	• Find, select, and integrate information from a wider variety of sources, enabling greater extension and elaboration of ideas and selection of methods and processes from a variety of approaches to solving problems; and facilitate understanding of the relationship of these sources to the generation of ideas, alternatives, and various problem-solving approaches.

(Continued)

Visual Arts Processes	Fourth-grade students at the basic level in visual arts:	Fourth-grade students at the proficient level in visual arts:	Fourth-grade students at the advanced level in visual arts:
	• Demonstrate a limited ability to recognize personal strengths and weaknesses in their own work.	• Recognize personal strengths and weaknesses, and select and discuss own work.	• Recognize personal strengths and weaknesses; can select, discuss, and give specific examples from own work; and identify works of varying quality while reflecting on personal artistic processes.
Responding	• Demonstrate a limited ability to use vocabulary that describes visual experiences and/or phenomena.	• Can respond to works of art/design using a general vocabulary that describes visual experiences and/or phenomena.	• Can articulately respond to works of art/design using a specialized vocabulary that describes visual experiences and/or phenomena and support assertions.
	• Respond to questions about works of art/design (their own and others) with answers that focus on basic description rather than interpretation.	• Respond to questions about works of art and design (own and others) with answers that demonstrate an ability to interpret.	• Respond to questions about works of art and design (their own and others), offering multiple interpretations that provide evidence of curiosity.
	• Identify obvious patterns of similarity (i.e., style, subject/theme, function) in works of art/design but are unable to articulate basis for the judgment.	• Identify obvious patterns of similarity (i.e., style, subject/theme, function) in works of art and design, and can articulate some similarities in ways that show the relationships between the parts and the whole.	• Identify obvious and not-so-obvious patterns of similarity (i.e., style, subject/theme, function) in works of art and design and forms of response, and find inventive ways to articulate some similarities that show the relationships between the parts and the whole.

(Continued)

Visual Arts Processes	Fourth-grade students at the basic level in visual arts:	Fourth-grade students at the proficient level in visual arts:	Fourth-grade students at the advanced level in visual arts:
	• Cannot recognize obvious differences and similarities between works of art/design, and cannot defend their judgments.	• Recognize obvious differences and similarities between works of art/design, defending how similarities and differences relate to history, culture, and human needs.	• Recognize both obvious and not-so-obvious differences and similarities between works of art/design, defending how similarities and differences relate to history, culture, and human needs.

In creating and responding to works of art and design, the eighth-grade student shows emerging abilities to make intellectual and visual selections and decisions based on personal values and intent to construct or interpret meaning.

Grade 8

Visual Arts Processes	Eighth-grade students at the basic level in visual arts:	Eighth-grade students at the proficient level in visual arts:	Eighth-grade students at the advanced level in visual arts:
Creating/Performing	• Operate within a limited definition of context in design-related problems that focus on immediate, real-life situations with prescribed problem-solving approaches.	• Operate within an expanded definition of context in design-related problems that include broader issues of environment, human factors, and social behavior with diverse problem-solving approaches.	• Operate within an expanded definition of context in design-related problems that incorporates under-standing of the relationship between the process of design and the solutions that result from it, using inventive problem-solving approaches.
	• Do not recognize competing priorities or performance criteria in the definition of the problem; address only one aspect of the problem at a time; and cannot recognize principles guiding organization of form, content, or function.	• Recognize competing priorities or performance criteria in the definition of the problem; identify alternative solutions; and recognize principles guiding organization of form, content, or function.	• Recognize competing priorities in the definition of the problem; predict outcomes of solutions that reflect alternative needs of users/audience; and recognize and apply principles guiding the organization of form, content, or function.

(Continued)

Visual Arts Processes	Eighth-grade students at the basic level in visual arts:	Eighth-grade students at the proficient level in visual arts:	Eighth-grade students at the advanced level in visual arts:
	• Exhibit limited technical skill with tools and media with a tendency to prefer one media to another, more from a sense of proficiency with the material or tool rather than because it is the best choice for the communication of the idea.	• Demonstrate increased control of media and tools with a desire to learn specific techniques to gain greater ability to communicate ideas, and make conscious choices that are appropriate to the problem.	• Demonstrate greater control of media and tools, often choosing to specialize and practice to develop expertise, enabling greater facility in the communication of ideas; make conscious choices that are appropriate to the problem; and experiment with less obvious characteristics of the medium.
	• Develop one or two methods for judging ideas in planning or simulation (thumbnail sketches, models, maquettes) before reaching closure on concepts, visual organization, meaning, or production.	• Devise and employ several methods for judging ideas in planning or simulation (thumbnail sketches, models, maquettes) before reaching closure on concepts, visual organization, meaning, or production.	• Devise and employ many methods for judging ideas in planning or simulation, using both actual images (thumbnail sketches, models, maquettes) and mental images while decoding meaning before reaching closure on concepts, visual organization, meaning, or production.
	• Cannot weigh ideas against individually determined or group-determined criteria in the creation of works of art/design.	• Weigh ideas against individually determined or group-determined criteria in the creation of works of art/design.	• Weigh ideas against individually determined or group-determined criteria in the creation of works of art and design, reinterpreting and extending group-shared criteria.
	• Find, select, and integrate information from a few sources, precluding much extension or elaboration of ideas.	• Find, select, and integrate information from a variety of sources, enabling some extension and elaboration of	• Find, select, and integrate information from a wider variety of sources, enabling greater extension and elaboration of

(Continued)

Visual Arts Processes	Eighth-grade students at the basic level in visual arts:	Eighth-grade students at the proficient level in visual arts:	Eighth-grade students at the advanced level in visual arts:
		ideas and selection of methods and processes from several approaches to solving problems.	ideas and selection of methods and processes from a variety of approaches to solving problems; and facilitate understanding of the relationship of these sources to the generation of ideas, alternatives, and various problem-solving approaches.
	• Cannot identify personal strengths and weaknesses; and within process reviews, provide limited positive and realistic evaluation of work.	• Identify personal strengths and weaknesses, selecting and discussing their own work; and within process reviews, identify and comment on works of varying quality, demonstrating some ability to reflect criteria and insights.	• Identify and analyze personal strengths and weaknesses, selecting, justifying, and discussing their own work; within process reviews, identify and compare works of varying quality with insight; and demonstrate high-level ability to discuss the relationship of these works to personal creative and technical development.
	• Inappropriately use visual and verbal vocabulary of form and principles of organization as a way to construct meaning.	• Appropriately use visual and verbal vocabulary of form and principles of visual organization to make inferences and construct meaning.	• Appropriately and articulately use the visual and verbal vocabulary of form and principles of visual organization to make inferences and construct meaning.
Responding	• Respond to questions of art/design through literal discussion, debate, writing, and visual analysis, confining inferences made to obvious physical characteristics.	• Respond to questions of art/design through literal and metaphorically expanded discussion, supported debate,	• Respond to questions about art/design through extended and metaphorically embellished discussion, supported debate,

(Continued)

Visual Arts Processes	Eighth-grade students at the basic level in visual arts:	Eighth-grade students at the proficient level in visual arts:	Eighth-grade students at the advanced level in visual arts:
		expository writing, and visual analysis, making inferences on the obvious and not-so-obvious physical, as well as some abstract, characteristics.	expository writing, and visual analysis, making inferences on the obvious and not-so-obvious physical and many abstract characteristics, revealing a philosophical position.
	• Cannot apply criteria to interpretation of works of art/design but can recognize one or two obvious connecting patterns, shared concepts, and inferences or connections among works of art and other types of experience or ideas.	• Apply criteria to the interpretation of works of art/design and can recognize most obvious connecting patterns, shared concepts, and inferences or connections among works of art and other types of experience or ideas.	• Apply criteria to the interpretation of works of art/design; and search for and recognize obvious and subtle connecting patterns, shared concepts, and inferences or connections among works of art and other types of experience or ideas.
	• Do not judge or defend the various dimensions of context in which art and design are created and interpreted.	• Judge the various dimensions of context in which art and design are created and interpreted.	• Judge and defend the various dimensions of context in which art and design are created and interpreted.
	• Identify literal ways in which works of art reflect and influence the way people perceive experiences in their lives and how people's experiences influence the development of specific works.	• Identify and describe literal ways in which works of art reflect and influence the way people perceive experiences in their lives and how people's experiences influence the development of specific works.	• Identify and describe literal and abstract ways in which works of art reflect and influence the way people perceive experiences in their lives and how people's experiences influence the development of specific works.

(Continued)

In creating and responding to works of art and design, students in the 12th grade show evidence of increased awareness about thinking about and processing concepts and judgments.

Grade 12

Visual Arts Processes	Twelfth-grade students at the basic level in visual arts:	Twelfth-grade students at the proficient level in visual arts:	Twelfth-grade students at the advanced level in visual arts:
Creating/ Performing	• Recognize one or two predictable approaches to the organization of form, theories of meaning, and dimensions of context.	• Recognize and analyze several different predictable and inventive approaches to the organization of form, theories of meaning, and dimensions of context.	• Recognize, analyze, and synthesize many different inventive approaches to the organization of form, theories of meaning, and dimensions of context and understand how they impact the content of the work.
	• Generate a single solution to a problem that replicates an existing solution; and show little understanding of context, audience, and performance criteria.	• Generate several solutions to a problem, some of which depart from known solutions; and show an emerging understanding of context, audience, and performance criteria.	• Generate many solutions to a problem, most of which depart from known solutions; and show a high degree of originality and sensitivity to context, performance criteria, and theoretical frameworks of design.
	• Generate one or two alternatives with little recognition of personal, conceptual, and critical development across an accumulated body of work.	• Generate several alternatives while recognizing personal, conceptual, and critical development across an accumulated body of work.	• Generate multiple alternatives with a high level of recognition of personal, conceptual, and critical development across an accumulated body of work.
	• Use media, tools, and technical processes with some evidence of focused selection and personalization, control in communicating meaning, and testing of limits; and work against the medium without understanding its limits and capacity.	• Use media, tools, and technical processes with greater evidence of focused selection, personalization, control in communicating	• Use media, tools, and technical processes with competence and considerable interest in selection, personalization, control in communicating meaning, and

(Continued)

Visual Arts Processes	Twelfth-grade students at the basic level in visual arts:	Twelfth-grade students at the proficient level in visual arts:	Twelfth-grade students at the advanced level in visual arts:
		meaning, and testing of limits; and can work with the medium, understanding its capacity and limits.	testing of limits; and work and experiment with the medium's more subtle aspects, inventing new limits and capacities.
	• Respond to a few simple components of challenging problems; define superficial, physical dimensions of the problem, proceeding haphazardly through the problem-solving process; and are unable to assess the impact of process on solutions.	• Respond to some complex components of challenging problems; define most physical and some abstract dimensions of the problem, proceeding consciously through a linear problem-solving process but not extending or elaborating upon it; and can assess the impact of process on the solution.	• Respond to multiple complex components of challenging problems; define most physical and abstract dimensions of the problem, proceeding intentionally through a lateral problem-solving process, extending and elaborating upon it; and use analogies and abstract principles to understand and assess the impact of process on the solution.
	• Make limited use of simulation techniques but are unable to predict the outcome of possible solutions.	• Develop some use of simulation techniques and predict the outcome of some possible solutions.	• Develop a variety of simulation techniques, determine appropriateness for specific problems, and predict the outcome of most simulated solutions.
	• Develop design solutions that respond to a partial list of performance criteria but are unable to weigh criteria or resolve competing demands within the same problem.	• Develop design solutions that respond to a broad range of performance criteria and can weigh criteria or resolve competing demands within the same problem.	• Respond to a full range of performance criteria; define problems in differing ways and are likely to redefine the problem in terms of specific orientation, context, or indepth focus that

(Continued)

Visual Arts Processes	Twelfth-grade students at the basic level in visual arts:	Twelfth-grade students at the proficient level in visual arts:	Twelfth-grade students at the advanced level in visual arts:
			meets students' need for personal growth; and weigh criteria and articulate reasons for weighting certain aspects of the problem more heavily than others.
	• Recognize one or two personal strengths and weaknesses in creating and responding but are unable to select and discuss their own work or identify works of varying quality related to the progression of personal creative development.	• Recognize some personal strengths and weaknesses in creating and responding; and select and discuss their own work, identifying works of varying quality related to the progression of personal creative development.	• Recognize most personal strengths and weaknesses in creating and responding; and select, identify, and justify works of varying quality through the insightful and focused analysis of the relationship of these works to progression of personal creative development.
Responding	• Do not refer to the visual and verbal vocabulary of form and principles of visual organization in the construction of meaning; and recognize obvious, literal relationships of ideology, theory, and context to the formal principles.	• Refer to the visual and verbal vocabulary of form and principles of visual organization in the construction of meaning; and recognize obvious literal and abstract relationships of ideology, theory, and context to the formal principles.	• Refer to and integrate the visual and verbal vocabulary of form and principles of visual organization in the construction of meaning; and recognize and articulate abstract and subtle relationships of ideology, theory, and context to the formal principles.
	• Understand and manage simple, obvious relationships between context and the creation and interpretation of works of art/design.	• Understand and manage simple, not-so-obvious, and abstract relationships between context and the	• Understand and manage abstract, complex, and subtle relationships between context and the creation

(Continued)

Visual Arts Processes	Twelfth-grade students at the basic level in visual arts:	Twelfth-grade students at the proficient level in visual arts:	Twelfth-grade students at the advanced level in visual arts:
		creation and interpretation of works of art/design.	and interpretation of works of art/design.
	• Develop predictable and common theoretical constructs and methods for decisionmaking among competing priorities or opinions.	• Develop predictable and inventive theoretical constructs and methods for decisionmaking among competing priorities or opinions.	• Develop inventive and unusual theoretical constructs and methods for decisionmaking among competing priorities or opinions.
	• Place singular and obvious personal comments within an elementary critical process, with little engagement in criticism by explaining meaning; identifying, describing, and recognizing critical models; and forming belief systems.	• Place varied and thoughtful personal comments within a compound critical process, with conscious engagement in criticism by explaining meaning; identifying, describing, and recognizing critical models; and forming belief systems.	• Place multiple and discerning personal comments within a complex critical process, with perceptive engagement in criticism by explaining meaning; identifying, describing, and recognizing critical models; and forming belief systems.
	• Cannot identify where design solutions do not function well and show limited ability to transfer learning from one problem to another.	• Identify where design solutions do not function well and transfer learning from one problem to another.	• Identify and articulate where design solutions do not function well; make adjustments in their own problem-solving process; and transfer learning from one problem to another.

APPENDIX A. THE CONTENT OUTLINES

The content outlines for the disciplines of dance, music, theatre, and visual arts are based on the work of the NAEP planning committee and on the *National Standards* in each of the arts disciplines. The *National Standards* in dance, music, theatre, and the visual arts were developed by professionals in those disciplines who are members of the National Consortium of Arts Organizations. The consortium was funded to develop content standards in the arts by the U.S. Department of Education, the National Endowment for the Arts, and the National Endowment for the Humanities.

The connection between the work of the *National Standards* task forces and the work of the NAEP planning committee is a strong one. Through each phase of the NAEP project, the planning committee in each arts discipline based its assessment discussions on the concurrent work of the *National Standards* task force in that discipline.

For purposes of assessment, the NAEP planning committee (composed of specialists in dance, music, theatre, and the visual arts) identified major categories in which the content of the arts could be organized. Thus, in assessing what students know and are able to do in each of the arts, the content was formulated around the processes of creating, performing, and responding.

In developing standards in the arts, the *National Standards* task forces initially organized their work around the processes of creating and performing, perceiving and analyzing, knowing historical and social contexts, and understanding the nature and the meaning of each of the arts. Although these categories are not specifically delineated in the final document, they can be used to approach and understand the work of each discipline.

In the content outlines, the NAEP planning committee content categories appear in boldface Roman numerals I, II, or III followed by each discipline group's assessment recommendation, which is labeled in boldface capital letters. The Achievement Standards from the proposed *National Standards* that delineate the content to be assessed in that discipline are cited. For reference purposes, the Achievement Standards number and letter from the proposed voluntary *National Standards* are noted in parentheses at the end of each statement.

In unfolding the standards for the purposes of assessment, it was sometimes necessary for the NAEP planning committee to modify the wording (but not the intent) of an achievement standard to provide the level of detail needed by assessment developers. These modifications occur in italics to indicate the changes made for assessment purposes. At the 12th-grade level, reframing the standards in this way also made them more inclusive and therefore more appropriate in the assessment of general students. Asterisks are used in music and theatre to indicate the standards that are particularly useful for measurement of the student who has had less than 2 years of specific arts instruction at the high school level.

At grade 12, following the pattern of the *National Standards,* the standards designated as proficient are abbreviated with "Pro" and advanced standards are abbreviated with "Adv." Both are followed by the number and letter of the standard being addressed, as in grades 4 and 8.

Not all of the proposed *National Standards* are included in the content outlines. Some standards cannot be appropriately evaluated in a large-scale assessment and are more appropriately addressed in state level, district level, or classroom-based assessments.

In some assessment examples in the content outline, the music group cited the six levels of difficulty as defined in the music glossary in the *National Standards*. These levels were adapted for use in the standards with permission from *NYSSMA Manual,* Edition XXIII, published by the New York State School Music Association in 1991.

The following general comments made by the visual arts group of the NAEP planning committee reflect circumstances that called for changes necessary to meet the demands of the assessment:

1. In the *National Standards,* the term "design" refers to "composition," whereas in the NAEP Arts Education Assessment Framework and specifications the term "design" refers to the disciplines of architecture, interior design, industrial design, and graphic design, all of which are included in the NAEP visual arts assessment. Therefore, the NAEP visual arts group replaced the word "design" with "composition."
2. The NAEP Arts Education Assessment content outline deals with cognitive skills implied but not specified in the standards. Specifically mentioned are areas related to visual thinking, the construction of meaning, and representation.
3. The NAEP visual arts group's rewording of the *National Standards* clearly differentiates content that is about "syntax" (organization of visual elements) from content that is about "semantics" (selection of subject matter) so that these two aspects of content can be considered separately. The standards combine these two aspects of content in a single statement.
4. The NAEP Arts Education Assessment framework and specifications use the word "form" rather than "image" to include more spatial and temporal considerations. Where there are references to "visual" characteristics, the NAEP visual arts group added "spatial and temporal" to include three-dimensional art and time-based media.
5. The NAEP visual arts group was more specific in its use of terminology to provide information to the assessment development contractor. For example, when the standards refer to "characteristics," the group added words such as "characteristics of materials" or "formal and symbolic characteristics" to clarify the intended meaning.
6. The NAEP visual arts group felt it necessary to elaborate on issues related to application of the arts to daily life and on criticism. Because the standards did not address these issues explicitly, the group augmented the content outline to provide a focus for assessment.
7. The standards use "art forms" and "arts disciplines" to refer to the same concept. The NAEP visual arts group standardized that concept under the term "arts disciplines" or "other arts," reserving "visual art forms" for cases in which there is a need to distinguish painting from printmaking (for example, in the exercise design).

Dance Content Outline

Dance, Grade 4

I. Creating

A. **Invent Solutions to Movement Problems, Generating and Selecting from Alternatives (A movement problem is a task that requires effort, thought, and practice to solve.)**
   1. *Given a movement problem that requires an original response, devise and test out two to three movement solutions;* students choose their favorite solution and discuss the reasons for that choice (4a).
B. **Follow Improvisational and Compositional Structures**
   1. Create *an original dance of at least 30 seconds* with a beginning, middle, and end *expressing* the student's own idea (2a, 2b).
   2. Create an *original* dance phrase *of 20 seconds,* repeat *the phrase accurately,* and vary it (making changes in the time, space, and/or force or energy) (2d).
C. **Collaborate To Achieve Solutions**
   1. *Create and perform an original dance of at least 30 seconds with a partner, expressing an idea agreed upon by the partner* (2e).

II. Performing

A. **Accurately Recall and Reproduce Movement**
   1. *Given verbal direction,* demonstrate the nonlocomotor movements of bend, stretch, twist, and swing (nonlocomotor movements are done in place) (1a). *Given a live demonstration, perform a combination of these movements.*
   2. *Given verbal direction,* demonstrate eight basic locomotor movements (walk, run, hop, jump, leap, gallop, slide, skip) traveling forward, backward, sideward, diagonally, and turning (locomotor movements travel from one place to another) (1b). *Given a live demonstration, perform a combination of these movements.*
   3. *Given verbal direction,* demonstrate movements in straight and curved pathways (1e).
   4. *Given verbal direction and changes in rhythmic accompaniment (e.g., drumbeat tempo changes), demonstrate changes in movement that respond to* changes in tempo (1f).
B. **Demonstrate Physical Technique (Physical technique is defined as skills that allow the dancer to move with appropriate skeletal alignment, body part articulation, strength, flexibility, balance, and coordination in locomotor and nonlocomotor movements.)**
   1. *Given verbal directions to move through space as part of a large group,* demonstrate the ability to define and maintain personal space, distance from others, and spatial arrangement (form) (1d).
   2. *While following the movements of a facilitator,* demonstrate physical technique, concentration, and focus while performing movement skills in a group (1g).

3. *Given verbal direction,* demonstrate the following partner skills: copying, leading and following, mirroring (2f).
C. **Communicate through Movement (Expression)**
1. With competence and confidence, *perform* their own dances *for* peers and discuss their meanings (3c).
2. With competence and confidence, *perform for peers* folk dances from various cultures, *learned previously through demonstrations by a facilitator* (5a).

III. Responding

A. **Identify Compositional Elements and Notice Details**
1. *After viewing a brief movement study,* describe the *movements* (e.g., skip, gallop) and the movement elements (such as levels and directions) *and suggest ideas being communicated in the study* (1h).
B. **Identify Contexts (Stylistic, Cultural, Social, Historical) of Dance**
1. *After viewing three dances from* particular specific cultures and/or time periods (such as Colonial America), describe the cultural and/or historical contexts of each dance (5c).
C. **Make Informed Critical Observations about the Dance's and Dancer's Technical and Artistic Components**
1. Observe and discuss *how dancers differ from others who move (such as athletes, pedestrians)* (3 a).
2. Take an active role in a discussion *of a dance, offering personal reactions and interpretations* (3b).
3. Observe two dances and discuss how they are similar and different in terms of one element of dance (such as space, shapes, levels, pathways) (4b).

Dance, Grade 8

I. Creating

A. **Invent Solutions to Movement Challenges, Generating and Selecting from Alternatives**
1. Create a warmup exercise and explain how that exercise prepares the body and mind for expressive purposes (6c).
B. **Follow Improvisational and Compositional Structures**
1. *Given verbal direction,* demonstrate *in movement* the principles of contrast and transition (2a).
2. *Given verbal direction, demonstrate movements that exemplify choreographic processes such as* reordering (2b).
3. *Given verbal direction,* demonstrate *movements in the following* forms of AB, ABA, canon, call and response, and narrative (2c).
C. **Collaborate to Achieve Solutions**
1. Demonstrate the following partner skills in a visually interesting way: creating and complementary shapes, taking and supporting weight (2e).

2. Demonstrate the ability to work cooperatively in a *group of three or four* during the choreographic process (2d).

II. Performing

A. Accurately Recall and Reproduce Movement
1. Memorize and reproduce *dance sequences that are at least 32 counts in length* (1 g).
2. *Given the prompt of a rhythmic pattern drumbeat, reproduce* that rhythmic pattern in movement (1d).
3. *Given the prompt of a spatial pattern drawn on paper, reproduce that pattern by traveling through space* (1c).
4. *Given verbal prompts, demonstrate two previously learned dances, each at least 32 counts in length, representing two different styles, including* basic dance steps, *body* positions, and *spatial* patterns in demonstration (1b)(5b)(5a).

B. Demonstrate Physical Technique
1. *Given verbal prompts*, demonstrate *through movement sustained, percussive, and vibratory* qualities (1e).
2. *While following the demonstrated movements of a facilitator,* demonstrate the skills of alignment, balance, articulation of isolated body parts, weight shift, elevation and landing, fall, and recovery (1a).

C. Communicate Through Movement (Expression)
1. Create a dance *of at least 32 counts* that successfully communicates a topic of personal significance (3d).

III. Responding

A. Identify Compositional Elements and Notice Details
1. *After viewing a dance,* describe the *movements* and movement elements using appropriate dance vocabulary (i.e., level, direction) (1h).

B. Identify Contexts (Stylistic, Cultural, Social, Historical) of Dance
1. Describe the role of dance in two different cultures and/or time periods (5d).

C. Make Informed Critical Observations About the Dance's and Dancer's Technical and Artistic Components
1. *After observing a dance,* discuss *personal* opinions about *both the choreography and the performers* (4b).
2. Identify *and use* criteria for evaluating dance (such as skill of performers, originality, visual and/or emotional impact, variety, and contrast) (4d).
3. Compare and contrast two dance compositions in terms of space (such as shape and pathways), time (such as rhythm and tempo), and force/energy (such as movement qualities) (4c).

Dance, Grade 12

Proficient and Advanced

* Denotes expectations appropriate for the general 12th-grade student.

The Standards Dance Task Force has identified both "proficient" and "advanced" levels of achievement for grades 9–12 to address the level of attainment for a student who has received instruction in the skills and/or knowledge of dance for 1 to 2 years beyond grade 8 and the level of attainment for a student who has received instruction for 3 to 4 years beyond grade 8.

I. Creating

A. **Invent Solutions to Movement Challenges, Generating and Selecting from Alternatives**
   *1. Create and perform a *dance that includes two or more dynamic qualities (such as percussive) and expresses personal meaning* (Pro–1d).
   *2. Use improvisation to generate movement for choreography (Pro–2a).
   3. *Create a dance, then manipulate it by applying a different form, describing how the meaning of the dance was changed* (Adv–2e).

B. **Follow Improvisational and Compositional Structures**
   1. *Create a movement sequence that illustrates one of the following* structures or forms: theme and variation, rondo, or round (Pro–2b).
   2. Create a dance *of at least 1 minute, describing* the reasons for the *choreographic* decisions (Pro–4a).
   *3. *Observe a dance on video, describe the choreographic style, then create a dance of at least 1 minute in the style of the choreography observed.*

C. **Collaborate to Achieve Solutions**
   1. *Working in groups of three or four, choreograph a dance of at least 32 counts, then describe the choreographic principles, processes, and structures used* (Pro–2c).
   2. *Working with a partner, choreograph and perform a duet of at least 64 counts discussing the use of choreographic principles, processes, and structures* (Pro–2c).

II. Performing

A. **Accurately Recall and Reproduce Movement**
   *1. *After learning 32 counts of a dance taught by a facilitator, accurately recall and reproduce the movements and rhythmic patterns* (Pro–1f).
   2. *After learning two dances of different styles, accurately recall and reproduce each dance.*

B. **Demonstrate Physical Technique**

*1. *After learning 32 counts of a dance demonstrated by a facilitator,* demonstrate appropriate skeletal alignment, bodypart articulation, strength, flexibility, agility, and coordination in locomotor and nonlocomotor movement (Pro–1a).
2. *After learning a 64-count dance,* perform *the dance* with artistic expression, demonstrating clarity, musicality, and stylistic nuance (Adv–1h).

C. Communicate through Movement (Expression)

*1. Create a dance *of at least 32 counts* that communicates a contemporary social theme (such as isolation, poverty, relationships, the environment) (Pro–3c).
2. *Create a dance of at least 32 counts that conveys a contemporary social theme, vary the choreography so that it expresses a different theme, and discuss each idea and the ways it was expressed.*

III. Responding

A. Identify Compositional Elements and Notice Details

*1. *After observing a dance,* answer questions about how *the choreographer's choices communicate ideas* (Pro–3a).
2. After observing a dance on video, identify the choreographer's use of structure or form (i.e., theme and variation, rondo, round, canon call and response, narrative) (Pro–2b).
3. *After observing two different dances, compare how* the choreographers manipulate movement and movement *elements to express ideas* (Adv–2e).

B. Identify Contexts (Stylistic, Cultural, Social, Historical) of the Dance

*1. *After observing* a classical dance form (such as ballet), discuss the traditions and technique (Pro–5b).
2. Analyze how dance and dancers are portrayed in contemporary American media (Pro–5d).
3. Compare and contrast the role and significance of dance in two different social/historical/cultural/political contexts *(such as dance used for political devices in Communist China compared with dance used in Native-American ceremonies)* (Adv–5f).

C. Make Informed Critical Observations about the Dance's and Dancer's Technical and Artistic Components

1. Establish aesthetic criteria and apply them in evaluating own work and that of others (Pro–4b).
*2. Describe similarities and differences between two contemporary theatrical dances (Pro–5a).
3. Analyze issues of ethnicity, gender, social/economic class, age and/or physical condition in relation to dance *(what are the stereotypes in dance in reference to these issues? How does dance reflect such contemporary issues? etc.)* (Adv–4f).
4. Examine ways that dance creates and conveys meaning by considering the dance from a variety of perspectives *(such as the dance critic, the audience, the choreographer, the performer)* (Adv–3d).

Music Content Outline

Music, Grade 4

I. Creating

A. Compose
1. Create music to accompany readings or dramatizations, *manipulating dimensions such as the variety of sounds, tempo, loudness, and mood of a piece to enhance or match the readings or dramatizations and describing and explaining the choices made* (4a).
2. Create short songs and instrumental pieces *of 4 to 8 measures in length* within specified guidelines (e.g., a particular style, form *[call and response, ostinato, aba]*, instrumentation, compositional technique, *tonality [major, minor, pentatonic], meter [duple, triple]*) (4b).
3. Use a variety of sound sources (*e.g., classroom instruments, electronic instruments, body sounds*) when composing (4c).

B. Evaluate Own Composition
1. *Use* criteria *based on knowledge of the elements and style of music for comparing*, evaluating, and revising compositions (7a).
2. Explain, using appropriate music terminology *(e.g., describing dimensions such as tempo, text, instrumentation)*, personal preferences (*likes and dislikes*) for specific musical works or styles (7b).

C. Improvise
1. Improvise "answers" in the same style to given rhythmic and melodic phrases *from 2 to 4 measures long* (3 a).
2. Improvise simple rhythmic and melodic ostinato accompaniments (3b).
3. Improvise simple rhythmic variations and simple melodic embellishments on familiar melodies (3c).
4. Improvise short songs and instrumental pieces, using a variety of sound sources, including traditional sounds (e.g., voices, instruments); nontraditional sounds available in the classroom (e.g., paper tearing, pencil tapping); body sounds (e.g., hands clapping, fingers snapping); and sounds produced by electronic means (e.g., personal computers and basic MIDI devices, including keyboards, sequencers, synthesizers, and drum machines) (3d).

II. Performing

A. Sing: Competence and Expressiveness
1. Sing independently *(as a soloist singing familiar songs)*, on pitch and in rhythm, with appropriate timbre, diction, and posture and maintain a steady tempo (1a).
2. Sing expressively *(as a soloist singing familiar songs)* with appropriate dynamics, phrasing, and interpretation (1b).
3. Sing *familiar songs* from memory (1c).

4. Sing ostinatos, partner songs, and rounds *along with an ensemble on videotape that includes all parts* (1 d).
5. Sing in groups *along with a videotape that includes the conductor,* blending vocal timbres, matching dynamic levels, and responding to the cues of the conductor (1 e).

B. **Sight Singing (Read Unfamiliar Pieces From Notation)**
   1. Read whole, half, dotted half, quarter, and eighth notes and rests in 2/4, 3/4, and 4/4 *time* signatures (5a).
   2. *Sing at sight* simple pitch notation in the treble clef in major keys *(range of no more than an octave, primarily stepwise movement, no more than 4 measures)* (5b).

C. **Evaluate and Improve Own Singing**
   1. Use criteria *based on knowledge of the elements and style of music* for evaluating and *suggesting improvements* in performance (7a).
   2. Explain, using appropriate music terminology, personal preferences (*likes and dislikes*) for specific musical works or styles (7b).

D. **Play Instruments: Competence and Expressiveness**
   1. Perform *familiar music as a soloist* expressively (2c) on pitch, in rhythm, with appropriate dynamics and timbre, and maintain a steady tempo (2a).
   2. Perform *(in an ensemble or as a soloist)* easy rhythmic, melodic, and choral patterns accurately and independently on rhythmic, melodic, and harmonic classroom instruments, *either using own instrument or selecting an instrument from among those provided. The piece should be no more than 16 measures, with harmony limited to I and V chords and melody limited to range of an octave and stepwise movement* (2b).
   3. Echo short *(2–4 measure)* rhythms and melodic patterns (2d).
   4. Perform in groups *along with a videotape that includes the conductor,* blending instrumental timbres, matching dynamic levels, and responding to the cues of the conductor (2e).
   5. Perform independent instrumental parts while other students play *1–3* contrasting parts *on a videotape that includes a conductor* (2f).

E. **Sight Reading (Play an Unfamiliar Piece from Notation)**
   1. *Play from notation* whole, half, dotted half, quarter, and eighth notes and rests in 2/4, 3/4, and 4/4 *time* signatures (5a).
   2. *Play from notation* easy rhythmic, melodic, and chordal patterns on rhythmic, melodic, and harmonic classroom instruments (2b).

F. **Evaluate Own Playing**
   1. Use criteria *based on knowledge of the elements and style of music* for evaluating *and suggesting improvements* in performances (7a).
   2. Explain, using appropriate music terminology, personal preferences (*likes and dislikes*) for specific musical works or styles (7b).

III. Responding

A. Describe, Analyze, Compare, and Contrast
1. Identify simple music forms *(e.g., ABA, call and response)* presented aurally (6a).
2. Demonstrate perceptual skills by moving, answering questions about, and describing aural examples of various styles of music representing diverse cultures (6b).
3. Use appropriate terminology to explain music, music notation, music instruments and voices, and music performances (6c).
5. Identify the sounds of a variety of instruments, including many orchestra and band instruments, and instruments from various cultures, as well as male and female voices (6d).
6. Respond through purposeful movement to selected prominent music characteristics or to specific music events while listening to music (6e).

B. Use Notation (Connect What Is Seen with What Is Heard)
1. Read whole, half, dotted half, quarter, and eighth notes and rests in 2/4, 3/4, and 4/4 time signatures (5a).
2. Read simple pitch notation in the treble clef in major keys (5b).
3. Identify symbols and traditional terms referring to dynamics *(e.g., piano, forte, crescendo, diminuendo)*, tempo *(e.g., presto, ritard, accelerando)*, and articulation *(e.g., staccato, legato, marcato, accent)* (5c).
4. Use standard symbols to notate meter *(2/4, 3/4, and 4/4 time signatures)*, rhythm *(whole, half, dotted half, quarter, and eighth notes)*, pitch *(notes in treble clef)*, and dynamics *(p, f, < [crescendo], > [diminuendo])* in simple patterns (5d).

C. Evaluate Performances and Recommend Improvements
1. *Use criteria based on knowledge of musical elements and style* for evaluating performances (7a).

D. Evaluate Works
1. *Use criteria based on knowledge of musical elements and style* for evaluating compositions (7a).
2. Explain, using appropriate music terminology *(e.g., describing dimensions such as tempo, text, instrumentation)*, personal preferences *(likes and dislikes)* for specific musical works or styles (7b).

E. Place Works within Cultural and Historical Context
1. Identify, by genre or style, aural examples of music from various historical periods and cultures (9a).
2. Describe in simple terms how elements of music are used in music examples from various cultures of the world (9b).
3. Identify diverse uses of music in daily experiences and describe characteristics that make certain music suitable for each use (9c).
4. Identify and describe the roles of musicians in various music settings and cultures (9d).

Music, Grade 8

I. Creating

A. Compose
1. Compose short pieces *(8 to 12 measures)* within specified guidelines *(e.g., ABA form, limited range, and simple rhythms)*, demonstrating how the elements of music are used to achieve unity, variety, tension/release, and balance (4a).
2. Arrange simple pieces *(limit 12 measures)* for voices or instruments other than those for which the pieces were written *(e.g., create guitar accompaniment for folk song)* (4b).
3. Use a variety of traditional and nontraditional *(e.g., classroom instruments, body sounds, found sounds)* sound sources and electronic media *(synthesizer, sequencer)* when composing and arranging (4c).

B. Evaluate Own Composition
1. Evaluate the quality *(use of elements to create unity, variety, tension/release, and balance)* and effectiveness *(expressive impact)* of own and others' compositions and arrangements by applying specific criteria appropriate for the style of the music and offer constructive suggestions for improvement (7b).

C. Notate Personal Musical Ideas
1. Use standard notation to record their musical ideas and the musical ideas of others (5d).

D. Improvise
1. Improvise simple harmonic accompaniments (3a).
2. Improvise melodic embellishments and simple rhythmic and melodic variations on given pentatonic melodies and melodies in major keys (3b).
3. Improvise short melodies *(at least 12 measures)*, unaccompanied and over a given rhythmic accompaniment, each in a consistent style *(e.g., classical, blues, folk, gospel)*, meter *(e.g., duple, triple)*, and tonality *(e.g., major, pentatonic)* (3c).

E. Evaluate Own Improvisation
1. Evaluate the quality and effectiveness *(expressive impact)* of their own and others' improvisations by applying specific criteria appropriate for the style of the music and offer constructive suggestions for improvement (7b).

II. Performing

A. Sing: Competence and Expressiveness
1. *Sing familiar songs* accurately *(pitches, rhythms, expressions)* and with good *(consistent)* breath control throughout their singing ranges, alone and in small and large ensembles (1a).
2. Sing *familiar songs* with expression appropriate for the work being performed (1c).

3. Sing music written in two and three parts *(e.g., learn part through rote imitation and reading notation, then sing one part with a videotape of complete ensemble performance, including student's part, led by visible conductor)* (1d).
B. **Sight Singing (Read Unfamiliar Pieces from Notation)**
   1. Read whole, half, quarter, eighth, sixteenth, and dotted notes and rests in 2/4, 3/4, 4/4, 6/8, 3/8, and alla breve time signatures (5a).
   2. Read at sight simple melodies *(melodies appropriate to student's vocal range, no longer than 8 measures, mostly stepwise movement and rhythms specified above; sung using syllables, numbers, letters, or nonsense syllables)* in clef of student's choice (5b).
   3. Students who participate in a choral ensemble or class, sight-read, accurately and expressively, music with a level of difficulty of 2 (to be defined according to the piece selected for task) on a scale of 1 to 6 (5e).
C. **Evaluate and Improve Own Singing**
   1. Evaluate the quality *(technical)* and effectiveness *(expressive impact)* of their own performances by applying specific criteria appropriate for the style of the music and offer constructive suggestions for improvement (7b).
D. **Play Instruments: Competence and Expressiveness**
   1. Perform on at least one instrument accurately (technical and expressive) and independently, alone (familiar music) and in small and large ensembles (e.g., a part learned through rote imitation and reading notation, then sung with a videotape of complete ensemble performance that includes doubling of the student's part, led by a visible conductor), with good posture, good playing position, and good breath, bow, or stick control (2a).
   2. Play by ear simple melodies (e.g., *folk songs*) on a melodic instrument with simple accompaniments (e.g., *strummed I, IV, V, vi, ii chords*) on a harmonic instrument (2d).
   3. Perform music representing diverse genres and cultures, with expression appropriate for the work being performed (2c).
E. **Sight Reading (Play an Unfamiliar Piece from Notation)**
   1. Read whole, half, quarter, eighth, sixteenth, and dotted notes and rests in 2/4, 3/4, 4/4, 6/8, 3/8, and alla breve time signatures (5a).
   2. Read at sight simple melodies *(limited to 8 measures, range determined by instrument, rhythms indicated above)* in the clef *appropriate to the instrument* (5b).
   3. Students who participate in instrumental ensemble or class, sight-read, accurately and expressively, music with a level of difficulty of 2 on a scale of 1 to 6 (5e).
F. **Evaluate Own Playing**
   1. Evaluate the quality *(technical)* and effectiveness *(expressive impact)* of their own performances by applying specific criteria appropriate for the style of the music and offer constructive suggestions for improvement (7b).

III. Responding

A. Describe, Analyze, Compare, and Contrast
1. Describe specific music events in a given aural example, using appropriate terminology (6a).
2. Analyze the uses of elements of music in aural examples representing diverse genres and cultures (6b).
3. Demonstrate knowledge of the basic principles of meter, rhythm, tonality, intervals, chords, and harmonic progressions in their analyses of music (6c).

B. Read Notation (Connect What Is Seen with What Is Heard)
1. Read whole, half, quarter, eighth, sixteenth, and dotted notes and rests in 2/4, 3/4, 4/4, 6/8, 3/8, and alla breve time signatures (5a).
2. Identify and define *(while looking at a score)* standard notation symbols for pitch, rhythm, articulation *(accents, legato, staccato, marcato)*, dynamics *(piano, forte, crescendo, diminuendo)*, tempo, and expression (phrasing) (5c).
3. Use standard notation to record their musical ideas and the musical ideas of others (5d).

C. Evaluate Performances and Recommend Improvement
1. Evaluate the quality *(technical and expressive)* and effectiveness *(expressive impact)* of their own and others' performances and improvisations by applying specific criteria appropriate for the style of the music and offer constructive suggestions for improvement (7b).

D. Evaluate Works
1. Evaluate the quality *(technical and expressive)* and effectiveness *(expressive impact)* of their own and others' compositions and arrangements by applying specific criteria appropriate for the style of the music and offer constructive suggestions for improvement (7b).

E. Place Works within Cultural and Historical Context
1. Describe distinguishing characteristics *(relating to instrumentation, texture, rhythmic qualities, melodic lines, form)* of representative music genres and styles from a variety of cultures (9a).
2. Classify by genre and style (and, if applicable, by historical period, composer, and title) a varied body of exemplary (that is, high-quality and characteristic) musical works and explain the characteristics that cause each work to be considered exemplary (9b).
3. Compare the functions music serves, the roles of musicians, and the conditions under which music is typically performed in several cultures of the world (9c).

Music, Grade 12
* Denotes expectations appropriate for the general 12th-grade student.

I. Creating

A. Compose
1. Compose music in several distinct styles *(classical, folk, pop, jazz, rock)*, demonstrating creativity in using the elements of music for expressive effect (Pro–4a) and imagination and technical skill in applying the principles of composition (Adv–4d).
2. Arrange *simple* pieces *(e.g., piano music, 4-part hymns, duets, trios, quartets)* for voices or instruments other than those for which the pieces were written, in ways that preserve or enhance the expressive effect of the music (Pro–4b).
3. Compose and arrange music for voices and various acoustic and electronic instruments, demonstrating knowledge of the ranges and traditional use of the sound sources (Pro–4c).

B. Evaluate Own Composition
*1. Apply specific criteria for making informed, critical evaluations of the quality *(technical)* and effectiveness *(expressive impact)* of compositions or arrangements in their personal participation in music (Pro–7a).
*2. Evaluate a composition or arrangement by comparing it to similar or exemplary models (Pro–7b).
3. Evaluate a given musical work in terms of its aesthetic qualities *(e.g., interplay of unity and variety, tension/release, balance, overall expressive impact)* and explain the musical means it uses to evoke feelings and emotions (Adv–7c).

C. Notate Personal Musical Ideas
*1. Use standard notation to record their musical ideas (Grade 8–5d).

D. Improvise
1. Improvise stylistically appropriate harmonizing parts in a variety of styles *(e.g., classical, hymn, folk, pop, jazz, blues, rock)* (Adv–3d).
2. Improvise rhythmic and melodic variations on given pentatonic melodies and melodies in major and minor keys *(e.g., folk songs, standard pop songs, hymn tunes)* (Pro–3b).
*3. Improvise original melodies in a variety of styles *(e.g., classical, folk, pop, jazz, blues, rock)*, over given chord progressions *(progressions typical of the styles)*, each in a consistent style, meter, and tonality (Adv–3e).

E. Evaluate Own Improvisation
1. Apply specific criteria for making informed, critical evaluations of the quality *(technical)* and effectiveness *(expressive impact)* of improvisations in their participation in music (Pro–7a).
2. Evaluate *(e.g., consider questions of unity or variety, consistency, appropriate use of resources)* an improvisation by comparing it to similar or exemplary models (Pro–7b).

II. Performing

A. **Singing: Competence and Expressiveness**
   *1. Sing *familiar* songs performed from memory with expression and technical accuracy (Pro–1a).
   2. Sing *(one of the parts in)* music written in four parts (Pro–1b) *and* more than four parts, *with and without accompaniment* (Adv–1e).
   3. Demonstrate well-developed ensemble skills *(e.g., balance, intonation, rhythmic unity)* (Pro–1c).
   4. Sing in small ensembles with one student on a part (Adv–1f).

B. **Sight Singing (Read Unfamiliar Pieces From Notation)**
   Students who participate in a choral or instrumental ensemble or class:
   1. Sight-read, accurately *(correct pitches and rhythms)* and expressively *(e.g., appropriate dynamics, phrasing)*, music with a level of difficulty of 3 on a scale of 1 to 6 (Pro–5b) or 4 on a scale of 1 to 6 (Adv–5e).
   2. Interpret nonstandard notation symbols used by some 20th-century composers (Adv–5d).

C. **Evaluate and Improve Own Singing**
   1. Apply specific criteria for making informed, critical evaluations of the quality *(technical)* and effectiveness *(expressive impact)* of performances in their participation in music (Pro–7a).
   *2. Evaluate a performance by comparing it to similar or exemplary models (Pro–7b).
   3. Evaluate the quality *(technical)* and effectiveness *(expressive impact)* of their own performances by applying specific criteria appropriate for the style of the music and offer constructive suggestions for improvement (Grade 8–7b).

D. **Play Instruments: Competence and Expressiveness**
   1. *Play* with expression *(e.g., appropriate dynamics, phrasing, rubato)* and technical accuracy a large and varied repertoire of instrumental literature with a level of difficulty of 4 on a scale of 1 to 6 (Pro–2a) or 5 on a scale of 1 to 6 (Adv–2d).
   2. Perform an appropriate part in an ensemble, demonstrating well-developed ensemble skills *(e.g., balance, intonation, rhythmic unity)* (2b).
   3. Perform in small ensembles with one student on a part (2c).

E. **Sight Reading (Play an Unfamiliar Piece From Notation)**
   Students who participate in a choral or instrumental ensemble or class:
   1. Sight-read, accurately and expressively, music with a level of difficulty of 3 on a scale of 1 to 6 (Pro–5b) or 4 on a scale of 1 to 6 (Adv–5e).
   2. Interpret nonstandard notation symbols used by some 20th-century composers (Adv–5d).

F. **Evaluate Own Playing**
   1. Apply specific criteria for making informed, critical evaluations of the quality *(technical)* and effectiveness *(expressive impact)* of performances, compositions, arrangements, and improvisations in their personal participation in music (Pro–7a).
   *2. Evaluate a performance by comparing it to similar or exemplary models (Pro–7b).

3. Evaluate the quality *(technical)* and effectiveness *(expressive impact)* of their own performances by applying specific criteria appropriate for the style of the music and offer constructive suggestions for improvement (Grade 8–7b).

III. Responding

A. **Describe, Analyze, Compare, and Contrast**
   1. Analyze aural examples of a varied repertoire of music, representing diverse genres and cultures, by describing the uses of elements of music and expressive devices (Pro–6a).
   2. Demonstrate knowledge of the technical vocabulary of music *(e.g., Italian terms, form, harmony, tempo markings)* (Pro–6b).
   3. Identify and explain composition devices and techniques *(e.g., motives, imitation, retrograde, inversion)* used to provide unity, variety, tension, and resolution in a musical work and give examples of other works that make similar uses of these devices and techniques (Pro–6c).
   4. Demonstrate the ability to perceive and remember music events by describing in detail significant events *(e.g., elements of form, order of themes or phrases, nature of variations)* occurring in a given aural example (Adv–6d).
   5. Compare ways in which musical materials *(e.g., melody, accompaniment, instrumentation, dynamics)* are used in a given example relative to ways in which they are used in other works of the same genre or style (Adv–6e).
   6. Analyze and describe uses of the elements in a given musical work that make it unique, interesting, and expressive (Adv–6f).

B. **Use Notation (Connect What Is Seen with What Is Heard)**
   1. Demonstrate the ability to read *(e.g., follow a score while listening)* an instrumental or vocal score of up to four staves by describing how the elements of music are used in the score (Pro–5a) and explaining all transpositions and clefs (Adv–5c).
   2. Interpret nonstandard notation symbols used by some 20th-century composers (Adv–5d).
   *3. Use standard notation to record the musical ideas of others (Grade 8–5d).

C. **Evaluate Performances and Recommend Improvement**
   1. Apply specific criteria for making informed, critical evaluations of the quality *(technical)* and effectiveness *(expressive impact)* of performances in their personal participation in music (Pro–7a).
   *2. Evaluate a performance by comparing it to similar or exemplary models (Pro–7b).
   *3. Evaluate the quality *(technical)* and effectiveness *(expressive impact)* of others' performances by applying specific criteria appropriate for the style of the music and offer constructive suggestions for improvement (Grade 8–7b).

D. **Evaluating Works**
   *1. *Apply* specific criteria for making informed, critical evaluations of the quality *(technical)* and effectiveness *(expressive impact)* of compositions, arrangements, and improvisations in their participation in music (Pro–7a).

*2. Evaluate a composition, arrangement, or improvisation by comparing it to similar or exemplary models (Pro–7b).
*3. Evaluate a given musical work in terms of its aesthetic qualities *(e.g., interplay of unity and variety, tension/release, balance, overall expressive impact)* and explain the musical means it uses to evoke feelings and emotions (Adv–7c).

E. **Place Works within Cultural and Historical Contexts**
  *1. Compare characteristics of two or more arts within a particular historical period or style and cite examples from various cultures (Pro–8b).
  *2. Classify by genre or style, and by historical period or culture, unfamiliar but representative aural examples of music and explain the reasoning behind their classifications (Pro–9a).
  *3. Identify sources of American music genres, trace the evolution of those genres, and cite well-known musicians associated with them (Pro–9b).
  *4. Identify several *distinct* roles that musicians perform, cite representative individuals who have functioned in each role, and describe their activities and achievements (Pro–9c).
  5. Identify and explain the stylistic features of a given musical work that serve to define its aesthetic tradition and its historical or cultural context (Adv–9d).
  6. Identify and describe several distinct music genres or styles that show the influence of two or more cultural traditions, identify the cultural source of each influence, and trace the historical conditions that produced the synthesis of influences (Adv–9e).

Theatre Content Outline

Theatre, Grade 4

I. **Creating and Performing**

A. **Develop Scripts and Scenarios From Adaptations of Storylines or Objects Presented in Groups of Two to Eight**
   (A scenario is an outline of a story.)
   1. Collaborate *(students contribute suggestions relevant to the improvisation; they listen and accept others' suggestions)* to select interrelated characters, environments, and situations for classroom dramatizations (1a).
   2. Describe characters, their relationships, and their environments *in the process of developing the script or scenario* (2a).
   3. Improvise dialog to tell stories (1b).

B. **Develop Characters in Groups of Two to Eight, Act Out Characters, Their Relationships, and Their Environments**
   1. Use variations of locomotor and nonlocomotor movement and vocal expression (pitch, tempo, and tone) *in creating* characters (2b).

2. Assume roles, exhibit concentration, and contribute to the action of classroom dramatizations based on personal experience and heritage, imagination, literature, and history (2c).

C. **Make Design Choices To Communicate Locale and Mood**
(Constructing designs, at this level, means creating an environment by arranging materials for classroom dramatizations. The materials could be a table, chairs, pieces of fabric, etc., or students might use materials to create objects or effects such as using two blocks of wood to sound like a door slamming.)
1. Construct designs *which reflect* environments *that* communicate locale and mood using visual elements (such as space, color, line, texture) and aural aspects using a variety of sound sources (such as making wind noises with the mouth, stamping feet to simulate an army marching) (3 a).
2. Collaborate to establish playing spaces for classroom dramatizations and to select and safely organize available materials that suggest scenery, properties, lighting, sound, costumes, and makeup (3b).

D. **Direct by Planning Classroom Dramatizations**
1. Collaboratively plan improvisations and a way of staging (organizing) classroom dramatizations (4a).

II. Responding

A. **Describe and Analyze Artistic Choices in Their Own Dramatic Work**
(Students know that they can and should make choices in all aspects of the creating and performing dramatic processes, and that in so doing, they will achieve different effects.)
1. Identify and describe the visual *(see)*, aural *(hear)*, oral *(say)*, and kinetic *(do with our bodies)* elements of classroom dramatizations and dramatic performances (7a).
2. *Describe and provide rationales for* personal choices in creative and performing work (7c).
3. Analyze classroom dramatizations and constructively suggest alternative ideas for dramatizing roles, arranging environments, and developing situations along with means of improving the collaborative process of planning, playing, and responding (7d).

B. **Describe and Compare Various Elements and Effects of Theatre to Dramatic Media (Film and Television)**
1. Describe visual, aural, oral, and kinetic elements in theatre and dramatic media *such as film and television* (6a).
2. Compare how ideas *(e.g., sibling rivalry, respect)* and emotions *(e.g., sadness, anger)* are expressed in theatre, film, and television (6b).

C. **Place Work in Context (Personal, Social, Historical, Cultural)**
(Students explain how context is reflected in and influences theatre, film, and television.)
1. Identify and compare similar characters and situations in dramas from and about various cultures, and discuss how *theatre and dramatic media (film and television)* reflect life (8a).

2. Explain how the wants and needs of characters are similar to and different from *other people they know* (7b).
   D. **Evaluate Performances as Audience**
      1. Articulate emotional responses to dramatic performances and *give reasons for those responses* (7c).
      2. State a personal preference *for certain* parts of a dramatic performance and provide reasons to support that preference (7c).
      3. *Compare whole performances, stating a personal preference for one over another and providing reasons to support that preference* (7c).

Theatre, Grade 8

I. Creating/Performing

   A. **Develop Scripts and Scenarios from Adaptations of Storylines or Create Original Work**
      1. Individually and in groups create characters, environments, and actions that create tension and suspense (1a).
      2. Refine and record dialog and action (1b).
   B. **Develop Character through Script Analysis and the Rehearsal Process**
      1. Analyze descriptions, dialog, and actions to discover, articulate, and justify character motivation and invent character behaviors based on the observation of interactions, ethical choices, and emotional responses of people (2a).
      2. Demonstrate acting skills (such as sensory recall, concentration, breath control, diction, body alignment, control of isolated body parts) to develop characterizations that suggest artistic choices (2b).
      3. In an ensemble (working compatibly together in groups of 3 or 4), interact as invented characters (ones created by students) (3c).
   C. **Make Design Choices to Communicate Locale and Mood and Understand the Use of Technical Theatre Elements**
      1. Explain the functions and interrelated nature of scenery, properties, lighting, sound, costumes, and makeup in creating an environment appropriate to drama (3 a).
      2. Analyze improvised and scripted scenes for technical requirements (necessary scenery, properties, special lighting, sound, costumes, and makeup) (3b).
      3. Work collaboratively and safely to select and create elements of scenery, properties, lighting, and sound to signify environments, and costumes and makeup to suggest character (3d).
   D. **Direct by Interpreting Dramatic Texts and Organizing Time and People in Small Groups (2 to 4) in Planning and Rehearsing Improvised and Scripted Scenes**
      1. Lead small groups in planning design elements and in rehearsing improvised and scripted scenes, demonstrating social and consensus skills (4a).

II. Responding

A. Describe and Analyze Artistic Choices and Construct Meaning
(Students should understand dramatic/artistic intentions and actions and their social and personal significance, selected and organized from the aural, oral, and visual symbols of a dramatic production.)
1. Articulate and support the meanings constructed from their and others' dramatic performances (7b).
2. Describe and evaluate the perceived effectiveness of students' contributions (as playwrights, actors, designers, and directors) to the collaborative process of developing improvised and scripted scenes (7d).
3. Explain the knowledge, skills, and discipline needed to pursue careers and avocational opportunities in theatre, *film, and television* (8b).

B. Describe and Compare Elements, Styles, Genres, Media, and Dramatic Literature
1. Describe and compare archetypal characters (those types that have emerged from centuries of storytelling, such as the trickster, the villain, the warrior, or the superhero) and situations in dramas from and about various *artistic styles, genres, and historical periods* (8a).
2. *Identify the elements of film (composition, movement, sound, editing).*

C. Place Work in Context (Personal, Social, Historical, and Cultural)
1. Analyze the emotional and social impact of dramatic events in their lives, in the community, and in other cultures (8c).
2. Explain how culture affects the content and production values of dramatic performances (8d).
3. Explain how social concepts such as cooperation, communication, collaboration, consensus, self-esteem, risk-taking, sympathy, and empathy apply in theatre and daily life (8e).

D. Evaluate Performances as Audience
1. Use articulated criteria to describe, analyze, and constructively evaluate the perceived effectiveness of artistic choices found in dramatic performances *and identify some exemplary artists and works* (7c).
2. Describe and analyze the effect of publicity, study guides, programs, and physical environments on audience response and appreciation of dramatic performances (7a).
3. Describe characteristics and compare the presentation of characters, environments, and actions in theatre, musical theatre, and dramatic media (6a).

Theatre, Grade 12

I. Creating and Performing

A. Develop Scripts and Scenarios
1. Construct imaginative scripts and collaborate with actors to refine scripts so that story and meaning are conveyed to an audience (Pro–1a).

2. Write theatre, film, and television scripts that include original characters with unique dialog that motivates action (Adv–1b).
B. **Develop Characters through an Acting Process**
   1. Analyze the physical, emotional, and social dimensions of characters found in dramatic texts *and* from various genres and media (Pro–2a).
   2. In an ensemble, create and sustain characters who communicate with audiences (Pro–2c).
   3. Create consistent characters from classical, contemporary, realistic, and nonrealistic dramatic texts in informal theatre productions (Adv–2e).
C. **Make Design and Technical Theatre Choices to Communicate Locale and Mood and Understand the Use of Technical Theatre Elements**
   1. *Sketch designs for a set, lights, costumes, props, or makeup appropriate for a scene or a scenario considering the* cultural and historical perspectives (Pro–3b).
   2. Select music and sound effects to convey environments that clearly support the text (Pro–3c).
   3. Design coherent stage management, promotional, or business plans *for a production* (Pro–3e).
   4. Explain how scientific and technological advances have impacted set, lights, sound, costume design, and implementation for theatre, film, and television productions (Adv–3f).
   5. Collaborate with a director to develop unified production concepts (a brief statement, metaphor, or expression of the essential meaning of a play which orders and patterns all parts of the play) that convey the metaphorical nature of the drama for theatre, film, or television productions (Adv–3g).
D. **Direct by Interpreting Dramatic Texts and Organizing Time and People in Small Groups (3 to 5) in Planning and Rehearsing Improvised and Scripted Scenes**
   1. Effectively communicate directorial choices to an ensemble for improvised or scripted scenes (Pro–4c).
   2. Explain and compare the roles and interrelated responsibilities of the various personnel involved in theatre, film, and television productions *(e.g., set designers, costumers, camera operators)* (Adv–4d).
   3. Collaborate with designers and actors to develop aesthetically unified production concepts for theatre, film, or television productions (Adv–4e).
   4. *Direct a scene* to achieve production goals (Adv–4f).

II. Responding

A. **Describe and Analyze Artistic Choices and Construct Meaning**
   1. Constructively evaluate personal and others' collaborative efforts and artistic choices in *theatre* productions (Pro–7d).
   2. Analyze the effect of personal cultural experiences on own dramatic work (Pro–8d).
   3. Articulate and justify personal aesthetic criteria that compare perceived artistic intent with the final aesthetic achievement (Pro–7b).

B. **Describe and Compare Elements of Styles, Genre, Media, and Dramatic Literature**
   1. Compare how similar themes are treated in drama from various cultures and historical periods, illustrate with informal performances, and discuss how theatre can reveal universal concepts (Pro–8a).
C. **Place Work in Context (Personal, Social, Historical, and Cultural)**
   1. Identify and compare the lives, works, and influence of representative theatre artists in various cultures and historical periods (Pro–8b).
   2. Identify cultural and historical influences on American theatre (Pro–8c).
   3. Analyze the social impact of underrepresented theatre and film artists (e.g., Native American, Hispanic) (Adv–8e).
D. **Evaluate Performances as Audience and Critic**
   1. Analyze and critique parts of dramatic performances, taking into account the context, and constructively suggest alternative artistic choices (Pro–7c).
   2. Analyze and evaluate critical comments about dramatic work, explaining which points are most appropriate to inform further development of the work (Adv–7h).
   3. Analyze how dramatic forms, production practices, and theatrical traditions in-fluence contemporary theatre, film, and television productions (Adv–8g).

Visual Arts Content Outline

Visual Arts, Grade 4

I. Creating

A. **Generate Subjects, Themes, Problems, and Ideas for Works of Art and Design in Ways That Reflect Knowledge and Understanding of Values (Personal, Social, Cultural, Historical), Aesthetics, and Context**
   1. Explore and understand prospective content for works of *art and design, selecting the subject matter, symbols, and ideas that are to be communicated* (3a).
   2. Demonstrate awareness that the visual arts and design have both a history and specific relationship to various cultures (4a).
   3. Demonstrate awareness *of* how history, culture, the visual arts, *and design* can influence one another in making and studying works of art/*design* (4c).
B. **Invent and Use Ways of Generating Visual, Spatial, and Temporal Concepts in Planning Works of Art and Design**
   1. *Show development of ideas over time.*
   2. *Demonstrate knowledge of* the difference between materials, techniques, and processes (1a).
   3. *Show familiarity with and ability to* use different media, techniques, and processes to communicate ideas, experiences, and stories (1c).
   4. Demonstrate *knowledge of* the differences among visual characteristics and purposes of art to convey ideas (2a).

5. *Plan compositions using specific placement or organization of elements, symbols, and images that communicate the intended meaning or function.*
6. *Provide reasons for specific selections and explain means for giving visual form to content expressed in words and other forms of communication.*

C. **Select and Use Form, Media, Techniques, and Processes to Achieve Goodness of Fit with the Intended Meaning or Function of Works of Art and Design**
   1. *Demonstrate ability to* use art *and design* materials and tools in a safe and responsible manner (1d).
   2. *Select and use basic media, techniques, and processes with qualities and characteristics that communicate specific ideas.*
   3. *Use different art and design materials in ways that result in the purposeful use of form (lines, shapes, colors, textures, space, etc).*
   4. Create *compositions using specific placement or organization of elements, symbols, and images.*

D. **Experiment with Ideas (Sketches, Models, etc.) before Final Execution as a Method of Evaluation**
   1. *Attempt multiple solutions to compositional and expressive problems.*
   2. *Analyze* how different *compositional* and expressive features cause different responses (2b).
   3. *Simulate, assess, and select prospective ideas (sketches, models, etc.) for development of final works of art and design* (3 a).

E. **Create a Product That Reflects Ongoing Thoughts, Actions, and New Directions**
   1. Use different media, techniques, and processes to communicate ideas, experiences, and stories (1c).
   2. *Discuss* how different materials, techniques, and processes cause different responses (1b).

F. **Reflect Upon and Evaluate Their Own Works of Art and Design (i.e., students judge the relationship between process and product; the redefinition of current ideas or problems; and the definition of new ideas, problems, and personal directions)**
   1. *Evaluate final compositions for use of compositional and expressive features.*
   2. *Demonstrate knowledge of the various purposes and reasons* for works of art and design based on people's experiences (cultural backgrounds, human needs, etc.) (5a and 5b).
   3. *Propose how works in the visual arts and design affect the way people perceive their experiences.*

II. Responding

A. **Describe Works of Art and Design in Ways That Show Knowledge of Form, Aesthetics, and Context (Personal, Social, Cultural, Historical)**
   1. *Identify characteristics of materials and visual, spatial, and temporal structures in their works and the works of others.*
   2. *Provide reasons for an artist's or designer's specific selections of content and the communication role of visual, spatial, and temporal form in specific works of art and design.*

3. Identify specific works of art as belonging to particular cultures, times, and places (4b).
4. Describe and *compare* how people's experiences *(cultural backgrounds, human needs, etc.)* influence the development of specific art works that *differ visually, spatially, temporally, and functionally* (5b).

B. **Analyze and Interpret Works of Art and Design for Relationships between Form and Context, Form and Meaning or Function, and the Work of Critics, Historians, Aestheticians, and Artists/Designers**
   1. *Analyze and interpret* how history, culture, *personal experiences,* and the visual arts *and design* can influence one another in making and studying works of art/*design* (4c).
   2. *Demonstrate knowledge* of various purposes and reasons for works of visual art and design based on people's experiences *(cultural backgrounds, human needs, etc.)* (5a and 5b).
   3. *Analyze and interpret* similarities and differences between characteristics of the visual arts *and design* and other arts disciplines (6a).
   4. *Interpret the ways other artists/designers use subject matter, symbols, and ideas and speculate on their influences on students' own work and the work of others.*
   5. *Analyze how factors of time and place (such as climate, resources, ideas, and technology) influence the visual characteristics that give meaning to a work of art and design.*
   6. *Analyze a variety of purposes for creating works of art and design.*

C. **Articulate Judgments about Works of Art and Design That Reflect Attitudes and Prior Knowledge (Description, Analysis, Interpretation)**
   1. *Judge art and design works that differ visually, spatially, temporally, and functionally and defend how similarities and differences are related to history and culture as expressed in human needs and beliefs of the times being considered.*

D. **Apply Judgments about Works of Art and Design to Decisions Made in Daily Life, Developing a Personal Belief System and World View That Is Informed by the Arts**
   1. *Use different responses to works of visual art and design to form, confirm, or change a personal belief system.*

Visual Arts, Grade 8

I. Creating

A. **Generate Subjects, Themes, Problems, and Ideas for Works of Art and Design in Ways That Reflect Knowledge and Understanding of Values (Personal, Social, Cultural, Historical), Aesthetics, and Context**
   1. *Speculate and discriminate among various ideas, making the most appropriate choices for specific artistic or design purposes.*
   2. *Interpret and speculate on the ways that others have used subject matter, symbols, and ideas in visual, spatial, or temporal expressions, and how these are used to produce meaning or function that is appropriate to their own works.*

3. *Analyze the characteristics of art and design works of various eras and cultures to discover possible expressions or solutions to problems.*
4. *Speculate on* how factors of time and place (such as climate, resources, ideas, and technology) influence the visual, *spatial, or temporal* characteristics that give meaning or *function* to a work of art or design (4c).

B. **Invent and Use Ways of Generating Visual, Spatial, and Temporal Concepts in Planning Works of Art and Design**
1. *Demonstrate the development of ideas across time.*
2. *Analyze and consider form*, media, techniques, *and* processes and analyze what makes them effective or *ineffective* in communicating *specific* ideas (1a).
3. *Demonstrate knowledge of how sensory qualities, expressive features, and the functions of the visual arts evoke intended responses and uses for works of art and design.*
4. *Speculate* about the effects of visual structures *(elements and principles of design) and reflect upon their influence on students' ideas* (2a).
5. *Evaluate and discriminate among various ideas, making the most effective choices for specific artistic purposes or design uses.*

C. **Select and Use Form, Media, Techniques, and Processes to Achieve Goodness of Fit With the Intended Meaning or Function of Works of Art and Design**
1. *Experiment,* select, *and employ form,* media, techniques, and processes and analyze what makes them effective or *ineffective* in communicating ideas (1 a).
2. *Utilize knowledge of characteristics of materials and visual, spatial, and temporal structures to solve specific visual arts and design problems.*
3. *Interpret the way that others have used form, media, techniques, and processes and speculate how these produce meaning or function.*

D. **Experiment with Ideas (Sketches, Models, etc.) Before Final Execution as a Method of Evaluation**
1. *Evaluate, discriminate, and articulate differences among various ideas and forms, making the most effective choices for specific artistic purposes or design uses.*
2. *Simulate and articulate new insights and changes in direction that result from representation or simulation of ideas.*
3. *Employ organizational structures and analyze what makes them effective or ineffective* in the communication of ideas (2b).

E. **Create a Product That Reflects Ongoing Thoughts, Actions, and New Directions**
1. *Use* media, techniques, and processes and analyze what makes them effective or *ineffective* in communicating ideas (1a).
2. *Integrate visual, spatial, and temporal concepts with content to communicate intended meaning in their art works* (3 a).
3. *Use subjects, themes, and symbols that demonstrate knowledge of contexts, values, and aesthetics that communicate intended meaning in art works* (3b).
4. *Evaluate ideas and artwork throughout the creating process, making the most effective choices for specific artistic purposes or design uses.*

F. **Reflect Upon and Evaluate Their Own Works of Art and Design (i.e., students judge the relationship between process and product; the redefinition of current**

ideas or problems; and the definition of new ideas, problems, and personal directions)
1. *Evaluate final compositions for use of compositional and expressive features.*
2. *Demonstrate knowledge of the various purposes and reasons for works of visual art and design based on people's experiences (cultural backgrounds, human needs, etc.).*
3. *Propose how works in the visual arts and design affect the way people perceive their experiences.*
4. Compare *and evaluate* the characteristics of works in two or more art forms that share similar subject matter, historical period, or cultural context (6a).
5. *Describe new insights that have emerged from process and products of art and design that are meaningful to daily life.*

II. Responding

A. Describe Works of Art and Design in Ways That Show Knowledge of Form, Aesthetics, and Context (Personal, Social, Cultural, Historical)
1. Compare and *describe* the characteristics of *materials and visual, spatial, and temporal structures in their works and the works from* various eras and cultures (4a).
2. Describe and place a variety of art objects in historical and cultural contexts (4b).
3. Compare *and describe* multiple purposes for creating works of art *and design* (5 a).
4. Describe contemporary and historic meanings in specific art works through cultural and aesthetic inquiry (5b).
5. Describe and compare *multiple critical* responses to their own art works and to art works from various eras and cultures (5c).
6. Compare the characteristics of works in two or more art forms *and arts disciplines* that share similar subject matter, historical period, or cultural context (6a).

B. Analyze and Interpret Works of Art and Design for Relationships Between Form and Context, Form and Meaning or Function, and the Work of Critics, Historians, Aestheticians, and Artists/Designers
1. Compare *and analyze* the characteristics of art *and design* works in various eras and cultures (4a).
2. *Analyze and* place a variety of art *and design* objects in historical and cultural contexts (4b).
3. Analyze how factors of time and place (such as climate, resources, ideas, and technology) influence the visual characteristics that give meaning and value to a work of art *and design* (4c).
4. Compare *and analyze a variety* of purposes for creating works of art and design (5 a).
5. Analyze contemporary and historic meanings in specific art works through cultural and aesthetic inquiry (5b).
6. Compare *and analyze* multiple *critical* responses to their own art works and to art *and design* works from various eras and cultures (5c).

7. *Compare and analyze* the characteristics of works in two or more *arts disciplines* that share similar subject matter, historical period, or cultural context (6a).

C. Articulate Judgments about Works of Art and Design That Reflect Attitudes and Prior Knowledge (Description, Analysis, Interpretation)
1. Compare *and describe attitudes implicit in their art and design works with* the characteristics of art works of various eras and cultures (4a).
2. Compare the characteristics of works in two or more art forms *and arts disciplines* that share similar subject matter, historical period, or cultural context (6a).

D. Apply Judgments about Works of Art and Design to Decisions Made in Daily Life, Developing a Personal Belief System and World View That Is Informed by the Arts
1. *Propose and articulate how works in the visual arts and design might reflect and influence the way people perceive experiences in their lives; and conversely, how people's experiences influence the development of specific works.*
2. *Use different responses to works of art and design to form, confirm, or change a personal belief system.*

Visual Arts, Grade 12

I. Creating

A. Generate Subjects, Themes, Problems, and Ideas for Works of Art and Design in Ways That Reflect Knowledge and Understanding of Values (Personal, Social, Cultural, Historical), Aesthetics, and Context
1. *Identify a variety of sources for subject matter, symbols, and ideas they wish to convey in works of art and design, and select the sources that are most appropriate for the meaning they want to express.*
2. *Determine the origin of the ideas and images they have chosen, and explain how and why specific choices were made.*
3. *Speculate upon* multiple solutions to specific visual arts *and design* problems that demonstrate competence in producing effective relationships between *intent* and artistic *choices* (Adv–2e).
4. *Hypothesize,* initiate, and define challenging visual arts problems independently using intellectual skills such as analysis, synthesis, and evaluation (Adv 1–d).

B. Invent and Use Ways of Generating Visual, Spatial, and Temporal Concepts in Planning Works of Art and Design
1. *Show development of ideas across time.*
2. *Generate ideas for* works of art *and design* that demonstrate an understanding of how the communication of ideas relates to the media, techniques, and processes used (Pro–1b).
3. *Demonstrate skills with several media and processes sufficient to execute plans for specific works and reflect on the effectiveness of the result.*
4. Create and *use relationships among sensory elements,* organizational *principles, expressive features,* and functions to solve specific visual arts *and design* problems (Pro–2c).

5. Demonstrate the ability to form and defend judgments about the use of characteristics and structures to accomplish specific personal, communal, economic, intellectual, and other purposes in works of art *and design* (Pro–2a).
6. *Integrate subject matter and symbols, art forms, media, composition, and expressive qualities to define and convey their ideas.*
7. Create multiple solutions to specific visual arts problems that demonstrate competence in producing effective relationships between structural choices and artistic functions (Adv–2e).

C. **Select and Use Form, Media, Techniques, and Processes to Achieve Goodness of Fit With the Intended Meaning or Function of Works of Art and Design**
1. Demonstrate an understanding of how the communication of their ideas relates to the media, techniques, and processes used (Pro–1b).
2. Communicate ideas *effectively* in at least one visual arts medium (Adv–1c).
3. *Integrate subject matter and symbols, art forms, media, composition, and expressive qualities to define and convey own ideas.*
4. Create multiple solutions to specific visual arts problems that demonstrate competence in producing effective relationships between structural choices and artistic functions (Adv–2e).

D. **Experiment with Ideas (Sketches, Models, etc.) before Final Execution as a Method of Evaluation**
1. *Simulate and analyze sketches, models, etc., for insight into own overall thinking about ideas and problems.*
2. *Formulate and articulate changes in direction.*
3. *Inform later decisionmaking through the synthesis of insight gained from analysis of previous sketches, models, etc., created in response to other problems or ideas.*

E. **Create a Product That Reflects Ongoing Thoughts, Actions, and New Directions**
1. Apply media, techniques, and processes with sufficient confidence and sensitivity that their intentions are carried out in their art works (Pro–1a).
2. *Assess ideas and art works, making choices that are most effective for specific artistic purposes or design use.*
3. Create *a series of multiple works in response to* specific visual arts *and design* problems that demonstrates competence in producing effective relationships between structural choices and artistic functions (Adv–2e).

F. **Reflect Upon and Evaluate Their Own Works of Art and Design (i.e., students judge the relationship between process and product; the redefinition of current ideas or problems; and the definition of new ideas, problems, and personal directions)**
1. Identify intentions of those creating works of visual art *and design,* explore the implications of various choices, and justify their analyses of choices in particular works (Pro–5a).
2. Describe the meanings *and functions* of *works of art and design through* analyses *that incorporate knowledge of how* specific works are created and structured and how they relate to historical, cultural contexts, *and aesthetics* (Pro–5b).

3. Reflect analytically on various interpretations as a means for understanding and evaluating works of visual art *and design* (Pro–5c).
4. Compare the materials, technologies, media, and processes of the visual arts to those of other arts disciplines (Pro–6a).
5. Correlate responses to works of visual art with various techniques for communicating meanings, ideas, attitudes, views, and intentions (Adv–5d).
6. Synthesize the creative and analytical principles and techniques of the visual arts and selected other arts disciplines, the humanities, or the sciences (Adv–6c).

II. Responding

A. **Describe Works of Art and Design in Ways That Show Knowledge of Form, Aesthetics, and Context (Personal, Social, Cultural, Historical)**
   1. Describe the function and explore the meaning of specific art *and design* objects within varied cultures, times, and places (Pro–4b).
   2. *Identify and* differentiate among a variety of historical and cultural contexts in terms of characteristics and purposes of works of art *and design* (Pro–4a).
   3. Analyze and interpret art works for relationships among form, context, purposes, and critical models, showing understanding of the work of critics, historians, aestheticians, and artists (Adv–4d).
   4. Analyze common characteristics of visual arts evident across time and among cultural/ethnic groups to formulate analyses, evaluations, and interpretations of meaning (Adv–4e).

B. **Analyze and Interpret Works of Art and Design for Relationships between Form and Context, Form and Meaning or Function, and the Work of Critics, Historians, Aestheticians, and Artists/Designers**
   1. Differentiate *and analyze* a variety of historical and cultural contexts in terms of characteristics and purposes of works of art *and design* (Pro–4a).
   2. Analyze relationships of works of art to one another in terms of history, aesthetics, and culture, and justify analyses (Pro–4c).
   3. *Analyze,* evaluate, and defend the validity of sources for content and manner in which subject matter, symbols, and images are used in the students' works and in significant works by others (Adv–3d).
   4. Analyze and interpret art works for relationships among form, context, and purposes, showing understanding of the work of critics, historians, aestheticians, and artists/*designers* (Adv–4d).
   5. Analyze common characteristics of visual arts evident across time and among cultural/ethnic groups to formulate analyses, evaluations, and interpretations of meaning (Adv–4e).

C. **Articulate Judgments about Works of Art and Design That Reflect Attitudes and Prior Knowledge (Description, Analysis, Interpretation)**
   1. Identify intentions of those creating art works, explore the implications of various purposes, and justify their analyses of purposes in particular works (Pro–5a).
   2. Reflect analytically on various interpretations as a means for understanding and evaluating works of visual art *and design* (Pro–5c).

3. Synthesize *and judge* the creative and analytical principles and techniques of the visual arts *and design* and selected other arts disciplines, the humanities, or the sciences (Adv–6c).

D. **Apply Judgments about Works of Art and Design to Decisions Made in Daily Life, Developing a Personal Belief System and World View That Is Informed by the Arts**
   1. *Use different responses to works of art and design to form, confirm, or change a personal belief system.*
   2. *Propose and articulate how works in the visual arts and design might reflect and influence the way people perceive experiences in their lives, and conversely, how people's experiences influence the development of specific works.*

APPENDIX B. PUBLIC HEARINGS

Report on the February Public Hearings: The Issues Paper

San Francisco National Hearing

February 4, 1993

The first national hearing for the 1997 NAEP Arts Education Framework Project was held at the San Francisco Hilton and Towers in conjunction with a conference organized by the Getty Center for Education in the Arts. Notification for the hearing was disseminated through conference mailings and was timed to coincide with the publication and dissemination of the Issues paper that invited testimony at all three hearing sites. The press and electronic media in the San Francisco Bay area were informed through traditional media information releases from the public information office of CCSSO. The hearing took place from 9:30 a.m. to 12:30 p.m., and 36 individuals provided oral testimony. A total of 354 individuals attended the program.

The invitation to provide testimony was broad and relied on self-identification rather than soliciting specific individuals or organizations. The individuals providing oral testimony included artists, educators, parents, and administrators. Each was given 5 minutes for a presentation, which was scheduled through the project office in Washington, DC. The allotted time for the presentation was monitored fairly and adhered to strictly.

The testimony provided could be classified in three categories of comments: advocacy for arts education, comments pertaining to the development of the *National Standards,* and comments that addressed the issues surrounding the development of NAEP. The hearings also demonstrated some of the difficulty on the part of those providing the testimony in clearly differentiating the roles of the standards development project and the assessment framework development project.

In addition to the panelists representing the contractor, subcontractors, and the Governing Board, the panel invited members of the steering and planning committees who were present to join the panel on a rotating basis to hear the testimony and be recognized as part of the assessment framework development process.

A complete list of individuals who provided the testimony in San Francisco and their affiliations, along with a complete transcript of the proceedings, is available from the project office.

Orlando National Hearing

February 9, 1993

The second national hearing for the 1997 NAEP Arts Education Framework Project was held at the Orlando Marriott in conjunction with a conference organized by NCES and the Florida State Department of Education. The press and electronic media in the Orlando area were informed through traditional media releases from the public information office of CCSSO. Notification for the hearing was also disseminated through local arts education and other education leaders. In addition, project staff participated in local radio features discussing the hearings and the development of the assessment framework. The hearing took place from 4:30 p.m. to 8:30 p.m., and 29 individuals provided oral testimony. An effort was made to encourage classroom teachers, parents, and university students to attend and provide testimony. More than 60 individuals attended the program.

The individuals providing verbal testimony included an international opera star, a representative from the Disney organization in charge of talent recruiting, 9 teachers, 5 parents, 11 students, and 2 administrators. Each was given 5 minutes for a presentation, which was scheduled through the project office in Washington, DC. The allotted time for the presentation was monitored fairly and adhered to strictly.

The testimony could be classified in three categories of comments: advocacy for arts education, comments pertaining to the development of the *National Standards,* and comments that addressed the issues surrounding the development of NAEP. The hearings again demonstrated some of the difficulty in clearly differentiating the roles of the standards development project and the assessment framework development project.

Many of the concerns voiced in Orlando were similar to those heard in San Francisco. The presence of 11 university arts education majors from Central Florida University added unique viewpoints from recent graduates of a K–12 educational system. The Florida hearings provide an interesting contrast to the broad, general nature of the San Francisco group and to the urban contributions from New York City.

A complete list of individuals who provided the testimony in Orlando and their affiliations, along with a complete transcript of the proceedings, is available from the project office.

New York City National Hearing

February 24, 1993

The third national hearing for the 1997 NAEP Arts Education Framework Project was held at the corporate headquarters for New York Metropolitan Life Insurance. The press and electronic media in the New York metropolitan area were informed through traditional media releases from the public information office of CCSSO. Notification for the hearing was also disseminated through local arts education leaders, with help from the American Council for the Arts and the New York Foundation for the Arts. John Merrow from the Public Broadcasting System series "Education Matters" collected some interview material during the proceedings, which were aired on his program in March. The hearing took place from 1 p.m. to 4 p.m., and 32 individuals provided oral testimony. The effort in New York was directed at attracting a broad spectrum of individuals and organizations to attend and provide testimony. More than 150 individuals attended the program.

The individuals providing oral testimony included 19 people representing arts organizations and associations and 8 arts educators. The rest of the testimony was provided by people representing special interest groups, from arts education organizations to special learner needs. Each was given 5 minutes for a presentation, which was scheduled through the project office in Washington, DC. The allotted time for the presentation was monitored fairly and adhered to strictly by A. Graham Down, the moderator for the hearing.

As in the previous two hearings, the testimony could be classified in three categories of comments: advocacy for arts education, comments pertaining to the development of the *National Standards,* and comments that addressed the issues surrounding the development of NAEP. The testimony in this hearing again demonstrated the difficulty in clearly differentiating the standards development project and the assessment framework development project.

A complete list of individuals who provided the testimony in New York and their affiliations, along with a complete transcript of the proceedings, is available from the project office.

Report on the October Public Hearings

National Review of the Assessment Framework Draft Seattle, Washington, Hearing

October 1, 1993

The first national hearing to gather public input on the draft of the assessment framework was held at the Seattle Art Museum, with assistance from the Office of the Superintendent for Public Instruction for the State of Washington. The hearing was also held in conjunction with a meeting of the Superintendent's Arts Education Advisory Commission and a statewide meeting of the Washington Alliance for Arts Education. The press and electronic media in the Seattle area were informed through traditional media information releases from the public information office of CCSSO. The hearing took place from 2 p.m. to 6 p.m., and 30 individuals provided oral testimony. A total of 67 individuals attended the program.

The invitation to provide testimony was included in the mailing of the draft framework document to approximately 3,500 individuals and organizations and was supplemented by a special distribution by Gina May, arts education specialist for the Office of the Superintendent for Public Instruction. Individuals providing verbal testimony included artists, educators, parents, and administrators. Each was given 5 minutes for a presentation, which was scheduled through the project office in Washington, DC. The allotted time for the presentation was monitored and adhered to by the chair of the hearing panel, Ramsay Selden of CCSSO. The panel also included Deborah Brzoska from Vancouver, Washington, member of the NAEP planning committee; Barbara Wills from Seattle, Washington, and Kelvin Yazzie from Flagstaff, Arizona, members of the NAEP steering committee; Joan Peterson, representing the College Board; Gina May from the Office of the State Superintendent of Public Instruction; and Frank Philip, the NAEP project coordinator from CCSSO.

The hearing began with a welcome from Judith Billings, the Washington State Superintendent of Public Instruction.

A complete list of individuals who provided testimony in Seattle and their affiliations, along with a complete transcript of the proceedings, is available from the project office.

Chicago, Illinois, Hearing

October 5, 1993

The second hearing to gather public input on the draft of the assessment framework was held at the Art Institute of Chicago, with assistance from the Office of Museum Education (Ronne Hartfield, executive director). The press and electronic media in the Chicago area were informed through traditional media information releases from the information office of CCSSO. The hearing took place from 1 p.m. to 5 p.m., and 25 individuals provided oral testimony. A total of 61 individuals attended the program.

The invitation to provide testimony was included in the mailing of the draft framework document to approximately 3,500 individuals and organizations and was supplemented by special invitations from the project staff and the Illinois Alliance for Arts Education (Nadine Saitlin, executive director). Individuals providing verbal testimony included artists, educators, parents, and administrators. Each was given 5 minutes for a presentation, which was scheduled through the project office in Washington, DC. The allotted time for the presentation was monitored and adhered to by the chair of the hearing panel, A. Graham Down, president of the Council for Basic Education and cochair of the NAEP steering committee. The panel also included Jerry Hausman, Ronne Hartfield, and Adrienne Bailey, members of the NAEP steering committee from Chicago; Laurel Serleth, Laura Salazar, and Ruth Ann Teague, members of the NAEP planning committee; Carol Myford, representing the Educational Testing Service and the College Board; and Frank Philip, the NAEP project coordinator from CCSSO.

The hearing began with a welcome from Ronne Hartfield and an explanation of the process by Frank Philip before being turned over to the chair, A. Graham Down.

A complete list of individuals who provided testimony in Chicago and their affiliations, along with a complete transcript of the proceedings, is available from the project office.

Washington, DC, Hearing

October 7, 1993

The third and final hearing to gather public input on the draft of the assessment framework was held in Washington, DC, at the American Film Institute Theatre at the John F. Kennedy Center for the Performing Arts, with assistance from the Alliance for Arts Education and the Arts Education Partnerships Working Group. The hearing coincided with a national meeting of state representatives for the Alliance for Arts Education that was held in Washington on October 7–9, 1993. The press and electronic media in the Washington area were informed through traditional media information releases from the public information office of CCSSO. The hearing took place from 1 p.m. to 5 p.m., with 14 individuals providing oral testimony. Apparently due to a musicians' strike at the Kennedy Center, many of the individuals who originally signed up decided not to cross the picket line. A total of 73 individuals attended the program.

The invitation to provide testimony was included in the mailing of the draft framework document to approximately 3,500 individuals and organizations and was supplemented by special invitations from the project staff and the office of the Alliance for Arts Education at the Kennedy Center. Individuals providing oral testimony included artists, educators, parents, and administrators. Each was given 5 minutes for a presentation, which was scheduled through the project office in Washington, DC. The allotted time for the presentation was monitored and adhered to by the chairs of the hearing panel: A. Graham Down, president of the Council for Basic Education, and Ramsay Selden of CCSSO, who also cochairs the NAEP steering committee.

The panel also included members of the NAEP steering committee: Harry Clark from Pittsburgh; Ed Gero, Tom Hatfield, Rebbecca Hutton, and David O'Fallon from the Washington, DC, area; Claudette Morton, a member of the NAEP planning committee from Montana; Michael Sikes, representing the National Endowment for the Arts; Mary Crovo, representing the Governing Board; Ruth Mitchell, a consultant to the project; and Frank Philip, the NAEP project coordinator from CCSSO.

The hearing began with a welcome from David O'Fallon from the Arts Education Partnerships Working Group and an explanation of the process by Ramsay Selden before beginning the testimony.

A complete list of individuals who provided testimony in Washington, DC, and their affiliations, along with a complete transcript of the proceedings, is available from the project office.

APPENDIX C. PLANNING: SCHEDULES AND TIMELINES

Significant Dates for the Steering and Planning Committees

Steering Committee Meetings

Dates	Location	Notes
January 19–20, 1993	Baltimore, MD	Organizational Meeting • Receive overview and charge • Formulate guidelines • Meet with planning committee
August 9–10, 1993	Washington, DC	Mid-Project Meeting • Review draft of framework for national review and public hearings • Provide suggestions for drafts

| January 11–12, 1994 | Washington, DC | of framework and review progress of documents for specifications, background variables, and reporting formats
• Meet with planning committee Final Meeting
• Review final draft of Framework and other documents
• Provide suggestions for drafts and conditional approval
• Meet with planning committee |

Planning Committee Meetings

Dates	Location	Notes
January 20–21, 1993	Baltimore, MD	Organizational Meeting • Meet with steering committee • Receive overview and charge • Formulate structure for working
March 9–11, 1993	Crystal City, VA	Second Meeting • Initial development of framework • Working group sessions
May 2 1–23, 1993	Washington, DC	Third Meeting • Draft development
August 10–12, 1993	Washington, DC	Mid-Project Meeting • Meet with steering committee • Review suggestions for refinement • Finalize framework for national review and public hearings
November 1–3, 1993	Washington, DC	Fifth Meeting • Review input from the public hearings • Refine draft of framework • Review and refine drafts of the specifications, background variables, and reporting formats
January 12–14, 1994	Washington, DC	Final Meeting

- Meet with steering committee
- Finalize all documents for final approval or acceptance by the Governing Board

End Notes

[1]*Arts subgroup leaders.
[2]*Arts subgroup leaders.
[3]*Arts subgroup leaders.

In: Arts Education: Assessment and Access
Editor: Olivia M. Wilson

ISBN: 978-1-61728-266-9
© 2010 Nova Science Publishers, Inc.

Chapter 2

THE NATION'S REPORT CARD: ARTS 2008 - MUSIC AND VISUAL ARTS

National Assessment of Educational Progress at Grade 8

EXECUTIVE SUMMARY

This chapterpresents the results of the 2008 National Assessment of Educational Progress (NAEP) in the arts, which was given to a nationally representative sample of 7,900 eighth-grade public and private school students. Approximately one-half of these students were assessed in music, and the other half were assessed in visual arts.

The **MUSIC** portion of the assessment measured students' ability to respond to music in various ways. Students were asked to analyze and describe aspects of music they heard, critique instrumental and vocal performances, and demonstrate their knowledge of standard musical notation and music's role in society. One question, for example, asked students to identify the instrument they heard in the beginning solo of "Rhapsody in Blue" that was played for them.

The average responding score for music was reported on a NAEP scale of 0 to 300. Scores ranged from 105 for the lowest-performing students to 194 for the highest-performing students.

The **VISUAL ARTS** portion of the assessment included questions that measured students' ability to respond to art as well as questions that measured their ability to create art. Responding questions asked students to analyze and describe works of art and design. For example, students were asked to describe specific differences in how certain parts of an artist's self-portrait were drawn. The average responding score for visual arts was reported on a NAEP scale of 0 to 300 with scores ranging from 104 for the lowest- performing students to 193 for the highest-performing students.

Creating questions, on the other hand, required students to create works of art and design of their own. For example, students were asked to create a self-portrait that was scored for identifying detail, compositional elements, and use of materials. The average creating task score for visual arts was reported separately as the average percentage of the maximum possible score from 0 to 100 with a national average of 52. In general, students who performed well on the responding questions also performed well on the creating questions.

Racial/Ethnic and Gender Gaps Evident in both Music and Visual Arts

Although the results for music and visual arts are reported separately and cannot be compared, some general patterns in differences between student groups were similar in the two disciplines.

- *Average responding scores in both music and visual arts were 22 to 32 points higher for White and Asian/Pacific Islander students than for Black and Hispanic students. The creating task scores in visual arts were also higher for White and Asian/ Pacific Islander students than for their Black and Hispanic peers.*
- *Average responding scores for female students were 10 points higher than for male students in music and 11 points higher in visual arts. Female students also outperformed male students in creating visual art.*

Frequency of Arts Instruction Remains Steady

In 2008, fifty-seven percent of eighth-graders attended schools where music instruction was offered at least three or four times a week, and 47 percent attended schools where visual arts instruction was offered at least as often. There were no statistically significant changes since 1997 in the percentages of students attending schools offering instruction in music or visual arts with varying frequency.

There were also no significant differences found between the percentages of students in different racial/ethnic or gender groups attending schools with varying opportunities for instruction in either music or visual arts in 2008.

COMPARISONS BETWEEN 1997 AND 2008

Although the questions in the 2008 assessment were taken from those administered in the 1997 arts assessment, some of the scoring procedures could not be replicated in 2008. Therefore, comparisons cannot be made between students' scores in those two years. However, comparisons can be made for the percentages of students who responded correctly to the multiple-choice questions in the assessment, and the percentages of students based on responses to background questions that were asked in both years.

EXAMPLES OF WHAT STUDENTS KNOW AND CAN DO IN THE ARTS

Music

71% correctly identified a symphony orchestra as the type of ensemble that played a piece of music

52% were able to identify Africa as the region of origin for a musical excerpt and could describe a characteristic of the music's style

20% were able to identify the name of a piano dynamic marking and explain its meaning

Visual Arts

53% were able to describe specific differences in how certain parts of an artist's self-portrait were drawn

34% were able to describe two characteristics of the medium of charcoal as used in an artist's self-portrait

19% were able to connect the formal characteristics of an artist's self-portrait with what the artist was trying to communicate

More Students Writing Down Music and Writing about Their Artwork in Arts Classes

The percentage of eighth-grade students who reported being asked by their teacher to write down music in music class showed an increase from 26 percent in 1997 to 33 percent in 2008 (gure A). However, the percentages of students who reported engaging in other activities such as listening to music, singing, playing instruments, working on group assignments, and making up their own music in 2008 were not found to be signicantly different from the percentages of students in 1997.

The percentage of eighth-grade students who were asked by their teacher to write about their artwork in visual arts class increased from 21 percent in 1997 to 27 percent in 2008 (figure B). The percentage of students whose teacher had them choose their own art project, on the other hand, decreased from 47 percent to 39 percent over the same period. Additionally, the percentage of students who reported visiting an art museum, gallery, or exhibit with their class decreased from 22 percent in 1997 to 16 percent in 2008. There were no signicant changes for other activities such as painting or drawing, making things out of clay or other materials, or working in pairs or groups.

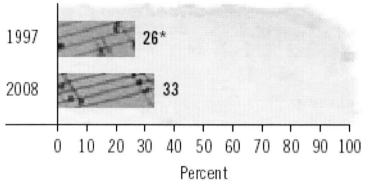

* Significantly different (p < .05) from 2008.

Figure A. Percentage of students at grade 8 who are asked to write down music at least once a month in music class: 1997 and 2008

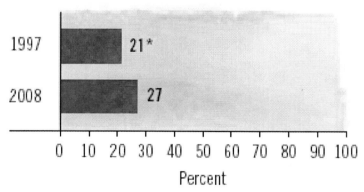

* Significantly different (p < .05) from 2008.
Source: U.S. Department of Education, Institute of Education Sciences, National Center for Education Statistics, National Assessment of Educational Progress (NAEP), 1997 and 2008 Arts Assessments.

Figure B. Percentage of students at grade 8 who are asked to write about their artwork at least once a month in art class: 1997 and 2008

INTRODUCTION

The 2008 NAEP arts assessment measured students' knowledge and skills in the arts by asking them to observe, describe, analyze, and evaluate existing works of music and visual art and to create original works of visual art.

The Eighth-Grade Arts Assessment

The Arts Framework

The NAEP arts framework serves as the blueprint for the assessment, describing the specific knowledge and skills that should be assessed in the arts disciplines. Developed under the guidance of the National Assessment Governing Board, the framework reflects the input of arts educators, artists, assessment specialists, policymakers, representatives from the business community, and members of the public. The *National Standards for Arts Education*[1] also served as an important reference in the development of the NAEP arts framework.

The framework specifies that students' arts knowledge and skills be measured in four *arts disciplines*: dance, music, theatre, and visual arts. Additionally, three *arts processes*—responding, creating, and performing—are central to students' experiences in these disciplines. While the responding process refers to observing, describing, analyzing, and evaluating works of art, the creating process refers to expressing ideas and feelings in the form of an original work of art. Due to budget constraints, only the responding process in music and both the responding and creating processes in visual arts were assessed in 2008.

To learn more about the arts framework, visit http://www.nagb.org/publications/frameworks/ arts-framework08.pdf.

Assessment Design

Because of the breadth of content covered in the NAEP arts assessment, each student was assessed in only one arts discipline, either music or visual arts.

The responding process in music and visual arts was assessed with multiple-choice questions and constructed-response questions that required students to produce answers of a few words or sentences. The constructed-response questions that assessed the creating process included questions that required students to generate written answers and to create original works of visual art.

Scoring Students' Work in the Arts

One of the challenges of the arts assessment was scoring students' work. Specific scoring guides were developed for the responding questions in music and the responding and creating questions in visual arts. Scorers were then trained to apply these criteria appropriately when evaluating students' responses that demonstrated a wide range of skill levels in music and visual arts.

The scoring guides for the sample questions presented in this report, and other released questions from the assessment, are available in the NAEP Questions Tool at http://nces.ed.gov/ nationsreportcard/itmrls/.

Reporting Arts Results

The results in this chapterare based on a nationally representative sample of 7,900 eighth-grade students from 260 public and private schools. Approximately one-half of these students were assessed in music, and the other half were assessed in visual arts.

Because music and visual arts are two distinct disciplines, results are reported separately for each area and cannot be compared. The average responding scores for music and visual arts are reported on two separate NAEP scales, each ranging from 0 to 300. The average creating task score for visual arts is reported as the average percentage of the maximum possible score ranging from 0 to 100. The arts assessment results cannot be reported in terms of the NAEP achievement levels (*Basic, Proficient,* and *Advanced*) given the complex and diverse nature of the assessment tasks both within and across the arts disciplines.

Comparisons between 1997 and 2008

Although the questions in the 2008 assessment were taken from those administered in the previous arts assessment in 1997, not all of the results can be compared between the two years (see the Technical Notes for more information). While comparisons across years cannot be made for the average responding and creating task scores, the percentages of students' correct responses to the multiple-choice questions in 2008 can be compared to those in 1997. These results are provided in appendix table A-3 for music and table A-4 for visual arts.

Accommodations and Exclusions in NAEP

Testing accommodations (for example, providing students with extra testing time or administering the assessment to students individually rather than in a group) are made available for students with disabilities and for English language learners participating in NAEP. Even with the availability of accommodations, a portion of these students was excluded from the NAEP arts assessment by their schools. In the 2008 arts assessment, overall exclusion rates for students with disabilities and/or English language learners were 2 percent of all students for music and for visual arts (see appendix table A-6).

More information about NAEP's policy on the inclusion of special-needs students is available at http://nces.ed.gov/nationsreportcard/about/ inclusion.asp.

Interpreting Results

NAEP uses widely accepted statistical standards for presenting and discussing results. Findings are reported based on statistical significance at the .05 level using t-tests with appropriate adjustments for multiple comparisons (using the False Discovery Rate procedure). Results that are reported to be "higher" or "lower" have been found to be statistically significant.

In addition to the overall results for eighth-graders in the nation, performance is presented for different student groups. These results should not be used to establish a cause-and-effect relationship between background characteristics and achievement. A complex mix of education and socioeconomic factors may affect student performance.

MUSIC

The 2008 arts assessment in music measured students' ability to respond to music. There were a total of four music sections in the arts assessment, each of which contained between 8 and 16 multiple-choice and constructed-response (or open-ended) questions. Many of the music questions in the assessment included multiple parts. Each student who was assessed in music was presented with two of the four sections. Because the length of the recorded music that was played for students varied in each section, the amount of time provided for students to complete two music sections ranged from 58 minutes to 63 minutes.

Students were asked to analyze and describe aspects of music they heard, critique instrumental and vocal performances, and demonstrate their knowledge of standard musical notation and music's role in society. Examples of the different types of music questions are presented later in this section.

Eighty-Nine-Point Score Gap between Lowest- and Highest-Performing Students in Music

While the overall average responding score in music was set at 150 in 2008, students at grade 8 exhibited a wide range of responding scores (figure 1). For example, scores ranged from 105 for lower-performing students at the 10th percentile to 194 for higher-performing students at the 90th percentile. Students at the 50th percentile had a score of 151.

CREATING MUSIC

A constructed-response question that asked students to write two measures of rhythmic music notation was included in one of the four music sections. Due to budget constraints, this was the only question in the assessment that asked students to create music; therefore, an average creating task score for music could not be reported. However, results for this question and other released questions from the 2008 arts assessment are available at http://nces.ed.gov/ nationsreportcard/itmrls/.

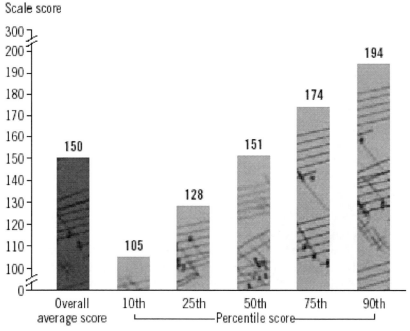

Source: U.S. Department of Education, Institute of Education Sciences, National Center for Education Statistics, National Assessment of Educational Progress (NAEP), 2008 Arts Assessment.

Figure 1. Average responding scale score and percentile scores in NAEP music at grade 8: 2008

Racial/Ethnic, Gender, and Socioeconomic Gaps in Music Scores

In addition to the overall average responding score in music, results are also available based on student characteristics such as race/ethnicity, gender, and eligibility for the National School Lunch Program.

In general, the same patterns in score gaps seen in other NAEP subjects were also evident in the results for music (figure 2). The percentages of students in each student group can be found in appendix table A-5.

Race/Ethnicity

In 2008, average responding scores in music for White and Asian/Pacific Islander students were 29 to 32 points higher than the scores for Black and Hispanic students. There were no significant differences between the average responding scores of White and Asian/Pacific Islander students or between the scores of Black and Hispanic students.

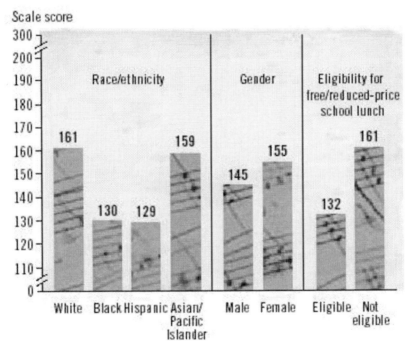

Note: Black includes African American, Hispanic includes Latino, and Pacific Islander includes Native Hawaiian. Race categories exclude Hispanic origin. Sample sizes were insufficient to permit reliable estimates for students whose race/ethnicity was American Indian/Alaska Native or unclassified. For the eligibility for free/reduced-price school lunch category, results are not shown for students whose eligibility status was not available.

Source: U.S. Department of Education, Institute of Education Sciences, National Center for Education Statistics, National Assessment of Educational Progress (NAEP), 2008 Arts Assessment.

Figure 2. Average responding scale score in NAEP music at grade 8, by selected student characteristics: 2008

Gender

On average, female students had a higher responding score in music than their male counterparts. There was a 10-point gap between the two groups in 2008.

Eligibility for Free/Reduced-Price School Lunch

NAEP uses students' eligibility for the National School Lunch Program as an indicator of poverty. Students from lower-income families are typically eligible for free/reduced-price school lunch (see the Technical Notes at the end of this chapter for eligibility criteria), while students from higher- income families typically are not. On average, the responding score for students who were eligible was 28 points[2] lower than the score for students who were not eligible.

Music Scores Vary by Type and Location of Schools

Results by selected school characteristics also show differences in average responding scores for music (figure 3). It is important to note that there may be many reasons students performed differently, on average, based on the type of school or its location. Differences in access to arts instruction and quality curricula, socioeconomic status, and other factors not measured in NAEP may influence student achievement in the arts.

Type of School

Public school students made up 93 percent of eighth-graders in the nation in 2008, while the other 7 percent of students attended private schools. The average responding score in music for eighth-graders in public schools was 14 points lower than the score for students in private schools.

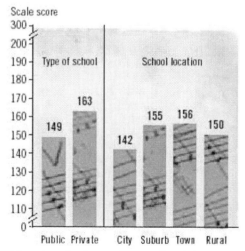

Source: U.S. Department of Education, Institute of Education Sciences, National Center for Education Statistics, National Assessment of Educational Progress (NAEP), 2008 Arts Assessment.

Figure 3. Average responding scale score in NAEP music at grade 8, by selected school characteristics: 2008

School Location

Results are available for four school location categories: city, suburb, town, and rural. Descriptions of how these school location categories are defined are included in the Technical Notes section of this report.

In 2008, eighth-graders who attended city schools had a lower average responding score in music than students who attended suburban, town, and rural schools. There were no significant differences in the average scores among students in suburban, town, and rural school locations.

Context for Arts Education in Music

Information collected from school and student questionnaires helps to provide the context in which arts learning takes place. For the music portion of the assessment, school administrators provided information on the availability and nature of music education in their schools. Students provided information on their participation in music activities.

Frequency of music instruction remains steady

School administrators were asked how often eighth-graders attending their schools might receive instruction in music. Fifty-seven percent of eighth- graders attended schools where students could have received music instruction at least three or four times a week in 2008 (figure 4). This was higher than the percentages of students attending schools where music was offered less frequently or not at all.

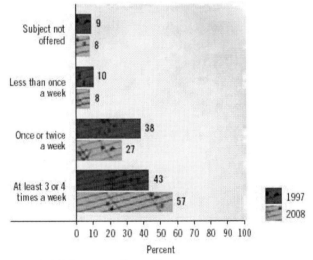

Note: Detail may not sum to totals because of rounding.
Source: U.S. Department of Education, Institute of Education Sciences, National Center for Education Statistics, National Assessment of Educational Progress (NAEP), 1997 and 2008 Arts Assessments.

Figure 4. Percentage of students at grade 8, by school-reported frequency with which instruction in music is available: 1997 and 2008

> **71** percent of eighth-graders attended schools where administrators reported that their state or district had a curriculum in music in 2008.
>
> **77** percent of students attended schools where music was taught by a full-time specialist.

Although the data are not shown here, access to music instruction, as reported by school administrators, did not differ significantly by race/ethnicity, gender, or eligibility for free/reduced-price school lunch. For example, the percentage of Black students attending schools where music was offered at least 3 or 4 times a week was not significantly different from the percentage of White students.

The same question was asked of school administrators in 1997, making it possible to look for changes in the instruction patterns over time. The apparent increase between 1997 and 2008 in the percentage of students attending schools where music was available at least three or four times a week was not statistically significant, nor were there any significant changes in the percentages of students attending schools where music was offered once or twice a week, less than once a week, or not at all.

More students writing down music in music class

Students responded to a series of questions about how often they did certain activities in music class. For each activity listed in figure 5, students indicated if they were asked by their teacher to do it almost every day, once or twice a week, once or twice a month, or never or hardly ever. Students were also given the option of indicating that they did not have music in school. The results summarized here show the combined percentages for all eighth- grade students who reported that they did various music-related activities at least once a month.

For the most part, students were as likely to be asked by their teachers to engage in these musical activities in 2008 as in 1997. There were no significant changes in the percentages of students who reported that teachers played music for them to listen to, or asked them to sing, play an instrument, work on group assignments, or make up their own music. Only the percentage of students who reported being asked to write down music showed a statistically significant increase from 26 percent in 1997 to 33 percent in 2008.

About one-third of students participate in musical performance activities at school

Students were also asked several questions about their participation in musical performance activities at school. These included whether or not they played in a band, played in an orchestra, or sang in a chorus or choir. Overall, 34 percent of eighth- graders reported participating in one or more of these musical activities at school in 2008 (figure 6). Although questions about participation in these musical activities were also asked in 1997, changes in the format of the questions prohibit comparing results from the two years.

What Eighth-Graders Know and Can Do in Music

The item map below is useful for understanding students' performance at different points on the responding scale. The scale scores on the left represent the average scores for students who were likely to get the questions correct or partially correct. Scores for the 25th and 75th percentiles are also noted. The descriptions of selected assessment questions are listed on the right.

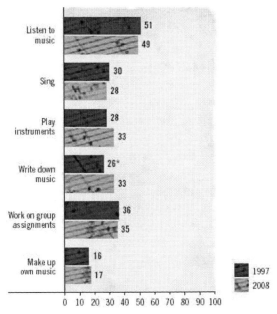

* Significantly different (p < .05) from 2008.

Figure 5. Percentage of students at grade 8, by student-reported in-school activities their teachers ask them to do in music class at least once a month: 1997 and 2008

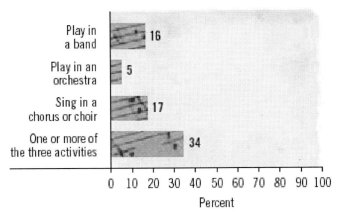

Note: Students were permitted to select more than one musical activity. The percentage for the category "One or more of the three activities" was derived from students' responses to each of the other three categories and was not a separate option by itself.

Source: U.S. Department of Education, Institute of Education Sciences, National Center for Education Statistics, National Assessment of Educational Progress (NAEP), 1997 and 2008 Arts Assessments.

Figure 6. Percentage of students at grade 8, by student-reported participation in musical activities in school: 2008

For example, the map shows that higher-performing eighth-graders in the upper range of the scale with an average score of 265 were likely to be able to identify one element of jazz present in "Rhapsody in Blue." Middle-performing students with an average score of 163 were likely to be able to describe one feature of a song that identifies it as a spiritual.

Constructed-response questions for which students could earn partial credit may appear on the map multiple times, once for each level of credit. For example, a question asking students to provide the name of a piano dynamic marking and to explain its meaning appears at the score of 192 for responses receiving full credit and at 183 for responses receiving partial credit.

Sample Question: Identifying the Texture of a Musical Example

The sample question below asked students to identify the texture of a musical example that was played. (The term "texture" was defined for the students as the blend of various musical sounds and the ways in which the lines of music in a piece are related.)

Grade 8 NAEP Music Responding Item Map

Scale score	Question description
300	
275	Identify piece of music as coming from twentieth century and provide limited justification why
265	Identify one element of jazz present in "Rhapsody in Blue"
239	Describe an emotion or mood created by a composition and describe two ways in which emotion or mood was created
237	Provide a partial identification and description of the errors in pitch in an instrumental solo
230	Describe a similarity and a difference between two written vocal parts
228	*Identify the solo instrument beginning "Rhapsody in Blue" (page 17)*
225	Provide a comparison between the tone color of two different singers
195	*Select a line drawing reflective of the texture of an example of music (page 15)*
195	*Identify the term for a fermata symbol*
192	Identify the name of a piano dynamic marking and explain its meaning (page 16)
183	Either identify the name of a piano dynamic marking or explain its meaning (page 16)
182	Provide a limited explanation of why spirituals were important in people's lives
176	*Identify a correct time signature for a piece of music*
174	**75th percentile**
172	Identify region of origin of African musical excerpt and provide a description of a characteristic related to its style (page 18)
167	*Identify a bass clef symbol*
166	*Identify the type of instrumental ensemble performing an excerpt*
163	Describe one feature of a song that identifies it as a spiritual
151	Identify the length of the introduction of "Shalom My Friends"
136	*Identify directional contour of part of melodic phrase*
128	**25th percentile**
124	Identify region of origin of African musical excerpt and provide partial explanation of its style characteristics (page 18)
84	Describe an emotion or mood created by a composition
49	Identify region of origin of African musical excerpt (page 18)
0	

Note: Regular type denotes a constructed-response question. Italic type denotes a multiple-choice question. The position of a question on the scale represents the average scale score attained by students who had a 65 percent probability of obtaining credit at a specific level of a constructed-response question, or a 74 percent probability of correctly answering a four-option multiple-choice question.

Source: U.S. Department of Education, Institute of Education Sciences, National Center for Education Statistics, National Assessment of Educational Progress (NAEP), 2008 Arts Assessment.

The music played for this question came from the beginning of "Contrapunctus 4" from *The Art of the Fugue* by J.S. Bach. In the recording, the fugue was played by a brass quartet. The fugue begins with one instrument entering and playing the subject (the initial melody) of the fugue, followed by the other members of the quartet, each playing the melody. The audio for this question is available in the NAEP Questions Tool at http://nces.ed.gov/nationsreportcard/itmrls/.

Each of the four diagrams below illustrates an example of a texture that could occur in a piece of music. In 2008, fifty-two percent of eighth-graders selected the correct answer (choice A), which shows the general pattern of musical lines that occurred in the music that was played. This was not found to be significantly different from the 52 percent who answered correctly in 1997. The other three choices are incorrect because they show patterns of musical lines that did not match the music that was played. Choice B shows a group of three voices in alternation with a solo line, choice C shows an alternation of two lines with no accompanying lines or voices, and choice D shows a solo line with a block chord accompaniment.

Percentage of Students in Each Response Category at Grade 8: 2008

Choice A	Choice B	Choice C	Choice D	Omitted
52	18	5	25	#

Rounds to zero.
Note: Detail may not sum to totals because of rounding.
Source: U.S. Department of Education, Institute of Education Sciences, National Center for Education Statistics, National Assessment of Educational Progress (NAEP), 2008 Arts Assessment.

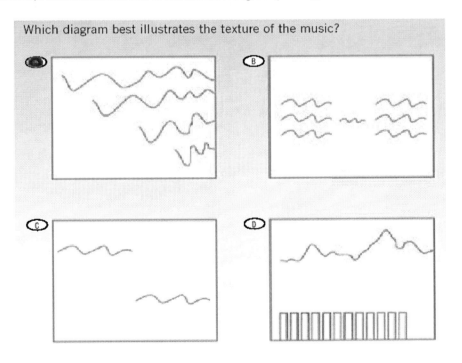

Sample Question: Reading Musical Notation

This two-part sample question was taken from a set of questions that asked students to demonstrate knowledge of standard musical notation. In the question below, students were asked to provide the name and meaning of the symbol indicated in circle 1 in the music shown here. No recorded music was played for this question. The question that pertains to the symbol indicated in circle 2 is not shown here but is available in the NAEP Questions Tool at http://nces.ed.gov/nationsreportcard/itmrls/.

Student responses for this two-part question were rated using three scoring levels: Adequate, Limited, and Inadequate. Examples of Adequate and Limited responses are shown here. Inadequate responses failed to provide correct information for either part of the question.

This sample response was rated "**Adequate**" because it provided the symbol's meaning (that the music should be performed softly) and the symbol's correct name (*piano*). Twenty percent of eighth- graders received a rating of "Adequate" on this question.

What does the symbol in circle 1 tell the performer to do?

Play or sing the music softly.

What is the musical (Italian) name for the symbol in circle 1?

Piano

This sample response was rated "**Limited**" because it provided the symbol's meaning but not its correct name. (*Pianissimo* refers to the symbol *pp,* which indicates that music should be performed *very* softly.) Nine percent of students' responses to this question were rated "Limited."

What does the symbol in circle 1 tell the performer to do?

Play soft

What is the musical (Italian) name for What is the musical (Italian) name for the symbol in circle 1?

Pianissimo

Percentage of Students in Each Response Category at Grade 8: 2008

Adequate	Limited	Inadequate	Omitted
20	9	62	#

Rounds to zero.
Note: Detail may not sum to totals because the percentage of responses rated as "Off-task" is not shown. Off-task responses are those that do not provide any information related to the assessment task.
Source: U.S. Department of Education, Institute of Education Sciences, National Center for Education Statistics, National Assessment of Educational Progress (NAEP), 2008 Arts Assessment.

Sample Question: Identifying the Sound of an Instrument

The sample question below asked students to identify the sound of an instrument. The music played for this question comes from the opening of "Rhapsody in Blue" by American composer George Gershwin. The audio is available in the NAEP Questions Tool at http://nces.ed.gov/ nationsreportcard/itmrls/.

In 2008, fifty percent of eighth-graders correctly identified the clarinet as the instrument on which the solo was played (choice D). This was not found to be significantly different from the 52 percent who answered correctly in 1997. Choices A, B, and C are also woodwind instruments like the clarinet but were not the instrument on which the solo at the beginning of the piece was played.

At the beginning of the piece, a solo is played on

Percentage of Students in Each Response Category at Grade 8: 2008

Choice A	Choice B	Choice C	Choice D	Omitted
12	15	22	50	#

Rounds to zero.
Note: Detail may not sum to totals because of rounding.
Source: U.S. Department of Education, Institute of Education Sciences, National Center for Education Statistics, National Assessment of Educational Progress (NAEP), 2008 Arts Assessment.

Sample Question: Identifying Origin of a Musical Style

The two-part sample question below asked students to identify music from a particular culture and to describe the features that help to characterize its style. The music played for this question came from an African song entitled "Drodope." The audio is available in the NAEP Questions Tool at http://nces.ed.gov/nationsreportcard/itmrls/.

Student responses for this two-part question were rated using four scoring levels: Developed, Adequate, Limited, and Inadequate. Examples of Developed and Adequate responses are shown here. Responses rated as Limited only provided a correct response to the first part of the question. Responses rated as Inadequate failed to provide a correct response for either part of the question.

This sample response was rated **"Developed"** because it both indicated the correct region of origin of the music and cited the "call and response" feature of the music that is common among many types of African songs. Mentioning the use of specific percussion instruments such as drums also contributed to this response receiving a rating of "Developed." Fifty-two percent of eighth-graders received a rating of "Developed" on this question.

From where does the music come?

    Ⓐ North America

    Ⓑ South America

    Ⓒ Asia

    ● Africa

Other than the language used in the song, describe one feature of the music that helps to identify it as coming from the part of the world you selected. Be specific in your description.

> The drums, also the call and response

This sample response was rated **"Adequate."** Although it indicated the correct region of origin of the music, the description of a feature of the music was vague. Twenty-four percent of students' responses to this question were rated "Adequate."

From where does the music come?

Other than the language used in the song, describe one feature of the music that helps to identify it as coming from the part of the world you selected. Be specific in your description.

> The music features instruments that are traditional to that part of the world.

Percentage of Students in Each Response Category at Grade 8: 2008

Developed	Adequate	Limited	Inadequate	Omitted
52	24	19	5	#

Rounds to zero.
Note: Detail may not sum to totals because the percentage of responses rated as "Off-task" is not shown. Off-task responses are those that do not provide any information related to the assessment task.
Source: U.S. Department of Education, Institute of Education Sciences, National Center for Education Statistics, National Assessment of Educational Progress (NAEP), 2008 Arts Assessment.

VISUAL ARTS

The 2008 arts assessment included four sections in visual arts that measured students' ability to respond to and create visual art. Students were given two of the four sections, each of which contained between 7 and 11 multiple-choice and constructed-response questions. Many of the visual arts questions in the assessment contained multiple parts. The amount of time provided for students to complete two visual arts sections ranged from 75 minutes to 104 minutes.

Responding questions asked students to analyze and describe works of art and design, thereby demonstrating their knowledge of media and techniques, visual organization, the cultural contexts of artworks, how works of art convey meaning, and the relationship between form and function in design. Creating questions assessed students' ability to communicate in works of art, think of different solutions to visual problems, and generate ideas for and then create works of art and design. These creating questions represented approximately one-half of the total assessment time in visual arts. Some examples of the different types of visual arts questions are presented later in this section.

Eighty-Nine-Point Score Gap between Lowest- and Highest-Performing Students in Visual Arts

The overall average responding score for visual arts was set at 150 in 2008 (figure 7). In addition to the overall average responding score, results are shown for students at selected percentiles on the responding scale. There was an 89-point gap between the scores for students at the 10th and 90th percentiles.

The assessment also included questions that asked students to create works of art and design. Results for these questions are presented as the average creating task score, which is expressed as the average percentage of the maximum possible score ranging from 0 to 100 (see the Technical Notes for an explanation of how the score was calculated). In 2008, the overall average creating task score for grade 8 students was 52 (figure 8).

Responding and Creating Results Related

Because the NAEP arts framework describes the integration among the arts processes, it is useful to explore the relationship between students' results on the responding and creating questions in visual arts. On average, students who performed well on the responding questions also performed well on the creating questions (figure 9). For example, students performing above the 75th percentile on the responding scale also had the highest average creating task score (62). Lower-performing students at or below the 25th percentile on the responding scale had the lowest average creating task score (40).

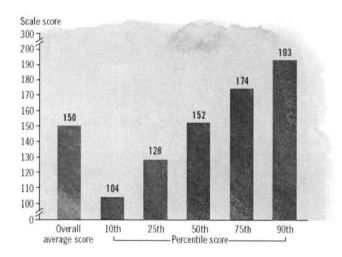

Figure 7. Average responding scale score and percentile scores in NAEP visual arts at grade 8: 2008

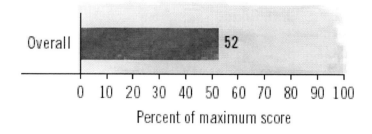

Figure 8. Average creating task score in NAEP visual arts at grade 8: 2008

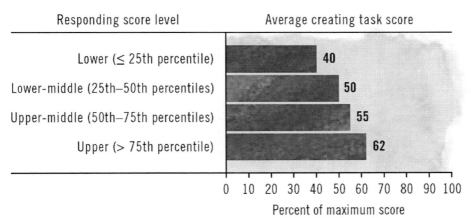

Figure 9. Average creating task score in NAEP visual arts at grade 8, by responding score level: 2008

Patterns in Score Gaps by Student Characteristics Similar for Responding to and Creating Visual Arts

In general, patterns in score differences based on student characteristics were similar for results in both responding (figure 10) and creating (figure 11).

Race/Ethnicity

In 2008, average responding scores in visual arts were 22 to 31 points higher for White and Asian/Pacic Islander students than for Black and Hispanic students. There were no signicant differences between the average responding scores of White and Asian/Pacific Islander students or between the scores of Black and Hispanic students.

Similarly, the average creating task scores of White and Asian/Pacific Islander students were higher than the scores of Black and Hispanic students, but there were no significant differences between the scores of White and Asian/Pacific Islander students or between the scores of Black and Hispanic students.

Gender

On average, female eighth-graders had a higher responding score in visual arts than their male counterparts. There was an 11-point[3] gap between the two groups in 2008. The average creating task score for female students was also 5 points higher than the score for male students.

Eligibility for Free/Reduced-Price School Lunch

On average, eighth-graders who were eligible for free/reduced-price school lunch had a lower responding score in visual arts than those who were not eligible. There was a 29-point gap between the two groups in 2008. Students who were eligible also had an average creating task score that was 9 points lower than the score for students who were not eligible.

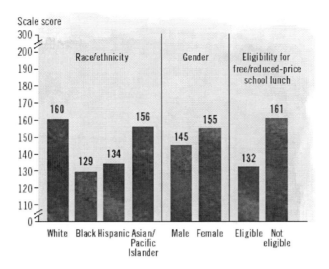

Figure 10. Average responding scale score in NAEP visual arts at grade 8, by selected student characteristics: 2008

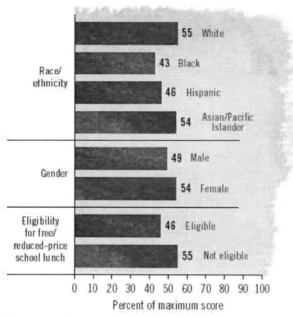

Note: Black includes African American, Hispanic includes Latino, and Pacific Islander includes Native Hawaiian. Race categories exclude Hispanic origin. Sample sizes were insufficient to permit reliable estimates for students whose race/ethnicity was American Indian/ Alaska Native or unclassified. For the eligibility for free/reduced-price school lunch category, results are not shown for students whose eligibility status was not available.

Source: U.S. Department of Education, Institute of Education Sciences, National Center for Education Statistics, National Assessment of Educational Progress (NAEP), 2008 Arts Assessment.

Figure 11. Average creating task score in NAEP visual arts at grade 8, by selected student characteristics: 2008

No Significant Difference in Responding Scores between Public and Private School Students

While the general patterns in results for responding to and creating visual arts by selected school characteristics were similar (figures 12 and 13), not all the apparent differences were found to be statistically significant.

Type of School

The apparent difference in 2008 between the average responding scores in visual arts for eighth- graders in public and private schools was not found to be statistically significant. However, the average creating task score was lower for public school students than for private school students.

School Location

Students attending suburban schools in 2008 had a higher average responding score in visual arts than students in city schools. There were no significant differences in the average responding scores between students from suburban schools and town or rural schools.

In the creating process of visual arts, students attending suburban schools had a higher average creating task score than students in both city and town schools. The average creating task score of students in suburban schools was not significantly different from the score of students in rural schools.

> Because responding results are presented as scale scores and creating results are presented as average percentages, it is not possible to compare the magnitude of differences between these scores. For example, an 11-point difference on the 0–300 responding scale between students attending schools in city and suburban locations is not necessarily greater than a 5-point difference between the same two groups on the 0–100 creating task scale.

Context for Arts Education in Visual Arts

To provide the context in which arts learning takes place, results are presented here based on school administrators' responses related to the availability and nature of visual arts education in their schools and students' responses about their participation in visual arts activities.

Frequency of visual arts instruction remains steady

School administrators were asked how often eighth- graders attending their schools might receive instruction in visual arts. Forty-seven percent of eighth-graders attended schools where students could possibly receive visual arts instruction at least three or four times a week in 2008 (figure 14). This was higher than the percentages of students attending schools where visual arts were offered less frequently or not at all.

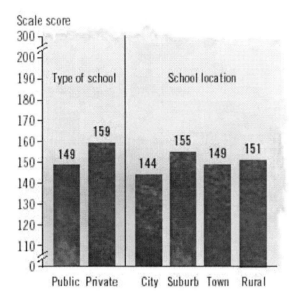

Figure 12. Average responding scale score in NAEP visual arts at grade 8, by selected school characteristics: 2008

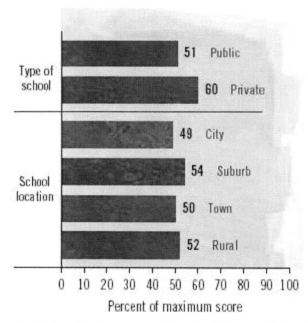

Source: U.S. Department of Education, Institute of Education Sciences, National Center for Education Statistics, National Assessment of Educational Progress (NAEP), 2008 Arts Assessment.

Figure 13. Average creating task score in NAEP visual arts at grade 8, by selected school characteristics: 2008

Although the data are not shown here, access to visual arts instruction did not differ significantly by race/ ethnicity, gender, or eligibility for free/reduced-price school lunch. For example, the percentage of students who were eligible for free/reduced-price school lunch attending schools where visual arts were offered once or twice a week was not significantly different from the percentage of students who were not eligible.

The same question was asked of school administrators in 1997, making it possible to look for changes in the instruction patterns over time. The results showed no significant changes between 1997 and 2008 in the percentages of students who attended schools where visual arts were available at least three or four times a week, once or twice a week, less than once a week, or not at all.

> **77** percent of eighth-graders attended schools where administrators reported that visual arts were taught by a full-time specialist.
> **69** percent of students attended schools that followed a state or district curriculum in visual arts.

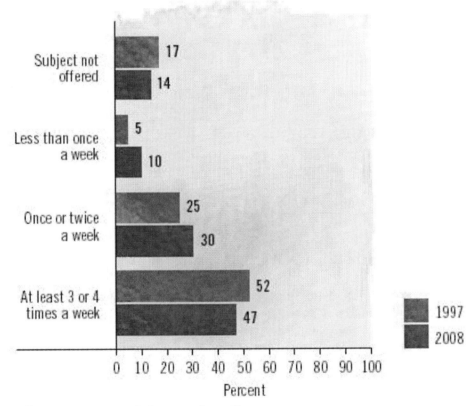

Note: Detail may not sum to totals because of rounding.
Source: U.S. Department of Education, Institute of Education Sciences, National Center for Education Statistics, National Assessment of Educational Progress (NAEP), 1997 and 2008 Arts Assessments.

Figure 14. Percentage of students at grade 8, by school-reported frequency with which instruction in visual arts is available: 1997 and 2008

More students writing about their artwork

Students responded to a series of questions about how often they did certain activities in visual arts class. For each activity listed in figure 15, students indicated if their teacher had them do it every day, once a week, once a month, or never or hardly ever. The results summarized here show the combined percentages for students who reported that they did various art- related activities at least once a month.

The percentage of students who reported that their teacher had them write about their artwork increased from 21 percent in 1997 to 27 percent in 2008. However, the percentage of students whose teacher had them choose their own art project decreased from 47 percent in 1997 to 39 percent in 2008. There were no significant changes between 1997 and 2008 in the percentages of students who reported that their teachers had them paint or draw; make things out of clay or other materials; work in a pair or group on an art project; talk with others about their own or others' artwork; or look at videotapes, filmstrips, slides, or television programs about art.

Fewer students visit art museums with class in 2008

Exposure to art museums and exhibits outside of school may help students learn about and engage in visual arts. Sixteen percent of students in 2008 reported that they had gone with their class to an art museum, gallery, or exhibit at least once in the last year, which was smaller than the 22 percent in 1997 (figure 16).

ABOUT HALF OF STUDENTS SAVE ARTWORK IN A PORTFOLIO

Although not presented here graphically, 54 percent of eighth-graders reported that they or their teacher saved their artwork in a portfolio in 2008, which was not significantly different from the 50 percent in 1997.

What Eighth-Graders Know and Can Do in Visual Arts

The item map below is useful for understanding students' performance at different points on the responding scale. The scale scores on the left represent the average scores for students who were likely to get the questions correct or partially correct. Scores for the 25th and 75th percentiles are also noted. The descriptions of selected assessment questions are listed on the right.

For example, the map shows that higher-performing eighth-graders in the upper range of the scale with an average score of 237 were likely to be able to identify the style of an artwork as surrealism. Middle-performing students with an average score of 144 were likely to be able to analyze the subject of five mother/child portraits of different genres.

Constructed-response questions for which students could earn partial credit may appear on the map multiple times, once for each level of credit. For example, a question asking students to describe two characteristics of charcoal in a self-portrait appears at the score of 201 for responses receiving full credit and at 134 for responses receiving partial credit.

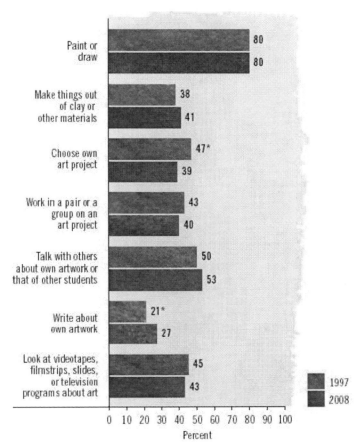

* Significantly different (p < .05) from 2008.

Figure 15. Percentage of students at grade 8, by student-reported in-school activities their teachers have them do in art at least once a month: 1997 and 2008

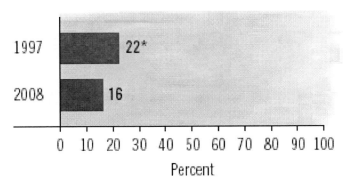

* Significantly different (p < .05) from 2008.
Source: U.S. Department of Education, Institute of Education Sciences, National Center for Education Statistics, National Assessment of Educational Progress (NAEP), 1997 and 2008 Arts Assessments.

Figure 16. Percentage of students at grade 8 who reported visiting an art museum, gallery, or exhibit with their class at least once a year: 1997 and 2008

Grade 8 NAEP Visual Arts Responding Item Map

Scale score	Question description
300	
∿	
285	Support plausible interpretation of Schiele self-portrait with observations about style, line, and color
280	Explain how an unusual/unexpected feature of a Bearden collage contributes to the work as a whole
256	Analyze and support with references to the work the narrative conveyed by a Bearden collage
241	Describe at least three aspects of own self-portrait that communicate something about you
240	Explain materials and design of own package idea for transporting fish on bicycle
237	*Identify the style of an artwork as surrealism*
229	Label and specifically describe one or two features of a Bearden collage that the artist wants you to notice
224	*Identify a technical similarity between Schiele and Kollwitz self-portraits (page 28)*
221	Explain how artist used light and shadow to create realism in mother/child portrait
220	Explain three ways an artist made some things look near and some far in mother/child portrait
213	Support plausible interpretation of Schiele self-portrait with observations about style, line, or color
205	Explain how Bearden creates contrast between interior and exterior areas in collage
202	Describe two aspects of own self-portrait that communicate something about you
201	Describe two characteristics of charcoal in Kollwitz self-portrait (page 29)
197	*Identify an example of Renaissance art*
197	*Identify compositional emphasis in a Bearden collage*
189	*Identify an example of 20th century western art*
176	Compare in specific terms how Kollwitz has drawn different parts of her self-portrait and offer plausible interpretation for differences (pages 30 and 31)
176	Explain where artist has used light and shadow to create realism in mother/child portrait
174	**75th percentile**
172	Describe and support how memory of place is shown in own collage
170	Explain how artist used light to create a lack of realism in mother/child portrait
144	Analyze subject of five mother/child portraits of different genres
136	Describe one aspect of own self-portrait that communicates something about you
134	Describe one characteristic of charcoal in Kollwitz self-portrait (page 29)
128	**25th percentile**
128	Identify an unusual/unexpected feature of the Bearden collage
62	Describe memory of place and/or aspect(s) of own collage
61	Describe what Schiele self-portrait is communicating or describe an aspect of style, line, or color
∿	
0	

Note: Regular type denotes a constructed-response question. Italic type denotes a multiple-choice question. The position of a question on the scale represents the average scale score attained by students who had a 65 percent probability of obtaining credit at a specific level of a constructed-response question, or a 74 percent probability of correctly answering a four-option multiple-choice question.

Source: U.S. Department of Education, Institute of Education Sciences, National Center for Education Statistics, National Assessment of Educational Progress (NAEP), 2008 Arts Assessment.

Self-portrait A: Kathe Kollwitz. Charcoal on brown laid paper. National Gallery of Art

Self-portrait B: Egon Schiele. Crayon and watercolor on buff paper. Galerie St. Etienne

Sample Questions for Visual Arts

Students were asked a series of questions related to two self-portraits shown here, one by Kathe Kollwitz (A) and one by Egon Schiele (B). These questions required students to apply their knowledge of aesthetic properties to the two artworks and to consider the relationships between these properties and the expressive qualities of each work. Students were then asked to create a self-portrait of their own.

Sample Question: Recognizing a Technical Similarity between Two Self-Portraits

The sample question below asked students to recognize a technical similarity between the Kollwitz and Schiele self-portraits. In both works, expressive, loose lines are combined with precise drawing.

In 2008, thirty-seven percent of students correctly identified this common feature of the two artworks (choice B). This was not found to be significantly different from the 36 percent who answered correctly in 1997. Choices A, C, and D do not accurately describe technical similarities between the two works.

Which statement describes a technical similarity between self-portraits A and B?

- Ⓐ The figure in each work is seen from the same point of view.
- ⬤ Both works combine loose gestural lines with careful drawing.
- Ⓒ The compositions in both works are symmetrical.
- Ⓓ Both works rely on light and shadow to emphasize depth.

Percentage of Students in Each Response Category at Grade 8: 2008

Choice A	Choice B	Choice C	Choice D	Omitted
8	37	8	46	#

\# Rounds to zero.
Note: Detail may not sum to totals because of rounding.
Source: U.S. Department of Education, Institute of Education Sciences, National Center for Education Statistics, National Assessment of Educational Progress (NAEP), 2008 Arts Assessment.

Sample Question: Characteristics of Charcoal

The sample question below asked students to describe characteristics of the medium of charcoal visible in the Kollwitz self-portrait. Student responses for this question were rated using three scoring levels: Acceptable, Partial, and Unacceptable. Examples of Acceptable and Partial responses are shown here. Responses rated as Unacceptable did not describe characteristics of the medium of charcoal evident in the self-portrait.

This sample response was rated "**Acceptable**" because it demonstrated the student's knowledge of charcoal as a medium. The student expressed what Kollwitz was able to accomplish with charcoal in her self-portrait. Thirty-four percent of eighth-graders received a rating of "Acceptable" on this question.

Self-portrait A is a charcoal drawing. Describe two characteristics of charcoal that you see in self-portrait A.

> 1. Charcoal can get very dark when you press harder than normal.
>
> 2. It leaves little white specks because it doesn't fill in every little bump or spot on the page.

This sample response was rated "**Partial**" because it provided only one example of how charcoal was used in the self-portrait. The student recognized that pressing harder on charcoal results in a darker mark, as is evident in the Kollwitz self-portrait. However, the second part of the response did not describe another characteristic of charcoal as a medium. Thirty-eight percent of students' responses to this question were rated "Partial."

Self-portrait A is a charcoal drawing. Describe two characteristics of charcoal that you see in self-portrait A.

> 1. One is the harder the charcoal is pushed down, the darker the markings will be.
>
> 2. It is not drawn straight but, like it was colored in.

Percentage of Students in Each Response Category at Grade 8: 2008

Acceptable	Partial	Unacceptable	Omitted
34	38	27	1

Note: Detail may not sum to totals because the percentage of responses rated as "Off-task" is not shown. Off-task responses are those that do not provide any information related to the assessment task.

Source: U.S. Department of Education, Institute of Education Sciences, National Center for Education Statistics, National Assessment of Educational Progress (NAEP), 2008 Arts Assessment.

Sample Question: Relationship between Technical Approach and Meaning

The two-part sample question below required students to analyze and interpret the Kollwitz self-portrait to explore relationships between technical approach and meaning. Part A of the question asked students about the work's formal characteristics, while part B asked them to connect those characteristics with what the artist was attempting to communicate. Student responses to each of the two parts were rated separately using three scoring levels: Acceptable, Partial, and Unacceptable. Examples of Acceptable and Partial student responses for each part of this question are shown here. Unacceptable responses for the question neither addressed differences in the way the parts of the self-portrait are drawn nor offered interpretations linked to observations.

Both parts of this sample response were rated "**Acceptable.**" This response accurately described the differences between the parts of the drawing and then used thes e o bser vati o ns t o offer an insightful and plausible interpretation of the reasons for those differences.

Fifty-three percent of students received a rating of "Acceptable" for part A, and 19 percent received an "Acceptable" rating for part B. Students who received the "Acceptable" rating were able to both comprehend the formal characteristics of the self-portrait and discuss the relationship between those characteristics and the artist's possible expressive goals.

Look at self-portrait A. Compare how Kollwitz has drawn her head and hand with the way she has drawn her arm. Be specific.

> A. Her head and hand are drawn carefully. They have shadings and fine details while her arm is a dark thick scribble.

Explain what you think Kollwitz may have been trying to communicate about herself by drawing these different parts of her self-portrait in different ways.

> B. She was showing expressions on her face. & that eventhough her body is weak, all she needs is her head & hands to keep drawing.

Both parts of this sample response received a "**Partial**" rating. This response accurately described the way the arm is drawn but did not specifically address the ways in which the head and hand are drawn differently from the arm. "Partial" credit was given for recognizing some characteristics of the artwork. While a few plausible interpretations about what Kollwitz was trying to communicate are provided in the second part of the response, none of these is clearly linked to the descriptions offered in the first part.

Fifteen percent of the student responses were rated "Partial" for part A, and 52 percent were rated "Partial" for part B.

Look at self-portrait A. Compare how Kollwitz has drawn her head and hand with the way she has drawn her arm. Be specific.

A. *Her arm is darker and it looks like she just scribbled it in the portrait.*

Explain what you think Kollwitz may have been trying to communicate about herself by drawing these different parts of her self-portrait in different ways.

B. *Shes trying to say she old, and that she is a good artist, and concentrates very well when shes drawing.*

Percentage of Students in Each Response Category at Grade 8: 2008

Part A

Acceptable	Partial	Unacceptable	Omitted
53	15	31	2

Part B

Acceptable	Partial	Unacceptable	Omitted
19	52	25	3

Note: Detail may not sum to totals because the percentage of responses rated as "Off-task" is not shown. Off-task responses are those that do not provide any information related to the assessment task.

Source: U.S. Department of Education, Institute of Education Sciences, National Center for Education Statistics, National Assessment of Educational Progress (NAEP), 2008 Arts Assessment.

Sample Question: Creating a Self- Portrait

After students had observed the Kollwitz and Schiele self-portraits and studied relationships between the technical and expressive qualities of the two artworks, they were asked to create a self-portrait of their own. Students were given a set of 12 Cray-pas (colored oil pastels), a charcoal pencil, a mirror, and a sheet of 12-inch by 18-inch white drawing paper and were asked to use these tools to create a self-portrait that would express something important about their personalities. These selfportraits were rated using four scoring levels: Sufficient, Uneven, Minimal, and Insufficient.

Characteristic of works rated "**Sufficient**," both of the students' responses presented here showed clear and specific observations that communicated something important about the artist. They incorporated identifying detail in terms of personal features and, in student response 1, an activity (art making). The self-portraits showed purposeful use of compositional elements and sophisticated use of materials. For example, in student response 1, the smudging of Cray-pas created an affinity among the head, arm, and hand, and loose, well-placed lines added definition to the body.

Both works also showed very good use of proportion, color, and line, and were fully developed and individualized. For example, in student response 2, the student skillfully used color to emphasize and create contrast between specific parts of her self-portrait. Both student responses 1 and 2 also showed evidence of the students having spent time observing the Kollwitz and Schiele self-portraits. Four percent of students' self-portraits were rated "Sufficient."

Percentage of Students in Each Response Category at Grade 8: 2008

Sufficient	Uneven	Minimal	Insufficient	Omitted
4	25	57	14	#

\# Rounds to zero.
Note: Detail may not sum to totals because the percentage of responses rated as "Off-task" is not shown. Off-task responses are those that do not provide any information related to the assessment task.
Source: U.S. Department of Education, Institute of Education Sciences, National Center for Education Statistics, National Assessment of Educational Progress (NAEP), 2008 Arts Assessment.

Works at the **"Uneven"** level made some specific observations. They sometimes employed pertinent compositional elements, gave attention to details such as facial features to convey expression, and/or effectively used materials to communicate. However, "Uneven" works were typically inconsistent or incomplete in parts.

In the sample presented here, the student gave her work individuality by vivid use of color, facial expression, and the symbols incorporated in her jewelry and the background. However, elements of her work seem inconsistent and lacking in deliberation, such as the placement and rendering of the symbols and colors in the background. Twenty-five percent of students' self-portraits were rated "Uneven."

As with many works rated at the **"Minimal"** level, in the sample self-portrait shown here, efforts at specific observations were apparent but relatively minimal (the red lines in the eyes). Compositional successes may seem more accidental than deliberate, and use of materials was unskilled. For example, while this student may have been attempting to convey some sense of an individual person by emphasizing only his eyes and mouth with color, he lacked the skill to make this choice distinctive enough to convey his message. Fifty-seven percent of students' self-portraits were rated "Minimal."

Most self-portraits rated **"Insufficient"** were generally so schematic as to convey little or nothing about the student. Like the sample self-portrait shown here, they showed unspecific observation, little awareness of composition, and highly unskilled use of materials. In contrast to the "Minimal" response, there were no features in this self-portrait that conveyed anything specific about a person, and it remained at a general level. Fourteen percent of students' self-portraits were rated "Insufficient."

Technical Notes and Data Appendix

Sampling and Weighting

The schools and students who participate in NAEP assessments are selected to form a representative sample of the nation. The national sample of eighth-graders in the 2008 arts assessment was chosen using a multistage design that involved drawing students from the sampled public and private schools across the country. The results from the assessed students were combined to provide accurate estimates of the overall performance of students in the nation.

Each school that participated in the assessment, and each student assessed, represents a portion of the population of interest. Results are weighted to make appropriate inferences between the student samples and the respective populations from which they are drawn. Sampling weights are adjusted for the disproportionate representation of some groups in the selected sample. This includes the oversampling of schools with high concentrations of students from certain racial/ethnic groups and the lower sampling rates of students who attend very small schools.

School and Student Participation Rates

The school and student participation rates for public and private schools in the 2008 arts assessment are provided in table A-1.

Table A-1. School and Student Participation Rates in NAEP Arts at Grade 8, by Subject and Type of School: 2008

Subject and type of school	School participation — Number of Schools participating	School participation — Weighted percent	Student participation — Number of Students assessed	Student participation — Weighted percent
Music				
Nation	260	97	4,000	93
Public	220	99	3,400	93
Private	30	76	500	97
Visual arts				
Nation	260	97	3,900	92
Public	220	99	3,400	92
Private	30	76	500	94

Note: The numbers of schools are rounded to the nearest ten, and the numbers of students are rounded to the nearest hundred. Detail may not sum to totals because of rounding.

Source: U.S. Department of Education, Institute of Education Sciences, National Center for Education Statistics, National Assessment of Educational Progress (NAEP), 2008 Arts Assessment.

NCES statistical standards require that a nonresponse bias analysis be conducted for any school or student group with a participation rate that falls below 85 percent. The participation rates for the 2008 NAEP arts assessment indicated a need for a school nonresponse bias analysis for the private school sample. The results showed that school substitution and nonresponse adjustments were not effective in reducing nonresponse bias for the percentage of Hispanic students enrolled and type of private schools (Catholic and other private schools). The disproportionate nonresponse resulted in an overestimation of the percentage of Hispanic students, an overestimation of the percentage of Catholic school students, and an underestimation of the percentage of other private school students.

Interpreting Statistical Significance

Comparisons over time or between groups in this chapter are based on statistical significance at the .05 level using t-tests with appropriate adjustments for multiple comparisons (using the False Discovery Rate procedure). These statistical tests consider both the size of the differences and standard errors of the two statistics being compared. Standard errors are margins of error, and estimates based on smaller groups are likely to have larger margins of error relative to estimates based on larger groups. Note, for example, that differences based on school-administrator-reported estimates have smaller sample sizes than differences based on student- reported estimates, resulting in smaller significant differences in the student-reported data than in the school-administrator-reported data. The size of the standard errors may also be influenced by other factors such as how representative the students assessed are of the entire population.

When an estimate has a large standard error, a numerical difference that seems large may not be statistically significant. Differences of the same magnitude may or may not be statistically significant depending upon the size of the standard errors of the estimates. For example, a 10-point difference between male and female students may be statistically significant, while a 10-point difference between students attending public and private schools may not be.

National School Lunch Program

NAEP collects data on student eligibility for the National School Lunch Program (NSLP) as an indicator of poverty. Under the guidelines of NSLP, children from families with incomes below 130 percent of the poverty level are eligible for free meals. Those from families with incomes between 130 and 185 percent of the poverty level are eligible for reduced-price meals. (For the period July 1, 2007 through June 30, 2008, for a family of four, 130 percent of the poverty level was an annual income of $27,000, and 185 percent was $38,000.) For more information on NSLP, visit http://www. fns.usda.gov/cnd/lunch/.

School Location

Results of the 2008 NAEP arts assessment were reported for four mutually exclusive categories of school location. These categories are based on standard definitions established by the Federal Office of Management and Budget using population and geographic information from the U.S. Census Bureau. The classification system is referred to as "urban-centric locale codes," which classifies territory into four major types: city, suburb, town, and rural. More details on the classification system can be found at http://nces.ed.gov/ccd/rural_locales.asp.

The Creating Task Score

Students' performance on questions assessing the creating process in visual arts is presented as the average creating task score in this report. The creating task score for each creating question (task) is the sum of the percentage of students receiving full credit and a fraction of the percentage of students receiving partial credit. The individual scores are then averaged together to report an average creating task score for the entire set of the visual arts creating questions.

An example of computing the creating task score is provided below for a sample question in this chapter that asks eighth-graders to draw a self-portrait. Responses to this question were scored "Sufficient," "Uneven," "Minimal," or "Insufficient." The percentages of students falling into these four scoring levels are 4 percent, 25 percent, 57 percent, and 14 percent, respectively (table A-2). Responses at these four levels receive score weights of 1, $\frac{2}{3}$, $\frac{1}{3}$, and 0, respectively. The creating task score for this question is computed as $1(4) + \frac{2}{3}(25) + \frac{1}{3}(57) + 0(14) = 40$.

Table A-2. Example Showing How the Creating Task Score Was Computed for a Sample Question in NAEP Visual Arts at Grade 8: 2008

Scoring level	Percentage of students	Score weight	Percentage of students × score weight
Sufficient	4	1	4
Uneven	25	$\frac{2}{3}$	17
Minimal	57	$\frac{1}{3}$	19
Insufficient	14	0	0
		Creating task score	$(4 + 17 + 19 + 0) = 40$

Source: U.S. Department of Education, Institute of Education Sciences, National Center for Education Statistics, National Assessment of Educational Progress (NAEP), 2008 Arts Assessment.

Comparing Results between the 1997 and 2008 Assessments

Although the assessment questions administered in 2008 were selected from those used in the 1997 assessment, due to changes in scoring procedures and materials, the 2008 score results in music and visual arts could not be directly compared to the results in 1997.

In the 2008 arts assessment, the scoring guides for constructed-response questions, the sample questions and student responses used to train scorers, and the standardized training procedures were updated to reflect changes in training and scoring procedures that have been adapted for use across all NAEP assessments since 1997. In addition, because the student artwork used as training samples for visual arts in 1997 had degraded over time and because of differences in the availability of certain types of art supplies and tools between 1997 and 2008, new samples were developed for scoring students' responses to the creating questions in 2008.

Table A-3. Percentage Correct for Multiple-Choice Questions in NAEP Music at Grade 8: 1997 and 2008

Question description	Percent correct 1997	Percent correct 2008
Overall	53*	51
Identify directional contour of part of melodic phrase	79	77
Identify form of vocal music in a recording (musical excerpt 1)	78	76
Identify the type of instrumental ensemble performing an excerpt	75	71
Identify form of musical examples as theme and variations	64	64
Identify a bass clef symbol	63	62
Identify pitch contour of melody in a recording	63*	56
Identify saxophone as instrument playing melody	66*	56
Identify a half note in printed music	52	56
Identify a correct time signature for a piece of printed music	55	52
Select a line drawing reflective of the texture of an example of music	52	52
Identify the solo instrument beginning "Rhapsody in Blue"	52	50
Identify form of vocal music in a recording (musical excerpt 2)	60*	49
Identify an appropriate texture drawing for a homophonic excerpt	51	48
Identify term best describing the texture	47	47
Identify an appropriate description of the texture of a recorded excerpt	50*	44
Identify correct time signature for recorded excerpt	42	43
Identify the name of a pitch shown in the treble clef	42	41
Identify an octave interval in a printed score	37	38
Identify the term for fermata symbol	38*	33
Identify which voices enter first in a choral excerpt	32	28
Identify the quality of a triad in a printed score	15*	21

* Significantly different ($p < .05$) from 2008.

Source: U.S. Department of Education, Institute of Education Sciences, National Center for Education Statistics, National Assessment of Educational Progress (NAEP), 1997 and 2008 Arts Assessments.

Table A-4. Percentage Correct for Multiple-Choice Questions in NAEP Visual Arts at Grade 8: 1997 and 2008

Question description	Percent correct 1997	Percent correct 2008
Overall	42	42
Identify purpose of insulating package material	61	62
Identify an example of 20th-century western art	55	59
Infer from photograph advantages of shrink-wrap packaging	57	57
Identify an example of a Renaissance painting	48	50
Identify compositional emphasis in a Bearden collage	49	46
Identify genre of a Bearden collage	34	37
Identify a technical similarity between Schiele and Kollwitz self-portraits	36	37
Identify an important compositional aspect of a Kollwitz self-portrait	40	37
Identify a stylistic emphasis in a Bearden collage	29	35
Identify a compositional feature of a medieval artwork	39*	32
Identify the style of an artwork as surrealism	27	31
Identify an artistic style that influenced cubism	25	23

* Significantly different ($p < .05$) from 2008.
Source: U.S. Department of Education, Institute of Education Sciences, National Center for Education Statistics, National Assessment of Educational Progress (NAEP), 1997 and 2008 Arts Assessments.

Table A-5. Percentage of Students in NAEP Arts Assessment at grade 8, by selected student and school characteristics: 2008

Student and school characteristics	Music	Visual arts
Race/ethnicity		
White	61	61
Black	15	14
Hispanic	18	17
Asian/Pacific Islander	5	5
American Indian/Alaska Native	1	2
Unclassified	1	1
Gender		
Male	50	51
Female	50	49
Eligibility for free/reduced-price school lunch		
Eligible	36	37
Not eligible	57	56
Information not available	7	8
Type of school		
Public	93	92
Private	7	8
School location		
City	29	29
Suburb	37	36
Town	12	13
Rural	22	22

Note: Black includes African American, Hispanic includes Latino, and Pacific Islander includes Native Hawaiian. Race categories exclude Hispanic origin. Detail may not sum to totals because of rounding.
Source: U.S. Department of Education, Institute of Education Sciences, National Center for Education Statistics, National Assessment of Educational Progress (NAEP), 2008 Arts Assessment.

Table A-6. Percentage of Students with Disabilities (SD) and/or English Language Learners (ELL) Identified, Excluded, and Assessed in NAEP Music and Visual Arts at Grade 8, as a Percentage of all Students: 2008

Student characteristics	Music	Visual arts
SD and/or ELL		
Identified	17	17
Excluded	2	2
Assessed	15	16
Without accommodations	6	6
With accommodations	8	10
SD		
Identified	12	12
Excluded	1	2
Assessed	10	11
Without accommodations	3	2
With accommodations	7	8
ELL		
Identified	6	6
Excluded	1	1
Assessed	5	6
Without accommodations	4	4
With accommodations	2	2

Note: Students identified as both SD and ELL were counted only once under the combined SD and/or ELL category, but were counted separately under the SD and ELL categories. Detail may not sum to totals because of rounding.

Source: U.S. Department of Education, Institute of Education Sciences, National Center for Education Statistics, National Assessment of Educational Progress (NAEP), 2008 Arts Assessment.

However, since the scoring method for multiple-choice questions was the same in 1997 and 2008, direct comparisons could be made between the two years on results for these questions in music and visual arts (tables A-3 and A-4). Because multiple-choice questions were only a portion of the assessment and only assessed certain types of topics in the responding process of music and visual arts, the changes in students' performance between 1997 and 2008 on these questions did not represent the performance changes for the constructed-response questions or the entire assessment.

U.S. DEPARTMENT OF EDUCATION

The National Assessment of Educational Progress (NAEP) is a congressionally authorized project sponsored by the U.S. Department of Education. The National Center for Education Statistics, a department within the Institute of Education Sciences, administers NAEP. The Commissioner of Education Statistics is responsible by law for carrying out the NAEP project.

Arne Duncan	John Easton	Stuart Kerachsky
Secretary	*Director*	*Acting Commissioner*
U.S. Department of Education	Institute of Education Sciences	National Center for Education Statistics

THE NATIONAL ASSESSMENT GOVERNING BOARD

In 1988, Congress created the National Assessment Governing Board to set policy for the National Assessment of Educational Progress, commonly known as The Nation's Report Card™. *The Governing Board is an independent, bipartisan group whose members include governors, state legislators, local and state school officials, educators, business representatives, and members of the general public.*

Darvin M. Winick, Chair
President
Winick & Associates
Austin, Texas

Amanda P. Avallone, Vice Chair
Assistant Principal and
Eighth-Grade Teacher
Summit Middle School
Boulder, Colorado

David J. Alukonis
Former Chairman
Hudson School Board
Hudson, New Hampshire

Gregory Cizek
Professor of Educational Measurement
University of North Carolina
Chapel Hill, North Carolina

Carol A. D'Amico
President and Chief Executive Ofcer
Conexus Indiana
Indianapolis, Indiana

Honorable David P. Driscoll
Former Commissioner of Education
Massachusetts Department of Education
Malden, Massachusetts

Louis M. Fabrizio
Director of Accountability Policy and Communications
North Carolina Department of
Public Instruction
Raleigh, North Carolina

Honorable Anitere Flores
Member
Florida House of Representatives
Miami, Florida

Alan J. Friedman
Consultant
Museum Development and Science Communication
New York, New York

David W. Gordon
County Superintendent of Schools
Sacramento County Ofce of Education
Sacramento, California

Robin C. Hall
Principal
Beecher Hills Elementary School
Atlanta, Georgia

Kathi M. King
Twelfth-Grade Teacher
 Messalonskee High School
Oakland, Maine

Kim Kozbial-Hess
Educational Technology Trainer
Hawkins Elementary School
Toledo, Ohio

Henry Kranendonk
Mathematics Curriculum Specialist
Milwaukee Public Schools
Milwaukee, Wisconsin

James S. Lanich
President
California Business for Education Excellence
Sacramento, California

Honorable Cynthia L. Nava *Senator*
New Mexico State Senate
Las Cruces, New Mexico

Honorable Steven L. Paine
State Superintendent of Schools
West Virginia Department of Education
Charleston, West Virginia

Honorable Sonny Perdue
Governor of Georgia
Atlanta, Georgia

Susan Pimentel
Educational Consultant
Hanover, New Hampshire

Andrew C. Porter
Dean
Graduate School of Education
University of Pennsylvania
Philadelphia, Pennsylvania

Warren T. Smith, Sr.
Vice President
Washington State Board of Education
Olympia, Washington

Mary Frances Taymans, SND
Executive Director
Secondary Schools Department
National Catholic Educational Association
Washington, D.C.

Oscar A. Troncoso
Principal
Anthony High School
Anthony, Texas

Eileen L. Weiser
General Public Representative
Ann Arbor, Michigan

John Easton (Ex officio)
Director
Institute of Education Sciences

U.S. Department of Education
Washington, D.C.

Mary Crovo
Interim Executive Director
National Assessment Governing Board
Washington, D.C.

SUGGESTED CITATION

Keiper, S., Sandene, B.A., Persky, H.R., and Kuang, M. (2009). *The Nation's Report Card: Arts 2008 Music & Visual Arts* (NCES 2009–488).
National Center for Education Statistics, Institute of Education Sciences, U.S. Department of Education, Washington, D.C.

End Notes

[1] *National Standards for Arts Education* (1994). Reston, Virginia: Music Educators National Conference.
[2] The score-point difference is based on the difference between the unrounded scores as opposed to the rounded scores shown in the figure.
[3] The score-point gap is based on the difference between the unrounded scores as opposed to the rounded scores shown in the figure.

Chapter 3

ACCESS TO ARTS EDUCATION: INCLUSION OF ADDITIONAL QUESTIONS IN EDUCATION'S PLANNED RESEARCH WOULD HELP EXPLAIN WHY INSTRUCTION TIME HAS DECREASED FOR SOME STUDENTS

United State Government Accountability Office

WHY GAO DID THIS STUDY

Under the No Child Left Behind Act (NCLBA), districts and schools must demonstrate adequate yearly progress (AYP) for all students. Because schools may spend more time improving students' academic skills to meet NCLBA's requirements, some are concerned that arts education might be cut back. To determine how, if at all, student access to arts education has changed since NCLBA, the Congress asked: (1) has the amount of instruction time for arts education changed and, if so, have certain groups been more affected than others, (2) to what extent have state education agencies' requirements and funding for arts education changed since NCLBA, (3) what are school officials in selected districts doing to provide arts education since NCLBA and what challenges do they face in doing so, and (4) what is known about the effect of arts education in improving student outcomes? GAO analyzed data from the U.S. Department of Education (Education), surveyed 50 state arts officials, interviewed officials in 8 school districts and 19 schools, and reviewed existing research.

WHAT GAO RECOMMENDS

To identify factors that may contribute to changes in access to arts education for certain groups, GAO recommends that the Secretary of Education require the department's planned study of NCLBA implementation to ask survey respondents why any changes in instruction time they report occurred. Education generally agreed with our recommendation.

WHAT GAO FOUND

According to data from Education's national survey, most elementary school teachers--about 90 percent--reported that instruction time for arts education stayed the same between school years 2004-2005 and 2006-2007. The percentage of teachers that reported that instruction time had stayed the same was similarly high across a range of school characteristics, irrespective of the schools' percentage of low-income or minority students or of students with limited English proficiency, or the schools' improvement under NCLBA. Moreover, about 4 percent of teachers reported an increase. However, about 7 percent reported a decrease, and GAO identified statistically significant differences across school characteristics in the percentage of teachers reporting that the time spent on arts education had decreased. Teachers at schools identified as needing improvement and those with higher percentages of minority students were more likely to report a reduction in time spent on the arts. Because Education's survey did not include questions about why instruction time changed, GAO was not able to determine the reasons for the disparities its analysis identified. A new study of NCLBA implementation that Education plans to undertake may collect information on the uses of instruction time, among other topics. However, Education has not yet determined if it will collect information on the reasons instruction time changed for certain groups.

While basic state requirements for arts education in schools have remained unchanged in most states, state funding levels for arts education increased in some states and decreased in others, according to GAO's survey of state arts officials. Arts education officials attributed the funding changes to state budget changes to a greater extent than they did to NCLBA or other factors.

Source: Art Explosion (image).

Elementary School Children Participating in Arts Education

School principals have used several strategies to provide arts education; however, some struggled with decreased budgets and competing demands on instruction time, according to those GAO interviewed. Strategies for maintaining arts education include seeking funding and collaborative arrangements in the arts community. Competing demands on instruction time were due to state education agency or school district actions taken to meet NCLBA proficiency standards.

Overall, research on the effect of arts education on student outcomes is inconclusive. Some studies that examined the effect of arts education on students' reading and math achievement found a small positive effect, but others found none.

ABBREVIATIONS

AEP	Arts Education Partnership
AYP	adequate yearly progress
CEP	Center on Education Policy
CPS	Chicago Public Schools
ERIC	Education Resources Information Center
ESEA	Elementary and Secondary Education Act of 1965
IASA	Improving America's Schools Act of 1994
NAEP	National Assessment of Educational Progress
NCLBA	No Child Left Behind Act
NEA	National Endowment for the Arts
NLS-NCLB	National Longitudinal Study of No Child Left Behind
SEAS	Student Enrichment in the Arts program
SES	supplemental education services

February 27, 2009

The Honorable Christopher J. Dodd
Chairman
The Honorable Lamar Alexander
Ranking Member
Subcommittee on Children and Families
Committee on Health, Education, Labor and Pensions
United States Senate

The federal government has invested billions of dollars in federal grants to states and school districts to improve educational opportunities for low- income students because their academic performance is substantially lower than that of other students. The No Child Left Behind Act of 2001 (NCLBA) sought to address this issue by building on the proficiency targets required by the Improving America's Schools Act of 1994 (IASA) and by establishing a deadline of 2014 for all students to reach proficiency in reading, math, and science. Under NCLBA, districts and schools must demonstrate adequate yearly progress (AYP) toward meeting state standards for all students and every key student subgroup, including low-income and minority students, students with disabilities, and students with limited English proficiency, toward annual state-established proficiency targets. When students in schools receiving funds under Title I of NCLBA do not make sufficient progress toward meeting state proficiency targets, their schools are identified as needing improvement, and both districts and schools are required to take certain actions.

Schools' efforts to improve students' academic performance and the school's NCLBA status can lead to changes in the amount of instruction time devoted to reading, math, and other subjects, including arts education. With NCLBA's 2014 deadline approaching, increased attention has been focused on the amount of time teachers are able to devote to other subjects, including the arts, which for this study includes four art forms: visual arts, music, theater, and dance. To the extent that schools spend more time improving students' reading, math, and science skills to meet NCLBA's accountability requirements, some are concerned that arts education might be reduced or eliminated.

To determine whether there have been any changes in student access to arts education since NCLBA, the Congress asked us to examine the following questions: (1) has the amount of instruction time for arts education changed and, if so, have certain groups been more affected than others, (2) to what extent have state education agencies' requirements and funding for arts education changed since NCLBA, (3) what are school officials in selected districts doing to provide arts education since NCLBA and what challenges do they face in doing so, and (4) what is known about the effect of arts education in improving student outcomes?

To identify changes in students' access to arts education, if any, we analyzed data on changes in instruction time between school years 2004-2005 and 2006- 2007 for all subjects, including the arts, from the Department of Education's (Education) National Longitudinal Study of No Child Left Behind (NLSNCLB).[1] Because this study collected data on changes in instruction time only from elementary school teachers, the nationally representative findings on students' access to arts education apply only to elementary schools. Although NLS-NCLB data did not allow us to answer the study question for middle and secondary schools, they were the only existing data on changes in instruction time available that met GAO's data quality standards. Our findings also apply only to the time between school years 2004-2005 and 2006-2007 and not to the full period of time since NCLBA's passage. As a further step in identifying changes in students' access to arts education by identifying any changes in state arts education requirements and funding, we surveyed arts officials in 49 states and the District of Columbia.[2] For the survey, an arts official was an official in a state department of education or other designated state agency who was knowledgeable about the states' role in shaping the provision of arts education in public schools. Forty-five state arts officials completed the survey. The survey collected data on state arts education requirements and funding in school years 2001-2002, the year NCLBA was passed, and 2006- 2007, changes made to state arts education requirements and funding between those school years, and factors contributing to any changes. To determine what district officials and school principals are doing to provide arts education since NCLBA and the challenges they face, we visited and interviewed officials in Illinois, Massachusetts, Florida, and New York. We selected states with large numbers of schools not meeting AYP and school districts and schools based on criteria that provide variation in the income level of the school district, schools' performance status under NCLBA, and schools' urban and rural location. Within each state, we visited 2 school districts and 4 to 6 schools in each district for a total of 8 school districts and 19 schools. In each state, we also interviewed officials representing at least one local arts organization that supported arts education in public schools. To determine what is known about the effect of arts instruction, we reviewed existing studies that examined the effect of arts instruction on student outcomes, such as academic achievement and graduation rates. Appendix I provides a detailed description of our methodology and its limitations, as well as our scope. We conducted this performance audit from September 2007 to February 2009, in accordance with generally accepted government auditing standards. Those standards require that we plan and perform the audit to obtain sufficient, appropriate evidence to provide a reasonable basis for our findings and conclusions based on the audit objectives. We believe that the evidence obtained provides a reasonable basis for our findings and conclusions based on our audit objectives.

RESULTS IN BRIEF

Most elementary school teachers—about 90 percent—reported that instruction time for arts education remained the same between school years 2004-2005 and 2006-2007. The percentage of teachers that reported that instruction time had stayed the same was similarly high across a range of school characteristics, irrespective of the schools' percentage of low-income or minority students or of students with limited English proficiency, or the schools' improvement under NCLBA. Moreover, about 4 percent of teachers reported an increase. However, about 7 percent reported a decrease, and we identified statistically significant differences across school characteristics in the percentage of teachers reporting that the time spent on arts education had decreased. Specifically, teachers at schools identified as needing improvement and those with higher percentages of minority students were more likely to report a reduction in time spent on the arts. In addition, when we examined the average amount of change in weekly instruction time among teachers that reported either an increase or a decrease, we found that teachers at elementary schools with high percentages of low-income or minority students reported larger average reductions than teachers at schools with low percentages of these students.[3] For example, teachers reporting decreases in arts education time at schools with a high percentage of low-income students reported an average decrease of 49 minutes per week while teachers reporting decreases in arts education time at schools with lower percentages of these students reported an average decrease of 31 minutes per week. Because Education's NLS-NCLB survey did not include questions for the teachers to identify why instruction time for arts education decreased at their school, we could not explore the reasons that might explain some of the disparities we identified in our analysis of the data. A new study of NCLBA implementation that Education plans to undertake may collect information on the uses of instruction time, among other topics. However, Education has not yet determined if it will collect information on the reasons instruction time changed for certain groups.

While basic state requirements for arts education in schools have stayed about the same in most states, state funding levels for arts education increased in some states and decreased in others, according to our survey of state arts officials. Basic state education requirements for arts education in schools—such as the number of hours a week that the arts must be taught or the number of courses that must be taken—have remained constant in most states since NCLBA was implemented. Of the 45 states that responded to our survey, 34 states had established the basic requirement that arts education be taught, and 28 states had included arts education as a high school graduation requirement by school year 200 1- 2002. By school year 2006-2007, most of these states had retained these requirements. While basic requirements for arts education remained nearly unchanged, state funding for arts education changed, with some states reporting decreases, and others reporting increases or funding levels that stayed about the same. For example, of the 32 states that awarded arts education grants in both school years 200 1-2002 and 2006-2007, funding decreased in 12 states and increased in 5 states. Arts education officials attributed the increases or decreases in funding to state budget changes to a greater extent than they did to NCLBA or other factors.

District officials and school principals have used several strategies to provide arts education; however, some struggled with decreased budgets and competing demands on instruction time, according to officials we interviewed. School principals that have been able to maintain arts education have used several strategies, including varying when the arts are offered, seeking funding and collaborative arrangements in the arts community, and integrating the arts into other subjects. For example, at one Boston school, the principal had eliminated arts education classes during the school day and purchased an after school arts program in drama and music production from an outside organization.

On the other hand, to ensure that students could attend arts education during the school day, one New York City school principal added an additional period to the end of the day to provide remedial instruction to students who required additional help. To expose his students to different international musical styles, one Broward County social studies teacher played music from other countries during geography lessons. Officials we met with told us that the main challenges to providing arts education have been decreased state or local funding and competing demands on instruction time due to requirements established by the state education agency or school district in order to meet NCLBA proficiency standards, such as doubling the amount of time low-performing students spend on reading and math. For example, at one school, the principal could not afford a full-time art teacher when the school's budget was reduced. In addition, some officials said that requirements established to meet NCLBA proficiency standards affected the time available for certain subjects. For example, at several schools, officials said that students not meeting state proficiency requirements could be pulled from art class to attend a remedial class in reading or math. Moreover, district officials and school principals told us that when trade-offs involving funding or instruction time had to be made, the school principal made the decision, and that principals' decisions differed. For example, some principals chose not to spend their limited discretionary funds on arts education, while other principals, even when their school had been identified as needing improvement several times, maintained their arts offerings.

Overall, research on the association between arts education and student outcomes is inconclusive. Some studies that examined the association between arts education and students' reading and math achievement found a small positive relationship, but others found none. For example, one study that combined the findings of several studies found that music education in elementary or high school had a small positive relationship with standardized math test scores. However, another similarly constructed study found that arts education had no significant relationship with standardized reading and math test scores. While some of the research on arts education has focused on special populations, such as students from low-income families, these studies did not meet GAO's criteria for methodological quality, and their findings were questionable.

To help identify factors that may contribute to changes in access to arts education for certain student subgroups, we are recommending that the Secretary of Education require that the department's planned study of NCLBA implementation include questions in its surveys asking survey respondents to describe the reasons for any changes in instruction time they report.

BACKGROUND

Since passage of the Elementary and Secondary Education Act of 1965 (ESEA), more than 40 years ago, the Congress has sought to improve student learning through several initiatives. Current legislation, NCLBA, builds upon previous legislation—the IASA—by adding provisions meant to strengthen accountability requirements for school districts and schools.[4] For example, both IASA and NCLBA required states to measure the performance of students in reading and math. NCLBA built upon this requirement by requiring annual testing in these subjects in each of grades 3 to 8 and added requirements that children's performance in science also be assessed.

Table 1. Time Line for Implementing Interventions for Schools That Do Not Make Adequate Yearly Progress

Adequate yearly progress	School status in the next year	NCLBA interventions for Title I schools
First year missed	Not applicable	None
Second year missed	Needs improvement (first year of improvement)	Required to offer public school choice[a]
Third year missed	Needs improvement (second year of improvement)	Required to offer public school choice and SES
Fourth year missed	Corrective action (third year of improvement)	Implement certain corrective actions and offer public school choice and SES
Fifth year missed	Planning for restructuring (fourth year of improvement)	Plan for a change in governance and offer public school choice and SES[b]
Sixth year missed	Implementation of restructuring (fifth year of improvement)	Implement a change in governance and offer public school choice and SES

Sources: GAO analysis of NCLBA and Education's regulations.
[a] At this stage, the school must also develop the school improvement plan.
[b] While NCLBA does not require that corrective actions must be continued after a school enters restructuring, Education officials noted that, in practice, many schools continue corrective actions after entering restructuring status.

Under NCLBA's accountability provisions, states are required to develop plans that include academic standards and establish performance goals for schools' meeting AYP that would lead to 100 percent of their students being proficient in reading, mathematics, and science by 2014.[5] To measure their progress, states were required to establish academic proficiency goals for making AYP and to administer an annual assessment to students in most grade levels.[6] In addition, each school's assessment data must be disaggregated in order to compare the achievement levels of students within certain designated groups, including low-income and minority students, students with disabilities, and those with limited English proficiency, with the state's proficiency targets. Each of these groups must make AYP in order for the school to make AYP. In addition to proficiency targets on state assessments, states must use another academic indicator to determine AYP. For high schools, the indicator must be graduation rates. States may choose what the other academic indicator will be for elementary and middle schools.

Title I of the ESEA, as amended and reauthorized by NCLBA, authorizes federal funds to help elementary and secondary schools establish and maintain programs that will improve the educational opportunities of economically disadvantaged children[7] For schools receiving Title I funds that do not achieve proficiency, a time line is required for implementing specific interventions based on the number of years the school missed AYP. If a school fails to meet AYP in reading, mathematics, or science for 2 consecutive years, districts must offer students in these schools the opportunity to transfer to a higher performing school in the district, and after the third year they must offer both school choice and supplemental education services (SES), such as tutoring. Prior legislation—IASA— required districts to take corrective action as a final intervention for schools that repeatedly missed AYP. While IASA allowed states to determine the appropriate corrective action for their districts and schools, NCLBA is more prescriptive in defining the corrective actions districts and schools must implement. In addition, a new intervention to change the governance of schools—school restructuring—was introduced for schools that miss AYP for 5 or more years. (See table 1.) Districts are responsible for selecting and implementing the corrective actions and restructuring options for these schools contained in the law. Schools exit improvement status if they make AYP for 2 consecutive years.

In prior work on implementation of NCLBA, GAO reported that the Title I schools in corrective action and restructuring status during school year 2005-2006 were more frequently located in urban school districts and a few states and served higher percentages of low-income, minority, and middle school students than other Title I schools.[8]

NCLBA Provisions and Funding Related to Arts Education in Public Schools

In its last two reauthorizations of the ESEA, the Congress has recognized the importance of arts education in public schools. Although the NCLBA does not include proficiency requirements for the arts, it does authorize Education to make grants for arts education. The purpose of these programs as set out in NCLBA includes helping students meet state academic achievement standards in the arts and supporting "the national effort to enable all students to demonstrate competence in the arts." In addition, arts education is identified by NCLBA as a core academic subject. Similarly, the Congress stated in IASA that the arts express "forms of understanding and ways of knowing that are fundamentally important to education." This finding incorporates the two prevailing perspectives on the role that arts education can play in public schools. One perspective sees arts education as having intrinsic value because of the insights into self and others that experiencing the arts can yield. A second perspective focuses on the association between arts education and development of cognitive, affective, and creative skills, including improved achievement in academic subjects such as reading and math. While NCLBA does not attempt to address these perspectives, it does affirm that arts education has a role in public schools.

Education administers a number of specific programs related to arts education, but two arts education grant programs authorized by NCLBA— the Model Development and Dissemination grants program and the Professional Development for Arts Educators program—are competitive grant programs that provide funding for arts education research projects that integrate arts disciplines into public school curricula, strengthen arts instruction, and improve students' academic performance and funding for art teachers' professional development, respectively. Total funding for these two programs in the last few years was $21.1 million in fiscal year 2006, $21 million in fiscal year 2007 and $20.7 million in fiscal year 2008.[9]

Research on Arts Education in Public Schools

Prior to passage of NCLBA, the National Endowment for the Arts twice collaborated with Education to determine the extent to which public schools offer arts education in the four major art forms: visual arts, music, theater, and dance. Through surveys of school principals and teachers that Education conducted in school years 1993-1994 and 1999-2000, Education found that visual arts and music were offered by 80 to 90 percent of public elementary and secondary schools, while theater and dance were offered by a smaller fraction—fewer than half. Education plans to conduct another such survey in school year 2009-2010. Education sponsored the National Assessment of Educational Progress (NAEP) arts assessment of students in the eighth grade during school year 1996-1997, which reported the frequency of arts offerings by art form, and how well public school students could respond to, create, and perform works of visual art, music, and theatre. Known as the *NAEP 1997 Arts Report Card*, the study report was issued in November 1998.[10] The assessment found that a high percentage of eighth grade students were offered music and visual arts in the schools they attended, but that instruction in theater and dance was more limited. Students' performance ranged from 78 percent who sang the song "America" rhythmically to 1 percent who created expressive collages. Two other studies focused primarily on NCLBA implementation but also included analyses of changes in instruction time for all subjects, including arts education. One study, reported in *Choices, Changes, and Challenges: Curriculum and Instruction in the NCLB Era*, sponsored by the Center on Education Policy (CEP) and issued in July 2007, asked school district officials in school year 2006-2007 whether instruction time for individual subjects, including arts education, had changed since school year 2001-2002 when NCLB was enacted.[11] The CEP study reported that 30 percent of school districts reported that instruction time for arts education in elementary schools had decreased since NCLBA was enacted. NLS-NCLB, also sponsored by Education, collected data in school years 2004- 2005 and 2006-2007 to describe major patterns in state, district, and school implementation of NCLBA's central accountability provisions, including changes in instruction time. To address study question 1 in our report concerning changes in students' access to arts education, if any, we analyzed the data on changes in instruction time and other school characteristics collected from elementary school teachers and principals during school year 2006-2007 by the NLS-NCLB.[12]

Education plans to undertake a new study, which is expected to build on previous research, including the NLS-NCLB study, to continue to examine NCLBA implementation issues. Among a broad range of topics the planned study likely will explore are the uses of instruction time for all academic subjects. Education expects to award a contract for the study in September 2009 and begin data collection in the 2011-2012 school year.

OVERALL TIME SPENT ON ARTS EDUCATION CHANGED LITTLE BETWEEN THE 2004-2005 AND 2006-2007 SCHOOL YEARS, BUT DECREASES WERE MORE LIKELY AT SOME SCHOOLS AND THE REASONS FOR THE DIFFERENCES ARE UNCERTAIN

Most elementary school teachers—90 percent—reported that instruction time for arts education stayed the same between the 2004-2005 and 2006-2007 school years. The percentage of teachers that reported that instruction time had stayed the same was similarly high across a range of school characteristics, irrespective of the schools' percentage of low-income or minority students or of students with limited English proficiency, or the schools' improvement under NCLBA. However, 7 percent of the teachers reported a reduction in the time spent on arts education. Moreover, when we looked at teacher responses across a range of school characteristics, we found some significant differences in the percentages of teachers reporting that the time spent on arts education had decreased and in the average amount of time that instruction had been reduced. In contrast, among teachers reporting increases in instruction time for the arts, we found no differences across different types of schools. Because Education's survey did not include questions for teachers to indicate why instruction time decreased at their school, in our analysis of Education's data, we were unable to identify factors that might help explain some of the apparent disparities in instruction time suggested by our findings.

Table 2. Percentage of Teachers across All Schools Reporting Whether Instruction Time Had Changed between the 2004-2005 and 2006-2007 School Years, by Subject

Subject	Increased	Stayed the same	Decreased	Total
Art/music	3.7	89.8	6.6	100
Physical education/ health	5.5	88.1	6.4	100
Social studies/ history	4.0	82.8	13.1	100
Science	5.6	82.0	12.4	100
Mathematics	18.1	77.8	4.1	100
Reading/language arts	21.9	75.4	2.7	100

Source: GAO analysis of Education data.
Note: Percentages across columns may not add to 100 percent due to rounding.

Teachers at Schools Identified as Needing Improvement and Those with a Higher Percentage of Minority Students Were More Likely to Report a Decrease in the Amount of Time Spent on Arts Education

According to Education's data, the vast majority of elementary school teachers surveyed reported that the amount of weekly instruction time spent across all subjects, including arts education, stayed the same in the 2006-2007 school year compared with the 2004-2005 school year.[13] Table 2 shows that about 89.8 percent of elementary school teachers reported that instruction time spent on arts education did not change between these school years, while about 3.7 percent reported the time had increased compared with about 6.6 percent that reported it had decreased. The percentage of teachers that reported increases in instruction time was higher for reading/language arts and mathematics than for other subjects, which is understandable since these were the two subjects for which the NCLBA held schools accountable for demonstrating student proficiency at that time. In contrast, the percentage of teachers that reported decreases in instruction time was higher for social studies and science than for other subjects, including arts education, even though the NCLBA required schools to begin testing student proficiency in science in the 2007-2008 school year.

When we looked at teacher responses across a range of school characteristics—including percentage of low-income and minority students and students with limited English proficiency, as well as improvement status, as indicated in table 3—we found no differences across characteristics in the percentages of teachers reporting that the time spent on arts education had increased. However, there were some significant differences across characteristics in the percentages of teachers reporting that the time spent on arts education had decreased, as shown in table 3. Elementary school teachers at schools identified as needing improvement, those at schools with higher percentages of minority students, and those at schools with higher percentages of students with limited English speaking skills, were significantly more likely to report a decrease in the amount of time spent on arts education compared with teachers at other schools. We might also point out that the vast majority of teachers reported that instruction time stayed the same, irrespective of their schools' percentage of low-income or minority students or students with limited English proficiency, or the schools' improvement status under NCLBA.

Teachers at Schools with Higher Percentages of Low-Income or Minority Students Reported Significantly Larger Average Decreases Compared with Other Teachers

When we looked at the average amount of change in instruction time among teachers that reported either an increase or decrease, we found significant differences among teachers that reported a decrease. Among teachers that reported a decrease, teachers at schools with higher percentages of low-income or minority students reported significantly larger average decreases in time spent on arts education compared with teachers at other schools. (See table 4.) For example, among teachers reporting a decrease, teachers at schools with a higher percentage of low-income students reported an average decrease of 49 minutes per week in the time spent on arts education compared with an average decrease of 31 minutes reported by teachers at schools with a low percentage of these students.[14] While this data might suggest that students at these types of schools are receiving less instruction time in arts education during the school day compared with students at other schools, we could not determine how this might affect their overall access to arts education without information on other opportunities, such as after-school programs in arts education.

Table 3. Percentage of Elementary Schools Teachers Reporting Whether Arts Education Instruction Time Had Changed between the 2004-2005 and 2006-2007 School Years, by School Characteristic

School characteristic	Increased	Stayed the same	Decreased
Percentage of low-income students[a]			
Schools with 75% or more	3	88	9
Schools with 35% or less	4	89	7
Percentage of minority students[b]			
Schools with 75% or more	6	84	10*
Schools with less than 25%	3	91	6*
Percentage of students with limited English proficiency			
Schools with greater than 5%	4	88	8*
Schools with 0%	3	92	4*
Improvement status[c]			
Schools identified for improvement	3	86	11*
Schools not identified for improvement	4	90	6*
School location[d]			
Urban	4	88	7
Rural	3	92	6

Legend
*=differences in percentage of teachers reporting a decrease were statistically significant (p<.05 level).
Source: GAO analysis of Education data.
Notes: Percentages across columns may not add to 100 percent due to rounding.
We also found statistically significant differences between the percentages of teachers reporting a decrease in arts education instruction at schools with a higher percentage of low-income students (9 % v. 5 %) or minority students (10 % v. 5 %) and those with a moderate percentage of these students.

[a]Schools were classified by Education as having "high—75 percent or more," "moderate—35 to less than 75," or "low—35 percent or less" percentages of low-income students using the number of students at the school that were eligible for the free and reduced-price lunch program.

[b]Schools were classified as having "high—75 percent or more," "moderate—25 to less than 75," or "low—25 percent or less" percentages of minority students, based on the school population that principals reported to be American Indian/Alaskan Native, Asian, Black, or African-American, Hispanic or Latino, and Native Hawaiian or other Pacific Islander. To see if certain groups were more affected than others, we also looked separately at the responses of teachers based on the percentages of African-American or Hispanic students enrolled at the school.

[c]Schools receiving funds under Title I of the NCLBA are identified as needing improvement when students do not make sufficient progress toward meeting state proficiency targets for 2 years or more.

[d]Schools were classified as central city (urban), urban fringe/large town (suburban), or small/fringe town (rural).

Table 4. Mean Decrease in the Amount of Instruction Time Spent on Arts Education among Teachers Reporting a Decrease from School Year 2004-2005 to 2006-2007

School characteristic	Minutes per week	
	Schools with a low percentage of these students	Schools with a high percentage of these students
Percentage of low-income students	31.2*	49.0*
Percentage of minority students	33.3*	48.5*
Percentage of limited English proficient Students	53.4*	40.2*
Percentage of African-American students	41.7*	52.3*
Percentage of Hispanic students	42.5*	52
	Schools not identified For improvement	Schools identified for improvement
Improvement status (Not IFI v. IFI)	37.6*	41.5*
	Urban schools	Rural schools
Location (urban v. rural)	43.4*	59

Legend
*=difference between the "low" and "high" range was statistically significant (p<.05 level).
Source: GAO analysis of Education data.

Note: All findings in the table are those reported by the fraction of teachers who reported a decrease. Because none of the differences in the percentages involving schools with teachers that reported an increase were statistically significant, findings for those schools are not included in the table.

Interestingly, while teachers at elementary schools identified for improvement and those with high percentages of limited English- proficient students were more likely to report a decrease in arts education as shown in table 3, when looking at the amount of change, as shown in table 4, the data shows that, on average, they reported about the same amount of change in instruction time as teachers from nonidentified schools and those with lower percentages of limited English-proficient students, respectively—that is, the differences were not statistically significant. It was difficult to determine which school characteristic had a stronger effect on the changes in arts education instruction time without a more advanced analysis.[15]

Education's NLS-NCLB Survey Does Not Currently Ask Questions That Might Explain the Disparities in Changes in Instruction Time across Different Types of Schools

Education's NLS-NCLB survey did not include questions for respondents to identify the reasons instruction time may have changed, which might help explain some of the apparent disparities in instruction time suggested by our analysis of Education's data. Although Education's survey asked questions regarding whether schools have implemented any of a variety of NCLBA-defined interventions,[16] such as extending the school day or adopting a new curriculum program, it did not specifically ask respondents to identify the reasons for any change in the amount of instruction time they reported for the respective subjects.

WHILE BASIC STATE REQUIREMENTS FOR ARTS EDUCATION IN SCHOOLS HAVE REMAINED CONSTANT IN MOST STATES, STATE FUNDING LEVELS FOR ARTS EDUCATION CHANGED

According to our survey of state arts officials, since passage of NCLBA, basic state requirements for arts education in schools, such as the number of hours a week that the arts must be taught, have remained virtually unchanged and more states have established funding for some type of arts education, such as providing grants to schools to promote arts education. However, while some states have increased funding, other states have reduced funding since NCLBA's passage. Arts officials attributed changes in funding to state budget changes to a greater extent than to NCLBA or other factors.

Table 5. Number of States with Arts Education Requirements in School Years 2001 - 2002 and 2006-2007

Arts education requirements	2001-2002 only	Both 2001-2002 and 2006-2007	2006-2007 only	No requirements in either year	Did not know	Total
General arts requirements	0	34	3	7	1	**45**
Arts requirements for high school graduation	0	28	5	11	1	**45**

Source: GAO analysis of GAO survey data.

Table 6. Number of States with Funding for Arts Education in School Years 2001-2002 and 2006-2007

Arts education funding	Funding in 2001-2002 only	Funding in both 2001-2002 and 2006-2007	Funding in 2006-2007 only	No funding in either year	Did not know	Total
Arts education grants	0	32	5	3	5	45
Artist-in-residence funding	2	33	0	5	4	44
Training funding	1	27	4	8	4	44
State-established arts school funding	0	11	1	29	4	45

Source: GAO analysis of GAO survey data.

The Basic Requirement for Arts Education Stayed about the Same in Most States and Additional States Have Established Funding for Some Type of Arts Education

By school year 2001-2002, the year NCLBA was enacted, most states had taken steps to establish arts education in their public school systems by developing basic arts education requirements, such as the number of hours a week that the arts must be taught or the number of courses that must be taken. As shown in table 5, of the 45 states that responded to our survey, 34 states had established the basic requirement that arts education be taught, and 28 states had included arts education as a high school graduation requirement by that school year. By school year 2006-2007, as shown in the third column of table 5, most of these states had retained these requirements. In addition, 3 more states had established basic arts education requirements, and 5 more states had included arts education as a high school graduation requirement by that school year. As table 5 also shows, a number of states did not have any requirements for arts education in place by the time NCLBA was passed. Specifically, 7 states had no basic requirement that arts education be taught, and 11 states had not included arts education as a high school graduation requirement by school year 2001-2002. State by state breakouts are provided in appendix III.

Many states had also provided funding to promote arts education in public schools and, as shown in the third column of table 6, most of the funding still was in place 5 years later, in school year 2006-2007. In addition, the number of states with arts education grants, training funding, and state established schools for the arts increased in school year 2006-2007.

State arts officials identified multiple sources of funding for arts education, including the state education agency, the state cultural agency, private foundations, the federal government, and other organizations, as shown in table 7. Of the 45 arts officials who responded to the survey, more identified the state cultural agency as a funding source than any other organization, including the state education agency.

Table 7. Sources of Funding for State Arts Education between School Years 2001-2002 and 2006-2007

Arts education funding	State education agency	State cultural agency	Private foundations	Federal government	Other	Number of states with funding[a]
Arts education grants	18	30	15	21	7	37
Artist-in-residence funding	8	33	12	16	9	35
Training funding	26	27	13	16	9	32
State-established arts school funding	8	0	1	2	2	12

Source: GAO analysis of GAO survey data.
[a]Total represents the number of states that provided funding in at least one of the 2 school years.

Table 8. Of States That Had Funding in Both School Years 2001-2002 and 2006-2007, Number of States with Changes in Funding for Arts Education and Number Where Funding Stayed about the Same

Arts education funding	Decreased greatly	Decreased somewhat	Stayed about the same	Increased somewhat	Increased greatly	Changes differed depending on school level[a]	Did not know
Arts in Education Grants	8	4	8	4	1	3	4
Artist-in-Residence Funding	6	6	7	5	0	5	4
Training Funding	4	6	6	4	3	4	0
State Arts Schools Funding	0	1	2	6	0	n/a	3

Source: GAO analysis of GAO survey data.

Notes: Five states had arts education grants only in school year 2006-2007.

Five states did not have artist-in-residence funding for either school year 2001-2002 or 2006-2007, and two states had artist-in-residence funding only in 2001-2002.

Four states had training funding only in 2006-2007, and one state had training funding only in 2001-2002.

Twenty-nine states did not have state-established arts schools in either school year 2001-2002 or 2006-2007.

[a] Arts officials were asked to answer questions about changes in funding for each school level (elementary, middle, and high). The frequencies in columns 2-6 and 8 represent the states that answered the same for each school level. The frequencies in column 7 show the number of states that gave mixed responses by school level.

Levels of State Financial Support for Arts Education Varied among the States, and States Reported That State Budget Changes rather than NCLBA Were the Major Factor Prompting the Funding Changes

While the number of states that had basic requirements for arts education remained nearly unchanged and most states maintained their arts education funding, levels of funding changed, with some states reporting decreases, and others reporting increases. For example, of the 32 states that awarded arts education grants in both years, funding decreased in 12 states, increased in 5 states, and stayed the about same in 8 states, as shown in table 8.

According to our survey, state arts officials attributed changes in funding for state arts education to state budget changes to a greater extent than to NCLBA or other factors. For example, of the states that provided arts education grants in both school years 2001-2002 and 2006-2007, 11 arts officials attributed changes in funding to state budget changes, and 18 reported that shifting funds to meet NCLBA needs had little or nothing to do with the funding changes. Table 9 shows the extent to which the arts officials attributed changes in funding to state budget changes, state policy changes, shifting funds to meet NCLBA needs, and other factors for each of the four types of state arts education funding.

Table 9. Number of States Identifying Factors That Contributed to Change in Funding of Arts Education between School Years 2001-2002 and 2006-2007

Factors that contributed to change	Very great extent	Great extent	Moderate extent	Some extent	Little or no extent	Cannot judge	Total response
Arts education grants							
State budget changes	11	6	2	2	8	5	34
State policy changes	4	1	4	2	18	4	33
Shifting funds to meet NCLB needs	3	0	2	0	18	9	32
Other	6	2	4	3	2	6	23
Artist-in-residence funding							
State budget changes	11	2	2	4	10	6	35
State policy changes	1	3	3	4	15	8	34
Shifting funds to meet NCLB needs	1	3	2	2	16	10	34
Other	3	0	2	1	6	8	20
Training funding							
State budget changes	11	4	4	0	7	5	31
State policy changes	2	3	2	3	14	4	28
Shifting funds to meet NCLB needs	4	0	5	1	14	6	30
Other	4	1	3	0	5	6	19
State-established arts school funding							
State budget changes	1	1	2	0	3	4	11
State policy changes	0	1	0	0	6	4	11
Shifting funds to meet NCLB needs	0	0	0	1	6	4	11
Other	0	0	1	1	3	4	9

Source: GAO analysis of GAO survey data.

SINCE NCLBA, DISTRICT OFFICIALS AND SCHOOL PRINCIPALS HAVE USED SEVERAL STRATEGIES TO PROVIDE ARTS EDUCATION; HOWEVER, SOME STRUGGLED WITH DECREASED BUDGETS AND COMPETING DEMANDS ON INSTRUCTION TIME

District officials and school principals have used several strategies to provide arts education, including varying when the arts are offered, seeking funding and collaborative arrangements in the arts community, and integrating the arts into other subjects; however, some struggled with decreased budgets and competing demands on instruction time, according to officials we interviewed. Faced with decreased funding or increased demands on instruction time, some principals told us that they had to make trade-offs.

District Officials and School Principals Have Used Several Different Strategies to Provide Arts Instruction

School principals we met with had found several ways to maintain arts education, including varying when the arts are offered. More than half of the 19 schools we visited offered some form of arts education outside of the regular school day. In a few schools, after school classes were the only arts education opportunity available to students. At one middle school in Boston that had not met AYP in school year 2006-2007, the principal had eliminated arts education classes during the school day and purchased an after-school arts program in drama and music production from an outside organization. The program is open to all students, but participation in the program is offered on a first-come-first-served basis. In contrast, one New York City middle school, which was not meeting AYP in English and language arts in school year 2007-2008, changed when other classes were offered, rather than changing when arts education was offered. This school extended the school day for students who required additional help by adding a period to the school schedule four times a week. The principal told us that this allowed all students to attend art class held during the regular school day. While many schools experienced changes to their arts programs, several of the schools we visited reported no changes in their arts education offerings. For example, the principal of the high school we visited in the Waltham school district, near Boston, which met AYP, said that the school had experienced a stable budget for the past 10 years and had made no changes to its arts education policies. The principal of a large high school in Chicago, which has not met AYP for 4 years, also said that the school had not changed its arts education policies. He explained that because the school's budget is determined by the enrollment level, his school had the resources to offer students arts education opportunities that smaller Chicago schools could not.

Several of the schools we visited also reported receiving grants and private funding and establishing collaborative relationships with organizations in the arts community that supplemented the arts education classes funded by general revenues. For example, one elementary school in Boston has developed partnerships with several companies, including a bank, that fund the school's instrumental music program. This elementary school also has obtained a grant from a television station to pay for instruments and participates in a city-funded program that sends seven selected students to the Boston Ballet once a week for lessons. A Chicago high school received a private grant that supported a student art project to do a mosaic on the walls outside the music rooms at the school.[17] The principal of this high school also said that he has informal arrangements with local artists to bring special projects to the school, such as the group that visited the school to teach a belly dancing class. A high school in Miami set up internships for its students at local music stores and solicited a donation of used equipment from the local news station when it moved to a new facility. The drama teacher also solicits donations of costumes for school dramatic productions. In Broward County, Florida, the school district provides funds each year to pay for the cost of transporting the school district's students to performances at the Broward Center for the Performing Arts (Center).[18] A New York City junior high school receives support for students to attend plays from a private program and sends the school's theater group to perform at Lincoln Center every year. A senior high school in the city has arranged music programs with Carnegie Hall, a local orchestra, and the Juilliard School of Music. The Museum of Modern

Art and the Metropolitan Museum of Art also cover the students' cost of admission for exhibits and performances.

Arts organization officials in Chicago, Miami, and Broward County, Florida, described the arts integration model of arts education as a strategy for maintaining the arts in school curricula and provided examples of arts integration programs in schools we did not visit. In Chicago, the Chicago Arts Partnerships in Education, a nonprofit arts education advocacy organization, is participating as a partner in a project that supports arts integration in the 55 fine and performing arts schools operated under Chicago Public Schools' (CPS) magnet school cluster program.[19] The project, funded by Education's Model Development and Dissemination grant program, funds teaching artists who work with art teachers and regular classroom teachers to incorporate the arts into teaching academic subjects. In Miami, Arts for Learning, a nonprofit that promotes arts integration through in-school and after-school programs, operates "GET smART," a yearlong professional development program that provides interdisciplinary training to teachers on how to effectively create and implement arts integration projects in the core academic subjects. About 18 Miami-Dade schools participated in this program in school year 2007-2008. Arts for Learning also offers "Early GET smART" a program that works with preschoolers aged 2 to 6 to provide an arts-based learning approach to literacy and school readiness. The Broward County Cultural Division, a publicly funded agency established by the Board of County Commissioners, promotes arts integration in the local schools. One initiative provides a block grant to the school board to implement artist-in-residencies and arts integration workshops in individual schools. Officials representing the division said that schools are increasing use of the arts to teach lessons in academic subject areas. For example, as his class learned about a particular country, a social studies teacher would play music from that country to expose the students to different musical styles from around the world. The teacher was also working with an artist to develop a visual presentation that could be incorporated into the lesson. In addition, the Ft. Lauderdale Children's Theater goes into schools and performs dramatic readings of plays with the children acting out the roles as part of their classroom reading lessons.

Officials Report That the Main Challenges to Providing Arts Instruction Have Been Decreased State or Local Funding and Competing Demands on Instruction Time

Officials we met with told us that the main challenges to providing arts education have been decreased state or local funding and competing demands on instruction time due to requirements established by the state education agency or school district to meet NCLBA proficiency standards, such as doubling the amount of time low-performing students spend on reading and math.

District officials and school principals in the Boston, Chicago, Miami- Dade, and New York City school districts all reported that state or local budget cuts created a challenge for arts education in the schools. The Boston school district expects an $11 million budget shortfall for the upcoming school year, a result of a declining population base. School district officials expect this shortfall to lead to a loss of 10 arts teachers across the school district. District officials and school principals in Chicago attributed funding shortages for arts education to the school district's arts personnel funding policy. The Chicago school district funds personnel positions on the basis of student enrollment and supports one half-time position for an arts teacher in primary schools with fewer than 750 students. To employ a full-time arts teacher on the staff, a school principal must supplement the arts teacher's salary from discretionary funds. Officials in both Florida school districts we visited reported budget pressures due to a state budget shortfall, but the consequences for arts education differed. Miami-Dade school district officials reported cuts in the district's arts education budget of as much as 70 percent, resulting in staff cuts. In Broward County, while acknowledging budget pressures, school district officials reported that the arts have not been cut. They said that the district had taken steps several years ago to prepare for this possible economic downturn. However, if cuts in content area programs are necessary, the district makes an across-the-board percentage cut in the budget allocated to each school rather than targeting individual subjects for reduction. New York City school district officials reported that a line item in the school district budget that provided schools a per capita allotment solely to support arts education was eliminated in 2007, and funds were incorporated into the school's general fund.[20] This change allowed school principals to allocate the funds to the arts or other subjects.

In addition to state and local budget cuts, district officials and school principals in the Boston, Chicago, Miami-Dade, and New York City school districts also agreed that competing demands on instruction time were a major challenge for providing arts education in their schools. These officials also identified NCLBA's proficiency standards—as well as requirements established by the state and school district to meet NCLBA proficiency standards—as a key source of the time pressure. Boston school district officials said that it is difficult to convince principals of the importance of continuing to provide arts education when it is not a tested subject. They said that the arts curriculum takes a back seat because school success is based on student performance on their state tests as required under NCLBA. Although they tried to avoid pulling students out of arts education classes for remedial work, one elementary and one high school principal interviewed in Boston, whose schools were not meeting AYP, agreed that NCLBA's testing requirements had increased the demands on instruction time for tested subjects and reduced time available for the arts, at least for students not meeting proficiency requirements. A Waltham school district official said that to meet the state and federal proficiency standards, the district added workshops in math, reading, and science, which led to cuts in arts staff and even eliminating arts field trips because they reduce the amount of available class time. She added that, 2 years ago, the district added a two-block period twice a week to keep up with state proficiency standards. This resulted in the loss of one full-time equivalent (FTE) arts teacher. A Chicago school district official affirmed that the priorities principals set for meeting AYP in reading and math affect the time available for the arts. In Florida, where the state requires that students who perform at the lowest two of five levels on the state NCLBA proficiency tests be placed in intensive classes for language arts and math, district officials agreed that time for arts education might be affected. In Broward County, officials said that the district follows the state policy that requires mandatory pull-out sessions for students performing at reading levels 1 and 2 on the state performance assessments. In some cases, the district will require some students to be pulled out for additional intensive instruction in math. These "pull-out" students receive double periods of reading or other intensive instruction that reduces the number of periods they have available to take elective classes, such as art or music. A New York City school district official acknowledged that schools not meeting AYP faced challenges in providing arts education but said that the responsibility for meeting instructional requirements was the school principal's. Principals in the elementary and middle schools we visited in New York, two of which were not meeting AYP, said they had taken steps to meet the time demands of NCLBA's testing requirements. The high school principal said that students not meeting proficiency requirements could attend their remedial classes and still meet the arts course requirement for graduation, but that they may not have an opportunity to take courses above the minimum credit requirement. This high school was not meeting AYP in school year 2007-2008.

Officials Report That When Trade-Offs Involving Funding or Instruction Time for Arts Education Had to Be Made, the School Principal Made the Decision

District officials and school principals told us that when they faced decreased budgets or increased demands on instruction time, trade-offs had to be made, and school principals made the decision. Principals' decisions differed, however. Some principals chose not to spend their limited discretionary funds on arts education, while other principals, even when their school had been identified as needing improvement several times, maintained their arts offerings. For example, one school principal in a Chicago elementary school chose to spend discretionary budget funds on special reading and math programs needed to improve students' performance rather than supplement half the salary of a full-time arts teacher. On the other hand, one Miami-Dade high school principal had allocated Title I funds to help retain and rebuild the school's arts education program as part of its NCLBA restructuring plan. New York City officials said that a new accountability system the school district had developed in part because of NCLBA, but also to evaluate progress toward meeting city instructional requirements, increased the discretionary authority vested in school principals. The district also developed an accountability initiative called ArtsCount. For this initiative, district arts officials developed measures to be incorporated in the district's evaluation of school performance and the quality of arts offerings. This information will be used to influence the scores that are incorporated into each school principal's report card. For middle and high schools, the results are incorporated into the measure of graduation requirements. Under the accountability system and this initiative, school principals are given greater authority to make trade-offs, such as the discretion to allocate funds formerly restricted to expenditures for the arts to other subjects, but the school district monitors the results of their decisions.

OVERALL RESEARCH ON THE ASSOCIATION BETWEEN ARTS EDUCATION AND STUDENT OUTCOMES IS INCONCLUSIVE

While some studies that have examined the association between arts education and students' academic achievement have found a small positive association with student outcomes, others have found none. One meta-analysis that combined the results of several studies found small positive relationships.[21] This study included two separate analyses: one that looked at the association between music instruction and math scores, and another that looked at the association between listening to music and math scores. The first analysis of six studies found that learning to play music had a small positive relationship with both standardized and researcher-designed achievement test scores in mathematics, regardless of whether or not the child learned to read music.[22] Music instruction in these studies included both instrumental and vocal performance for durations of at least 4 months and up to 2 years, and included children at the preschool through elementary level.[23] The second analysis, which included 15 studies, determined that there was a small positive relationship with math test scores when children listened to certain types of music while attempting to solve math problems. In contrast, another meta-analysis found no association with students' achievement. This analysis, which looked at 24 studies examining reading outcomes and 15 studies examining math outcomes, found no association between arts education and standardized reading or math test scores, regardless of the child's background or academic history. The students included in the studies had a wide range of academic abilities and came from a wide range of backgrounds. For example, some of the studies included academically at- risk students and students from lower-income families, while some of the studies included "academically gifted" students and students from higher- income families. The studies also included children of a variety of ages and several different types of arts instruction, including music, visual arts, drama, and dance. Moreover, some research has focused on special populations, such as students from low-income families; however, most of these studies did not meet GAO's criteria for methodological quality, and their findings are questionable.

Similarly, studies that examined the association between arts education and abilities associated with academic performance also were mixed. For example, two of the three analyses from one meta-analysis looking at the association between music education and certain spatial abilities found a positive relationship. One analysis, which was made up of 15 studies, and another that analyzed 8 studies, found that music education was associated with student performance on a wide range of spatial tasks. However, the third analysis, which included 5 studies, found no association between music education and one measure of spatial performance. In these studies, enhanced spatial performance referred to the ability to mentally recognize and manipulate patterns that fall into a certain logical order and are usually used in subjects such as music, geometry, and engineering. An example of spatial ability in a music course would be the ability to produce a piece of music based on memory alone, anticipating mentally the changes needed to play a certain piece of music. A complete list of the studies assessed is included in appendix IV.

CONCLUSIONS

Amid concerns about possible elimination of arts education, the national picture indicates that the vast majority of schools have found a way to preserve their arts education programs. However, a somewhat different story emerges for some schools identified as needing improvement under NCLBA, which include higher percentages of low-income and minority students. Among teachers reporting a decrease in instruction time for arts education, our study identified a more likely reduction in time spent on arts education at schools identified as needing improvement and those with higher percentages of minority students. While school officials in our site visit states told us that requirements established by the state and school district to meet NCLBA proficiency standards placed competing demands on instruction time for arts education, the reasons for the differences in instruction time our statistical analysis identified are difficult to establish nationally, given current limitations in Education's NLS-NCLB longitudinal data. Having national-level information about the reasons for these differences could add to the current body of research on arts education and help guide school decisions with respect to arts education.

RECOMMENDATION FOR EXECUTIVE ACTION

To help identify factors that may contribute to changes in access to arts education for certain student subgroups, we recommend that the Secretary of Education require that the department's planned study of NCLBA implementation include questions in its surveys asking survey respondents to describe the reasons for any changes in instruction time they report. Once the information has been collected and analyzed, Education could disseminate it to school districts and schools to help them identify and develop strategies to address any disparities in access.

AGENCY COMMENTS AND OUR EVALUATION

We provided a draft of the report to the Department of Education for review and comment. Education generally agreed with our findings and stated that, our finding that among the small percentage of teachers reporting a decrease in arts education instruction time, teachers in schools identified for improvement and those with high percentages of minority students were more likely to report reductions in time for arts education is cause for concern. Regarding our recommendation, Education agreed that further study would be useful to help explain why arts education instruction time decreased for some students. Education said that it will carefully consider our recommendation that the department's planned study of NCLBA implementation include questions in its surveys asking respondents to describe the reasons for any changes in instruction time they report. Education also provided technical comments, which have been incorporated in the report as appropriate. Education's comments appear in appendix V.

Cornelia M. Ashby

Cornelia M. Ashby
Director, Education, Workforce, and
Income Security Issues

APPENDIX I. SCOPE AND METHODOLOGY

This appendix discusses in more detail our methodology for examining any changes in students' access to arts education in public elementary and secondary schools that may have taken place since passage of the No Child Left Behind Act (NCLBA) and what is known about the effect of arts education on student academic performance. The study was framed around four questions: (1) has the amount of instruction time for arts education changed and, if so, have certain groups been more affected than others, (2) to what extent have state education agencies' requirements and funding for arts education changed since NCLBA, (3) what are school officials in selected districts doing to provide arts education since NCLBA and what challenges do they face in doing so, and (4) what is known about the effect of arts education in improving student outcomes?

Scope

As the Department of Education (Education), working in collaboration with the National Endowment for the Arts, determined first in school year 1993-1994 and again in school year 1999-2000, arts education in some form is provided in the vast majority of public schools nationwide.[24] Questions about changes in access thus need to be considered for the national population of public schools. However, because we recognized that states' and school districts' roles in school governance, funding, and implementation of NCLBA introduce variation in time devoted to individual subjects, including arts education, we determined that an in-depth look at state, district, and school policies and practices also was needed to help understand any systematic changes in instruction time for arts education that a national-level analysis might identify. Therefore, to examine any changes in students' access to arts education in public elementary and secondary schools that may have taken place since passage of NCLBA, we focused on time devoted to instruction in arts education and other subjects and any changes that occurred in a nationally representative sample of elementary schools. We also reviewed state arts education requirements and funding related to students' access to arts education and steps that school districts and schools in selected states had taken to provide arts education in the post-NCLBA environment. To determine what is known about the effect of arts education on student academic achievement and other outcomes, we reviewed and methodologically assessed existing research on arts education.

Methodology

We used separate sources of data for each study question, including nationally representative survey data collected by the Department of Education's (Education) National Longitudinal Study of No Child Left Behind (NLS-NCLB), which collected data on changes in instruction time by subject; a GAO survey of state arts education officials; on-site interviews with school district, school, and arts organization officials in selected states; and existing studies of the effect of arts education on student outcomes that met GAO's methodological criteria. Before deciding to use the NLS-NCLB data, we conducted a data reliability assessment. We discuss our assessment procedures and steps we took to mitigate any data limitations below, as part of the methodology for analyzing changes in instruction time. We provided specifications to Education for descriptive analyses of the NLS-NCLB data, and we conducted a descriptive analysis of our state survey data, a synthesis of our site visit data, and a methodological assessment of existing research on arts education.

Procedures for Analyzing Changes in Instruction Time

Because we were not able to obtain raw data files from Education to do a comprehensive analysis of the data ourselves, we asked Education to provide us with summary information from the Survey of Teachers component of the school year 2006-2007 NLS-NCLB. These data are from a nationally representative survey of teachers, as well as of schools and school districts. We requested tables that showed (1) the average (mean) amount of time that teachers reported devoting to arts education each week in 2006-2007; (2) the percentage of teachers that reported that the amount of time spent on arts education had increased, decreased, and remained the same over the past 2 years; and (3) for those teachers who reported a change, the average increase or decrease (in minutes per week) that was devoted to arts education. We obtained these estimates from Education for teachers in all schools, and separately for teachers in different categories of schools, defined by the percentages of students in the schools that were (1) minorities, (2) African-Americans, (3) Hispanics, (4) eligible for free/reduced lunches, and (5) in individualized education programs. We also compared the reports from teachers in schools that were (6) urban with those from rural teachers, and (7) that were and were not identified as being in need of improvement. We obtained from Education the standard errors associated with the estimates from the different types of schools and thus were able to test the statistical significance of the differences between what teachers from different types of schools reported.[25]

Before deciding to use the data, we reviewed guidance on the variable definitions and measures provided, documentation of the survey and sampling methodology used, and the data collection and analysis efforts conducted. We also interviewed Education officials about the measures they and their contractors took to ensure data reliability. We assessed the reliability of the NLS-NCLB data by (1) reviewing existing information and documentation about the data and the system that produced them and (2) interviewing agency officials knowledgeable about the data. On the basis of our efforts to determine the reliability of the estimates for which supporting information was provided, which included verifying calculations, we believe that they are sufficiently reliable for the purposes of this report.

State Survey Data Collection and Analysis Procedures

We designed and implemented a Web-based survey to gather information on states' role in shaping the provision of arts education in public schools and changes that may have occurred since NCLBA. Our survey population consisted of state arts officials in 49 states and the District of Columbia.[26] We identified these arts officials through searches of the Arts Education Partnership Web site, and verified the contact information provided through e-mails and phone contacts.

To develop survey questions, we reviewed existing studies on arts education and the state arts education policy data bases on the Web sites of the Education Commission of the States and the Arts Education Partnership. We also conducted interviews with representatives of these organizations. In addition, we interviewed the Arts Education Director and Research Director of the National Endowment for the Arts (NEA) to develop an understanding of federal and state roles in arts education in public schools and of the alternative funding sources for arts education that are available to schools. Finally, we conducted pretests of various drafts of our questionnaire with arts education officials in seven states to ensure that the questions were clear, the terms used were precise, the questions were unbiased, and that the questionnaire could be completed in a reasonable amount of time. We modified the questionnaire to incorporate findings from the pretests.

The survey was conducted using self-administered electronic questionnaires posted on the World Wide Web. In the questionnaire, we asked the state arts official to be the lead survey respondent and, if necessary, to confer with other representatives of state departments of education, state arts commissions, and state cultural agencies to answer questions requiring more detailed knowledge. We sent e-mail notifications to these officials beginning on April 22, 2008. To encourage them to respond, we sent two follow-up e-mails over a period of about 3 weeks. For those who still did not respond, GAO staff made phone calls to encourage the state officials to complete our questionnaire. We closed the survey on July 2, 2008. Forty-five state officials completed the survey.

Because this was not a sample survey, there are no sampling errors; however, the practical difficulties of conducting any survey may introduce errors. For example, difficulties in how a particular question is interpreted, in the sources of information that are available to respondents, or in how the data are entered into the database or were analyzed, can introduce unwanted variability into the survey results. We took steps in the development of this questionnaire, in the data collection, and in the data analysis to minimize such error. For example, a social science survey specialist designed the questionnaires in collaboration with GAO staff with subject matter expertise. Then, as noted earlier, the draft questionnaire was pretested in seven states to ensure that questions were relevant, clearly stated, and easy to comprehend. The questionnaire was also reviewed by an additional GAO survey specialist. Data analysis was conducted by a GAO data analyst working directly with the GAO staff with subject matter expertise. When the data were analyzed, a second independent data analyst checked all computer programs for accuracy. Since this was a Web-based survey, respondents entered their answers directly into the electronic questionnaires. This eliminated the need to have the data keyed into databases thus removing an additional source of error.

Site Visit Selection, Data Collection, and Analysis

To obtain information about what school officials are doing to provide arts education since NCLBA and the challenges, if any, they face in doing so, we visited school districts and schools in four states—Illinois, Massachusetts, Florida, and New York. Having learned from other studies of NCLBA implementation that schools not meeting AYP were difficult to recruit for site visits, to ensure that a sufficient number of schools would be selected, we identified states for our visits with large numbers of schools that were not meeting AYP in school year 2006-2007. Within each state, we selected school districts and schools that represented variation in income level of the school district, schools' performance under NCLBA, and schools' location as indicated in table 10.

Table 10. Criteria for Selecting School Districts and Schools

State	School districts' income level	Schools' NCLBA performance status	Schools' location
Massachusetts	1 low-income		4 urban
	1 moderate to upper income	3 not meeting AYP	1 suburban
		2 meeting AYP	
Illinois.	1 low-income	2 not meeting AYP	2 urban
	1 moderate income	2 meeting AYP	2 rural
Florida	1 low-income	2 not meeting AYP	2 urban
	1 moderate income	2 meeting AYP	2 suburban
New York	1 low-income		4 urban
	1 moderate to upper income	3 not meeting AYP	2 rural
		3 meeting AYP	

Source: GAO.

Within each state, we visited two school districts and 4 to 6 schools in each district for a total of eight school districts and 19 schools. We interviewed officials responsible for the arts education curriculum in each school district and school principals and, at the principal's discretion, art teachers in elementary, middle, and high schools. We also visited and interviewed officials representing local arts organizations that had undertaken arts education initiatives in the public schools.

Recruiting low-income school districts and schools for this study was especially challenging. For example, one district we initially selected to include in our study was in California, the state with the largest number of schools identified as needing improvement in school year 2006-2007. Officials representing that school district said that the district had placed a moratorium on all research in the district's schools. In other California school districts, we experienced long delays in receiving a response from both district and school officials to requests for initial or follow-up interviews. We ultimately decided to recruit school districts and schools in other states.

For the site visits, we developed structured interviews with a standard set of questions for school district and school officials including the following topics:

- *art forms included in the schools' arts education classes;*
- *daily or weekly schedule for all subjects, including arts education;*
- *changes in instruction time for all subjects, including arts education, occurring in the past school year and recent years;*
- *changes in students' access to arts education in the schools;*
- *challenges faced in providing arts education in the schools; and*
- *funding sources for arts education and how budget cuts are implemented when resource reductions occur.*

Our questions for arts organization officials asked them to describe their arts education initiatives in the local schools, what resources they contributed, if any, to arts education in the schools, and their perception of public school students' access to arts education and the challenges school districts and schools face in providing arts education.

To analyze the site visit data, we created matrices to summarize key findings from interviews with school district, school, and arts organization officials on changes in instruction time, changes in students' access to arts education, challenges faced, and experience with changes in funding.

Review of Existing Studies on the Effect of Arts Education on Student Outcomes

To determine what existing research says about the effects of arts education on student outcomes, we used several search strategies. To identify existing studies, we conducted searches of several automated databases, including the Education Resources Information Center (ERIC), Proquest, and Nexis. We also interviewed individuals familiar with available research, including the Research Director of the NEA and the former Director of the Arts Education Partnership (AEP). From these sources, we identified over 1,000 studies that were screened for relevance for our study. Using information about these studies that was readily available, we screened them using the following criteria:

- *published during or after 1998,*
- *research based on subjects within the United States,*
- *published in a peer reviewed journal, and*
- *employed an experimental or quasi-experimental design.*[27]

We selected the studies for our review based on their methodological strength and not on the generalizability of the results. Although the findings of the studies we identified are not representative of the findings of all studies of arts education programs, the studies consist of those published studies we could identify that used the strongest designs— experimental or quasi-experimental—to assess the effects of arts education. At the end of this screening process, 32 studies on the effects of arts education on student outcomes remained. We performed our searches for research and research evaluations between August 2007 and April 2008.

To assess the methodological quality of the 32 selected studies, we developed a data collection instrument to obtain information systematically about each study being evaluated and about the features of the evaluation methodology. We based our data collection and assessments on generally accepted social science standards. We examined such factors as whether evaluation data were collected before and after arts education implementation; how arts education effects were isolated, including the use of nonarts participant comparison groups or statistical controls; and the appropriateness of sampling, outcome measures, statistical analyses, and any reported results. A senior social scientist with training and experience in evaluation research and methodology read and coded the documentation for each evaluation. A second senior social scientist reviewed each completed data collection instrument and the relevant documentation for the outcome evaluation to verify the accuracy of every coded item. This review identified 7 of the 32 selected studies that met GAO's criteria for methodological quality.

APPENDIX II. AVERAGE AMOUNT OF INSTRUCTION TIME ELEMENTARY SCHOOL TEACHERS REPORTED SPENDING

Subject	Mean time spent per week (in hours)	Percentage of weekly instruction time
Reading/language arts/English	10.0	39
Mathematics	5.8	22
Science	2.5	10
Social studies/history	2.5	10
Art/music	1.6	6
Physical education/health	1.6	6

Source: GAO analysis of Education data.

APPENDIX III. ARTS EDUCATION REQUIREMENTS AND FUNDING, BY STATE, SCHOOL YEARS 2001-2002 AND 2006-2007

State	Arts education 2001-2002	Arts education 2006-2007	Artist-in-residence 2001-2002	Artist-in-residence 2006-2007	Training for arts education 2001-2002	Training for arts education 2006-2007	State-established arts schools 2001-2002	State-established arts schools 2006-2007	General state requirements For the arts 2001-2002	General state requirements For the arts 2006-2007	Minimum arts requirement For high school graduation 2001-2002	Minimum arts requirement For high school graduation 2006-2007
Alabama	Yes	Yes	Yes	Yes	Yes	Yes	Yes	Yes	Yes	Yes	Yes	Yes
Alaska	Yes	Yes	Yes	Yes	No	No	No	No	No	No	No	No
Arizona	Yes	Yes	Yes	Yes	Yes	Yes	No	No	Yes	Yes	Yes	Yes
Arkansas	Yes	Yes	Yes	Yes	Yes	Yes	Yes	Yes	Yes	Yes	Yes	Yes
California	Yes	Yes	No	No	Yes	Yes	No	No	Yes	Yes	No	No
Colorado	No	Yes	Yes	No	Yes	No	No	No	No	No	Yes	Yes
Connecticut	Yes	Yes	Yes	Yes	Yes	Yes	No	No	Yes	Yes	No	No
Delaware	Yes	Yes	Yes	Yes	Yes	Yes			Yes	Yes	No	No
Florida	Yes	Yes	Yes	Yes	No	No	No	No	Yes	Yes	No	Yes
Georgia	Yes	Yes	Yes	Yes	No	Yes	No	No	No	No	No	No
Hawaii	Yes	Yes	Yes	Yes	Yes	Yes	No	No	Yes	Yes	Yes	Yes
Idaho	Yes	Yes	Yes	Yes	No	Yes	No	Yes	Yes	Yes	Yes	Yes
Illinois	No	Yes	No	No	No	No	Yes	Yes	Yes	Yes	No	No
Indiana	Yes	Yes			No	No	No	No	Yes	Yes	No	No
Iowa	Yes	Yes			No	No	No	No	Yes	Yes	No	No
Kansas	Yes	Yes	No	No	Yes	Yes	No	No	No	Yes	No	Yes
Kentucky	Yes	Yes	Yes	Yes	Yes	Yes	No	No	Yes	Yes	Yes	Yes
Louisiana	Yes	Yes	Yes	Yes	Yes		Yes	Yes	No	No	Yes	Yes
Maine	Yes	Yes	Yes	Yes	Yes	Yes	No	No	No	No	Yes	Yes
Maryland	Yes	Yes	Yes	Yes	Yes	Yes	Yes	Yes	Yes	Yes	Yes	Yes
Massachusetts	Yes	Yes	Yes	Yes	Yes	Yes	No	No	No	No	No	No
Michigan	Yes	Yes	Yes	No	Yes	Yes	No	No			No	No
Minnesota	Yes	Yes	Yes	Yes	Yes	Yes	Yes	Yes	Yes	Yes	Yes	Yes
Mississippi			Yes	Yes	Yes	Yes	Yes	Yes	Yes	Yes	Yes	Yes

(Continued)

State	Arts education 2001-2002	Arts education 2006-2007	Artist-in-residence 2001-2002	Artist-in-residence 2006-2007	Training for arts education 2001-2002	Training for arts education 2006-2007	State-established arts schools 2001-2002	State-established arts schools 2006-2007	General state requirements for the arts 2001-2002	General state requirements for the arts 2006-2007	Minimum arts requirement for high school graduation 2001-2002	Minimum arts requirement for high school graduation 2006-2007
Montana	Yes	Yes	Yes	Yes	Yes	Yes	No	No	Yes	Yes	Yes	Yes
Nevada									No	No	No	No
New Hampshire	Yes	Yes	Yes	Yes	Yes	Yes	No	No	Yes	Yes	Yes	Yes
New Mexico	No	Yes	Yes	Yes	No	Yes	No	No	No	Yes		
New York			Yes	Yes	Yes	Yes	Yes	Yes	Yes	Yes	Yes	Yes
North Carolina			Yes	Yes	Yes	Yes	Yes	Yes	Yes	Yes	Yes	Yes
North Dakota	Yes	Yes	Yes	Yes	Yes	Yes	No	No	Yes	Yes	Yes	Yes
Ohio	Yes	Yes	Yes	Yes	Yes	Yes	No	No	Yes	Yes	Yes	Yes
Oklahoma	Yes	Yes	Yes	Yes	Yes	Yes	No	No	Yes	Yes	Yes	Yes
Oregon			Yes	Yes	Yes	Yes			Yes	Yes	Yes	Yes
Pennsylvania	Yes	Yes	Yes	Yes	Yes	Yes	Yes	Yes	Yes	Yes	No	No
Rhode Island	Yes	Yes							Yes	Yes	Yes	Yes
South Dakota	Yes	Yes	Yes	Yes	No	No	No	No	Yes	Yes	Yes	Yes
Tennessee	No	Yes	Yes	Yes	Yes	Yes	No	No	Yes	Yes	Yes	Yes
Texas	Yes	Yes	Yes	Yes	Yes	Yes	No	No	Yes	Yes	Yes	Yes
Utah	No	No	Yes	Yes	No	Yes	No	No	Yes	Yes	Yes	Yes
Vermont	No	No	Yes	Yes	Yes	Yes	No	No	Yes	Yes	Yes	Yes
Virginia	No	Yes	No	No	No	No	Yes	Yes	Yes	Yes	Yes	Yes
Washington	Yes	Yes	Yes	Yes	Yes	Yes	No	No	Yes	Yes	No	Yes
Wisconsin	No	No	No	No	No	No	No	No	Yes	Yes	No	No
Wyoming	Yes	Yes	Yes	Yes	Yes	Yes	No	No	No	Yes	No	Yes

Legend

Blank cell = either "don't know" or "no response"

Source: GAO analysis of GAO survey data.

APPENDIX IV. STUDIES MEETING GAO'S CRITERIA FOR METHODOLOGICAL QUALITY

Study title	Author	Source	Summary of findings
Does Studying the Arts Engender Creative Thinking? Evidence for Near but Not Far Transfer	Erik Moga, Kristin Burger, Lois Hetland, and Ellen Winner	*Journal of Aesthetic Education*, vol. 34, no. 3/4. Special Issue: The Arts and Academic Achievement: What the Evidence Shows, Autumn-Winter 2000, 149-166	Two meta-analyses: analysis 1 found no support for a causal relationship between arts study and verbal creativity. The second analysis found some equivocal support for a causal relationship between arts study and figural creativity.
Can Music Be Used to Teach Reading?	Ron Butzlaff	*Journal of Aesthetic Education*, vol. 34, no. 3/4. Special Issue: The Arts and Academic Achievement: What the Evidence Shows, Autumn-Winter 2000,167-178	Results varied and showed an extremely small positive overall association between the study of music and reading/verbal scores.
Learning to Make Music Enhances Spatial Reasoning	Lois Hetland	*Journal of Aesthetic Education*, vol. 34, no. 3/4. Special Issue: The Arts and Academic Achievement: What the Evidence Shows, Autumn-Winter 2000,179-238	Three meta-analyses: two of the analyses showed a positive relationship between music instruction and spatial-temporal tasks. The third analysis showed no relationship between music and a non spatial task.
Listening to Music Enhances Spatial-Temporal Reasoning:Evidence for the "Mozart Effect"	Lois Hetland	*Journal of Aesthetic Education*, vol. 34, no. 3/4. Special Issue: The Arts and Academic Achievement: What the Evidence Shows, Autumn-Winter 2000,105-148	Two meta-analyses: analysis 1 found a significant and robust relationship between listening to music and performance on all types of spatial tasks. Analysis 2 also found a significant, robust effect of music listening on spatial-temporal tasks.
Music and Mathematics: Modest Support for the Oft-Claimed Relationship	Kathryn Vaughn	*Journal of Aesthetic Education*, vol. 34, no. 3/4. Special Issue: The Arts and Academic Achievement: What the Evidence Shows,	Quasi-experimental studies showed that background music has a very minimal effect on math scores. Experimental instruction showed a small

(Continued)

Study title	Author	Source	Summary of findings
		Autumn-Winter, 149-166	association between music instruction and math skills.
Instruction in Visual Art: Can It Help Children Learn to Read?	Kristin Burger, Ellen Winner	*Journal of Aesthetic Education*, vol. 34, no. 3/4, Special Issue: The Arts and Academic Achievement: What the Evidence Shows. Autumn-Winter, 2000, 277-293	Analysis 1 did not demonstrate a reliable relationship between arts instruction and reading improvement. Analysis 2 found a positive, mode-rately-sized relationship between reading impro-vement and an integrated arts-reading form of instruction.
Mute Those Claims: No Evidence (Yet) for a Causal Link between Arts Study and Academic Achievement	Ellen Winner, Monica Cooper	*Journal of Aesthetic Education*, vol. 34, no. 3/4. Special Issue: The Arts and Academic Achievement: What the Evidence Shows, Fall-Winter 2000, 11-75	Showed no evidence for any educationally significant impact of arts on achievement (both verbal and math outcomes).

Source: GAO review of existing research.

Note: The autumn-winter 2000 issue of the Journal of Aesthetic Education was a special issue devoted to examining research evidence about the relationship between the arts and academic achievement.

Appendix V. Comments from the Department of Education

UNITED STATES DEPARTMENT OF EDUCATION

OFFICE OF PLANNING, EVALUATION AND POLICY DEVELOPMENT

February 23, 2009

Ms. Cornelia Ashby
Director, Education, Workforce,
 and Income Security Issues
U.S. Government Accountability Office
Washington, D.C. 20548

Dear Ms. Ashby:

Thank you for the opportunity to comment on the draft GAO report, *Access to Arts Education: Inclusion of Additional Questions in Education's Planned Research Would Help Explain Why Instruction Time Has Decreased for Some Students*. We were pleased to be able to share with your research team the teacher survey data from our study, the National Longitudinal Study of No Child Left Behind, which provided the basis for much of this report, and we reviewed your reanalysis of these data with great interest.

We agree that arts education is an important part of a well-rounded education for all students, and we were encouraged to see the survey findings that very few elementary teachers reported decreases in the amount of time spent on arts education. The findings that teachers in schools identified for improvement and high-minority schools are more likely to report reductions in time for arts education is cause for concern, but it is important to note that reductions in arts education time were reported by a small minority of teachers in these schools. We agree that further study would be useful to better understand the reasons behind changes in instruction time in certain types of schools.

As your report noted, the Department is currently planning to launch a new comprehensive evaluation of Title I implementation, and we will carefully consider your recommendations for collecting more detailed information on changes in instruction time when we develop the study design and survey instruments for that study.

We are attaching technical comments provided by Department staff on the text of the report. If you have any questions, we would be glad to discuss our comments with your research team.

Sincerely,

Thomas P. Skelly
Delegated to Perform Functions of
Assistant Secretary for OPEPD

400 MARYLAND AVE., SW, WASHINGTON, DC 20202
www.ed.gov

Our mission is to ensure equal access to education and to promote educational excellence throughout the nation.

GAO's Mission

The Government Accountability Office, the audit, evaluation, and investigative arm of Congress, exists to support Congress in meeting its constitutional responsibilities and to help improve the performance and accountability of the federal government for the American people. GAO examines the use of public funds; evaluates federal programs and policies; and provides analyses, recommendations, and other assistance to help Congress make informed oversight, policy, and funding decisions. GAO's commitment to good government is reflected in its core values of accountability, integrity, and reliability.

End Notes

[1] The NLS-NCLB's surveys collected data only in school years 2004-2005 and 2006-2007. Because the NLS-NCLB was a congressional mandate and conducted under contract, the time required to negotiate the mandate, solicit and award a contract, and design the study precluded collecting data before school year 2004-2005.

[2] One state has not designated an official to oversee arts education in the state's public schools, and the state education agency's director of curriculum and instruction did not respond to our contacts.

[3] The differences were statistically significant (p<. 05 level).

[4] IASA and NCLBA reauthorized and amended ESEA.

[5] This requirement applies to students in all public schools in a state regardless of whether the school receives Title I funding.

[6] Students in grades 3 to 8 must be annually assessed in reading and mathematics, while high school students are only required to be assessed once in these subjects. Assessments in science, which were first required under NCLBA in school year 2007-2008, are required at least once in grades 3 to 5, grades 6 to 9, and grades 10 to 12. 20 U.S.C. § 6311(b)(3)(C)(v) – (vii).

[7] In this report, we refer to Title I, Part A of the ESEA, as amended, as "Title I." Other parts of Title I (Parts B through I) are targeted at specific populations or purposes and are commonly referred to by their program names, such as Even Start.

[8] See GAO, *No Child Left Behind Act: Education Should Clarify Guidance and Address Potential Compliance Issues for Schools in Corrective Action and Restructuring Status,* GAO-07-1035 (Washington, D.C.: Sept. 5, 2007).

[9] Education also awards arts education grants to VSA arts—formerly known as Very Special Arts—and the John F. Kennedy Center for Performing Arts. These grants provide arts education activities for adults as well as school children. VSA arts supports the involvement of persons with disabilities in arts programs and promotes awareness of the need for such programs.

[10] The *NAEP 1997 Arts Report Card* cautions readers that, because of changes in the nature of the assessment, results are not comparable to assessments in music and visual arts that NAEP administered in 1974 and 1978.

[11] CEP is a national, independent advocate for public education and for more effective public schools.

[12] While findings of the CEP study were based on a survey of school district officials, the NLS-NCLB school year 2006-2007 survey collected detailed data on changes in instruction time from teachers, who are much closer than district officials to the point where instruction takes place.

[13] See appendix II for average amount of instruction time spent on individual subjects in school year 2006-2007.

[14] The average decrease in time spent on arts education among teachers reporting a decrease across all schools was 41 minutes per week.

[15] Because we were not able to obtain raw data files from Education to do a comprehensive analysis of the data ourselves, Education's research team generated a limited set of analyses from their survey data file for us, based on our specifications. Time and resources precluded a more advanced analysis to assess and control for the correlations between the variables and to estimate their effects net of one another. Moreover, the aggregated data we received from Education did not allow us to determine whether the larger declines in arts education instruction in selected schools resulted from their spending more time on those subjects than other schools to begin with or not.

[16] As part of Education's NLS-NCLB study, they administered separate surveys to school principals and elementary school teachers.

[17] The high school principal said that teachers are responsible for seeking and preparing grant proposals.

[18] In 1991, the Broward County school district established the Student Enrichment in the Arts (SEAS) program which provides $466,000 per year in funding for SEAS, with each school receiving about $2,400/year to pay for the costs of transporting students to attend, at no charge, educational performances held at the Center.

[19] The CPS Office of Academic Enhancement administers a magnet school cluster program, which involves about 300 schools. Each school focuses on one academic area or approach, including fine and performing arts, world language, literature and writing, math and science, International Baccalaureate, and Montessori. The International Baccalaureate program focuses on developing the intellectual, personal, emotional, and social skills to live, learn, and work in a rapidly globalizing world. The Montessori method is a child-centered alternative educational approach involving adapting the learning environment to a child's developmental level, and it emphasizes physical activity in absorbing both abstract concepts and practical skills. Magnet schools are located throughout Chicago, and they function as neighborhood schools. The magnet cluster program money is part of a desegregation decree between the federal government and CPS. Since CPS cannot bus, it uses the magnet cluster program as a tool to integrate schools and to bring quality programming to a large number of neighborhood schools.

[20] The line item for arts education provided all schools with approximately $63 per student annually.

[21] A meta-analysis is a statistical analysis of a collection of studies for the purpose of integrating the results.

[22] The author had predicted that learning music notation might be associated with higher test scores because practice in learning symbols in notation might generalize to practice in reading math symbols.

[23] Two studies included keyboard training, two included vocal training, one included violin training, and one included a variety of "school band instruments."

[24] Education plans to survey schools again in school year 2009-2010 to examine arts education.

[25] We obtained similar estimates from Education on the time devoted to other subjects, such as math, science, and reading, and whether and how much it had changed over the past 2 years.

[26] One state has not designated an official to oversee arts education in the state's public schools, and the state education agency's director of curriculum and instruction did not respond to our contacts.

[27] Meta-analyses were included as long as they met the stated criteria. For meta-analyses that included correlational research in addition to experimental and quasi-experimental studies, only the experimental and quasi-experimental research was reviewed for purposes of this report.

CHAPTER SOURCES

The following chapters have been previously published:

Chapter 1 – This is an edited, excerpted and augmented edition of a United States Department of Education, National Assessment Governing Board, National Assessment of Educational Progress (NAEP) Arts Education Framework Project, dated September 2008.

Chapter 2 – This is an edited, excerpted and augmented edition of a United States Department of Education, National Center for Education Statistics, Institute of Education Sciences Report, NCES 2009-488, dated June 2008.

Chapter 3 – This is an edited, excerpted and augmented edition of a United States Government Accountability Office (GAO), Report to Congressional Requesters. Publication GAO-09-286, dated February 2009.

INDEX

A

academic performance, 167, 168, 173, 186, 188
accountability, 168, 171, 173, 185, 199
achievement, vii, 1, 4, 18, 32, 44, 45, 51, 61, 63, 69, 71, 82, 87, 102, 124, 125, 167, 169, 170, 171, 172, 185, 188, 197
achievement test, 186
adaptations, 63
administrators, 4, 111, 112, 113, 114, 115, 129, 130, 141, 143
advocacy, 111, 112, 113, 183
aesthetic criteria, 27, 50, 69, 88, 102
aesthetics, 18, 22, 23, 30, 41, 106, 109, 110
age, 36, 41, 61, 88
alternatives, 24, 62, 76, 78
anger, 99
architects, 29
articulation, 3, 49, 52, 56, 84, 86, 88, 91, 94
assessment procedures, 189
assessment techniques, 35
athletes, 85
attitudes, 4, 108, 110
auditing, 169
authenticity, 33, 64
authority, 185
availability, 4, 33, 124, 129, 141, 158
awareness, 24, 71, 78, 103, 154, 199

B

background, 4, 5, 20, 37, 116, 121, 125, 153, 186
background information, 5
barriers, 40
behavior, 21, 31, 38
belief systems, 81
beliefs, 105
bias, 156

Black students, 130
blocks, 42, 99
body shape, 47, 48
bone, 17
brass, 133
budget cuts, 183, 184, 191
building blocks, 27

C

cadences, 53, 56
causal relationship, 196
cell, 23, 195
children, 16, 18, 20, 38, 156, 171, 183, 186, 199
choreographers, 50, 88
clarity, 38, 47, 49, 88
classes, 20, 60, 170, 182, 184, 191
classification, 157
classroom, 18, 41, 52, 62, 82, 89, 90, 92, 98, 99, 112, 183
classroom teacher, 112, 183
classroom teachers, 112, 183
classrooms, 21, 34
closure, 75
codes, 157
cognitive abilities, 31
collaboration, 15, 66, 101, 188, 190
collage, 159
communication, 17, 19, 30, 66, 75, 101, 104, 106, 108, 109
community, 3, 4, 15, 65, 66, 101, 123, 167, 170, 181, 182
competence, 78, 85, 108, 109, 172
competency, 44, 45, 51, 61, 71
complexity, 41
components, 22, 24, 27, 33, 79
composers, 25, 59, 96, 97

composition, 21, 30, 31, 43, 53, 54, 65, 83, 95, 97, 98, 101, 109, 154
compositional structure, 23, 24
computing, 42, 43, 44, 157
concentration, 61, 84, 99, 100
conductor, 51, 90, 93
confidence, 24, 45, 49, 58, 85, 109
conflict, 67
consensus, 5, 20, 64, 100, 101
construction, 4, 30, 31, 44, 71, 80, 83
consultants, 3
continuity, 4
contour, 158
control, 24, 46, 75, 78, 92, 93, 100, 199
correlations, 199
costs, 200
creative process, 22, 27, 30, 34, 41
creativity, 17, 18, 51, 54, 57, 58, 95, 196
credit, 132, 144, 146, 150, 157, 185
critical analysis, 57, 60
critical thinking, 35
criticism, 20, 29, 41, 50, 81, 83
cues, 51, 90
cultural tradition, 98
culture, 22, 27, 37, 46, 48, 66, 74, 98, 101, 103, 105, 110, 136
curiosity, 73
current limit, 187
curricula, 128, 173, 183
curriculum, 43, 130, 143, 178, 184, 191, 199, 200

D

dancers, 48, 85, 88
dances, 23, 36, 46, 47, 48, 49, 50, 85, 86, 87, 88
data analysis, 190
data collection, 36, 174, 189, 190, 192
database, 190
decisions, 18, 41, 44, 52, 74, 87, 170, 185, 187, 199
decoding, 75
definition, 19, 21, 35, 74, 104, 107, 109
designers, 20, 23, 29, 30, 31, 34, 101, 102, 105, 110
directors, 101
discipline, 16, 17, 20, 22, 23, 34, 35, 36, 42, 82, 101, 123
discrimination, 42
disseminate, 187
distribution, 42, 113
diversity, 20, 39
division, 183
donations, 182
draft, 3, 113, 114, 115, 116, 187, 190

drawing, 4, 29, 31, 41, 122, 147, 148, 149, 150, 151, 155, 158
duplication, 22
duration, 21

E

ears, 18
economic downturn, 184
education reform, 17
educational system, 16, 112
effective use of time, 45, 47, 48
elaboration, 72, 75
elementary school, 37, 166, 168, 169, 173, 174, 177, 182, 185, 188, 199
eligibility criteria, 128
e-mail, 189, 190
emotion, 27
emotional responses, 63, 100
emotions, 4, 95, 98, 99
empathy, 66, 101
encouragement, 17
energy, 5, 49, 84, 86
engagement, 21, 81
English Language, 160
enrollment, 182
environment, 20, 27, 30, 34, 37, 64, 67, 74, 88, 99, 100, 188
ethnic groups, 110, 155
ethnicity, 88, 127, 130, 140, 142, 159
evolution, 98
examinations, 16, 31
exclusion, 124
execution, 30, 31
exercise, 19, 33, 36, 39, 40, 42, 83, 85
expenditures, 185
experimental design, 192
expertise, 40, 75, 190
expressiveness, 26

F

fabric, 99
facial expression, 40, 153
facilitators, 34, 40, 42
family, 156
federal funds, 172
feelings, 21, 23, 28, 95, 98, 123
feet, 99
films, 29
financial resources, 19
flexibility, 17, 22, 24, 46, 47, 84, 88

focusing, 69
formal education, 38
freedom, 25
frustration, 18
fugue, 56, 133
funding, viii, 5, 15, 18, 165, 166, 167, 168, 169, 170, 173, 178, 179, 180, 181, 182, 183, 188, 190, 191, 192, 199, 200
funds, 168, 170, 172, 176, 180, 181, 182, 183, 184, 185, 199
furniture, 40

G

gender, 41, 61, 88, 121, 127, 130, 142
generation, 72, 76
genre, 25, 28, 53, 56, 57, 59, 60, 91, 94, 97, 98, 159
genres, 29, 53, 59, 65, 69, 93, 94, 97, 98, 101, 102, 144
geography, 170
gestures, 46
gifted, 186
goals, vii, 1, 20, 102, 150, 171
governance, 171, 172, 188
government, iv, 167, 169, 179, 199, 200
grades, vii, 1, 31, 37, 39, 42, 43, 44, 82, 87, 171, 199
grants, 167, 170, 172, 173, 178, 179, 180, 181, 182, 199
groups, viii, 2, 33, 36, 37, 40, 41, 61, 63, 64, 87, 90, 100, 120, 121, 122, 125, 128, 139, 141, 155, 156, 165, 166, 168, 169, 171, 176, 188, 192
growth, 17, 38, 63, 80
guidance, 2, 123, 189
guidelines, 5, 25, 38, 54, 89, 92, 115, 156

H

hands, 89
harm, 58, 59, 90, 97
harmony, 58, 59, 90, 97
health, 174, 193
high school, 17, 18, 32, 37, 82, 170, 172, 178, 179, 182, 184, 185, 191, 194, 195, 199
higher education, 2
higher-order thinking, 17, 22
house, 162
human condition, 28
human experience, 17, 28
human resources, 4

I

ideal, 17, 18
idealism, 4
identification, 111
identity, 67
ideology, 80
image, 18, 21, 31, 39, 83, 166
images, 40, 75, 104, 108, 110
imagination, 18, 25, 95, 99
imitation, 39, 45, 46, 48, 93, 97
implementation, 37, 68, 102, 166, 169, 171, 172, 173, 187, 188, 190, 192
incentives, 4
inclusion, 5, 16, 19, 124
income, 128, 156, 166, 167, 168, 169, 170, 171, 172, 174, 175, 176, 177, 186, 190, 191
independence, 51, 54
individuality, 153
industry, 19
inferences, 41, 76, 77, 155
injury, iv
insight, 24, 25, 41, 53, 57, 109
inspiration, 18
instruction time, viii, 165, 166, 168, 169, 170, 171, 173, 174, 175, 177, 181, 183, 184, 185, 186, 187, 188, 191, 192, 193, 199
instructional practice, 37
instructional time, 4, 43
instrumental music, 32, 182
instruments, 25, 26, 43, 52, 53, 54, 56, 57, 59, 60, 89, 90, 91, 92, 95, 122, 135, 136, 182, 200
integration, 33, 138, 183
integrity, 199
intellect, 4
intentions, 101, 109, 110
interaction, 28
interactions, 100
interest groups, 113
interval, 158
intervention, 172
interview, 113
intonation, 96
intrinsic value, 22, 172
inversion, 97
isolation, 19, 22, 33, 88

J

judgment, 4, 22, 31, 73
junior high school, 182

K

kindergarten, 18

L

labeling, 26
labor, 18
language, 15, 23, 31, 124, 136, 137, 174, 175, 182, 184, 193, 200
leadership, 2, 3, 62
learners, 124
learning, 4, 16, 17, 18, 20, 22, 27, 32, 34, 35, 36, 38, 41, 44, 81, 87, 88, 129, 141, 171, 183, 186, 200
learning environment, 200
legislation, 171, 172
life experiences, 4
line, 99, 115, 133, 158, 172, 184, 200
listening, 25, 26, 39, 43, 53, 56, 59, 91, 97, 122, 186, 196
literacy, 17, 183
locomotor, 45, 47, 84, 88, 98
lysis, 196

M

magnet, 4, 17, 20, 183, 200
management, 3, 68, 102
manipulation, 51
mastery, 41, 44, 45, 51, 61, 71
mathematics, 15, 36, 171, 172, 175, 186, 199
matrix, 31
meals, 156
meanings, 65, 85, 101, 107, 109, 110
measurement, 82
measures, 18, 89, 90, 92, 93, 126, 185, 189, 192
media, 16, 19, 21, 22, 28, 29, 30, 31, 33, 41, 57, 67, 69, 71, 75, 78, 83, 88, 92, 99, 101, 102, 103, 104, 106, 108, 109, 110, 111, 112, 113, 114, 137
melody, 90, 97, 133, 158
memory, 89, 96, 186
mental image, 75
meta-analysis, 185, 186, 200
metaphor, 102
minorities, 189
minority, 166, 167, 169, 171, 172, 174, 175, 176, 177, 186, 187
minority students, 166, 167, 169, 171, 174, 175, 176, 177, 186, 187
model, 2, 4, 18, 183
models, 30, 72, 75, 81, 95, 96, 97, 98, 104, 109, 110
money, 200
mood, 28, 51, 62, 64, 67, 89, 99
moratorium, 191
mosaic, 182
motion, 36
motivation, 21, 100
motives, 97
motor skills, 24, 26, 28, 30
movement, 5, 17, 19, 23, 24, 25, 26, 34, 38, 39, 45, 46, 47, 48, 49, 50, 53, 61, 65, 84, 85, 86, 87, 88, 90, 91, 93, 98, 101
multiple interpretations, 73
multiple-choice questions, 32, 121, 123, 124, 160
musicians, 20, 25, 34, 91, 94, 98, 115

N

nation, vii, 1, 29, 32, 125, 128, 155
National Center for Education Statistics (NCES), vii, 1
national policy, 4
new media, 29
No Child Left Behind, viii, 165, 167, 168, 188, 199

O

objectives, vii, 1, 35, 169
observations, 18, 24, 150, 153, 154
Office of Management and Budget, 157
oil, 151
order, 25, 32, 36, 97, 170, 171, 186
orientation, 79
originality, 71, 78, 86
ostinato, 51, 52, 89
oversight, 3, 199

P

packaging, 159
painters, 34
paints, 20
parameters, 38
parents, vii, 1, 3, 4, 111, 112, 113, 114, 115
pathways, 84, 85, 86
peer group, 67
peer review, 192
peers, 85, 120
percentile, 126, 138
performers, 25, 28, 29, 45, 47, 49, 57, 60, 65, 86
performing artists, 18
permit, 32, 127
personal computers, 89
personal values, 74

persons with disabilities, 199
physical activity, 200
physical environment, 66, 101
physics, 35
piano, 91, 94, 95, 121, 132, 134
pitch, 52, 55, 56, 60, 89, 90, 91, 94, 98, 158
planning, 2, 3, 5, 16, 28, 30, 31, 35, 37, 44, 64, 68, 72, 75, 82, 83, 99, 100, 111, 114, 115, 116
pluralism, 20
population, 3, 32, 155, 156, 157, 176, 183, 188, 189
portfolio, 19, 36, 37, 42, 144
portfolio assessment, 36
portfolios, 18, 19, 20, 36
portraits, 144, 154
positive relation, 170, 185, 186, 196
positive relationship, 170, 185, 186, 196
posture, 19, 89, 93
poverty, 88, 128, 156
power, 17
preference, 100
preschool, 186
preschoolers, 183
president, 2, 3, 114, 115
primary school, 184
prior knowledge, 30
privacy, 38
private schools, 124, 128, 141, 155, 156
probability, 132, 146
problem solving, 17
problem-solving, 29, 72, 74, 76, 79, 81
problem-solving strategies, 29
production, 18, 19, 20, 27, 28, 35, 37, 41, 46, 48, 50, 52, 55, 61, 66, 67, 68, 70, 75, 101, 102, 103, 170, 182
professional development, 173, 183
program, 15, 37, 111, 112, 113, 114, 115, 167, 170, 173, 176, 178, 182, 183, 185, 199, 200
programming, 200
public education, 199
public schools, 128, 168, 172, 173, 179, 188, 189, 190, 191, 199, 200

Q

qualifications, 4
quality standards, 168

R

race, 127, 130, 140, 142
radio, 112

range, 4, 5, 19, 20, 26, 35, 38, 41, 44, 52, 55, 58, 79, 90, 92, 93, 124, 126, 132, 144, 166, 169, 174, 175, 177, 186
reading, 36, 39, 93, 167, 168, 170, 171, 172, 175, 183, 184, 185, 186, 196, 197, 199, 200
realism, 17
reality, 4
reason, 35, 43
reasoning, 98
recall, 24, 27, 49, 87, 100
recognition, 4, 16, 78
recovery, 86
recruiting, 112
refining, 57
region, 121, 136
regulations, 171
rehearsing, 28, 64, 68, 100
relationship, 57, 60, 63, 65, 71, 72, 74, 76, 80, 103, 104, 106, 109, 125, 137, 138, 150, 170, 186, 196, 197
relevance, 192
reliability, 34, 36, 40, 189, 199
requirements, 178, 194
resolution, 63, 67, 97
resources, 4, 32, 35, 36, 37, 95, 105, 106, 107, 182, 191, 199
restructuring, 171, 172, 185
rhythm, 47, 48, 60, 86, 89, 90, 91, 94
risk, 18, 66, 101, 186
risk-taking, 101
rubrics, 36

S

sadness, 99
safety, 37
sample survey, 190
sampling, 31, 155, 189, 190, 192
sampling error, 190
satisfaction, 16
school activities, 131, 145
school community, 4
school performance, 185
search, 77, 192
searches, 189, 192
secondary schools, 168, 172, 173, 188
selecting, 24, 31, 33, 57, 76, 90, 103, 172
self-esteem, 66, 101
self-expression, 41
self-portrait, viii, 120, 121, 144, 147, 148, 149, 150, 151, 153, 154, 157, 159
self-portraits, 147, 148, 151, 153, 154, 159
semantics, 83

sensitivity, 78, 109
sequencing, 54
shape, 17, 20, 86
shaping, 168, 189
sharing, 2
shyness, 63
sibling, 99
simulation, 75, 79, 106
singers, 58
social behavior, 74
social context, 22, 33, 35, 63, 65, 82
social skills, 200
social structure, 35
socioeconomic status, 128
space, 28, 34, 39, 40, 41, 45, 47, 48, 49, 62, 84, 85, 86, 99, 104
spatial ability, 186
specific knowledge, 123
spectrum, 32, 113
sports, 38
standard error, 156, 189
standardization, 32
standards, 2, 3, 4, 15, 17, 20, 21, 35, 44, 82, 83, 111, 112, 113, 125, 156, 167, 169, 170, 171, 172, 183, 184, 187, 192
statistics, 156
stereotypes, 88
stimulus, 20, 31, 34, 36, 38, 39, 40
storytelling, 101
strategies, 5, 166, 170, 181, 187, 192
strength, 24, 46, 47, 84, 88, 192
student achievement, vii, 1, 15, 16, 20, 45, 51, 61, 71, 128
student enrollment, 184
student proficiency, 175
subgroups, 171, 187
substitution, 156
suspense, 63, 100
symbols, 25, 52, 53, 56, 59, 91, 94, 96, 97, 101, 103, 104, 105, 106, 108, 109, 110, 153, 200
sympathy, 66, 101
synthesis, 98, 108, 109, 189

T

talent, 112
targets, 167, 172, 176
teaching, 36, 183
television, 27, 28, 29, 41, 62, 63, 65, 66, 67, 68, 70, 99, 101, 102, 103, 144, 182
tension, 5, 17, 63, 92, 95, 97, 98, 100
territory, 157

test scores, 170, 186, 200
thinking, 24, 25, 29, 30, 32, 41, 78, 83, 109
thoughts, 30
time periods, 46, 48, 85, 86
time pressure, 184
tonality, 51, 89, 92, 94, 95
trade, 170, 181, 185
trade-off, 170, 181, 185
tradition, 98
traditions, 22, 27, 47, 49, 70, 88, 103
training, 32, 34, 37, 38, 42, 158, 179, 180, 183, 192, 200
transcendence, 17
transition, 85
translation, 38
trial, 71
tutoring, 172
twist, 84

U

uncertainty, 54
universities, 21
university students, 112

V

variability, 190
variables, 4, 20, 37, 116, 199
videotape, 33, 38, 90, 93
vocabulary, 23, 25, 33, 46, 47, 50, 53, 56, 57, 59, 60, 73, 76, 80, 86, 97
voice, 54, 55, 57

W

wants and needs, 100
wealth, 17
wind, 99
winter, 197
wood, 99
worry, 18
writing, 3, 4, 16, 19, 33, 35, 36, 41, 76, 77, 130, 144, 200

Y

young adults, 67